How to Become
a Really Good

PAIN
IN THE
ASS

How to Become
a Really Good

PAIN
IN THE
ASS

A Critical Thinker's Guide
TO ASKING THE
RIGHT QUESTIONS

10 Year Anniversary Edition

Christopher DiCarlo

 Prometheus Books

Guilford, Connecticut

PB Prometheus Books

An imprint of Globe Pequot, the trade division of
The Rowman & Littlefield Publishing Group, Inc.
4501 Forbes Blvd., Ste. 200
Lanham, MD 20706
www.rowman.com

Distributed by NATIONAL BOOK NETWORK

British Library Cataloguing in Publication Information Available

Library of Congress Cataloging-in-Publication Data

Names: DiCarlo, Christopher, 1962– author.
Title: How to become a really good pain in the ass : a critical thinker's guide to asking the right
    questions / Christopher DiCarlo.
Description: 10 year anniversary edition. | Lanham, MD : Prometheus Books, [2021] |
    Includes bibliographical references and index. | Summary: "In this witty, incisive guide to
    critical thinking the author provides you with the tools to allow you to question beliefs and
    assumptions held by those who claim to know what they're talking about"—Provided by
    publisher.
Identifiers: LCCN 2021018774 (print) | LCCN 2021018775 (ebook) | ISBN
    9781633887121 (paperback) | ISBN 9781616143985 (epub)
Subjects: LCSH: Reasoning. | Critical thinking. | Question (Logic) | Conduct of life.
Classification: LCC BC177 .D525 2021 (print) | LCC BC177 (ebook) | DDC 160—dc23
LC record available at https://lccn.loc.gov/2021018774
LC ebook record available at https://lccn.loc.gov/2021018775

∞™ The paper used in this publication meets the minimum requirements of American
National Standard for Information Sciences—Permanence of Paper for Printed Library
Materials, ANSI/NISO Z39.48-1992

33614082432880

CONTENTS

PREFACE

So why do you want to become a really good pain in the ass? What's in it for you? What do you expect to get out of a book that makes such a promise? Do you want to respond cleverly to your know-it-all relatives? Or do you want to put your obnoxious neighbor in his place? Do you want to have more meaningful discussions with your spouse, family, kids, coworkers, and friends? Or do you just want to become better at understanding and expressing your ideas? The purpose of this book is to provide tools to allow you to question beliefs held and assumptions made by others who claim to know what they're talking about. A really good pain in the ass is empowered with the ability to spot faulty reasoning and, by asking the right questions, can hold others accountable not only for what they believe but also for how they behave. There are many of these types of people whom we need to question—from politicians to lawyers and doctors, to professors and teachers, to car salespersons, to your boss and your bank manager. There are many different reasons why individuals would want tools to allow them to think more clearly about important things. In ancient Greece, people believed in all sorts of things: from many types of gods to different forms of politics, to developing expressions in art, to different forms of morality. People then, as they do today, believed that they had absolutely certain knowledge of such things. But it took people like Socrates and the ancient Skeptics to get them to think a little more carefully about their ideas, beliefs, and actions. One of the greatest problems in the world today has been with us for a long time: our inability to think carefully and responsibly about why it is we believe what we do and why we act on those beliefs. For example, if I think same-sex marriage should be illegal, what reasons do I have for this belief? How well have I thought this through? And how far am I willing to go in acting on this belief? Are my reasons based simply on a piece of documentation written in an ancient book? Or do I have reasons that are less religiously inspired? Like basic emotional responses: What if one of my kids wants a same-sex marriage? Would this affect the way I think and feel and act about the issue? And if I think same-sex marriage should be legal, what are my reasons in favor of it? The list could include the idea that the feeling of love is not limited exclusively to opposite-sex couples, or that it should be a right for any two consenting adults to marry each other if they so choose. I may also include other forms of evidence as further reasons for my belief regarding this particular issue, such as the scientific evidence supporting the idea that a person's sexuality is not chosen, that one is simply born with orientation already determined. Whether I'm for or against same-sex marriage, I need to be able to understand my emotional feelings and rational beliefs and coordinate them in ways that make sense to me and to others who might disagree with me.

It is extremely important to think carefully about why it is you believe what you do because what you believe often affects how you behave toward others. Your behavior is bound to affect others, and their behavior is going to affect you. To be a really good pain in the ass requires that you use the tools in this book to think about your thoughts, ideas, and beliefs and why you act—or don't act—on them. This process will help you understand why others might hold opposing views. When you have the right tools, you will know for yourself why your beliefs are what they are and can demonstrate to others any shortcomings in their beliefs. But be careful what you wish for, and be aware that many people do not like having their views and beliefs questioned and challenged. As a result, being a really good pain in the ass can be lonely. You may lose friends, pro-motions, jobs, or marriages; you could get hurt, beaten up, or even killed. However mundane or lofty your goals may be, this book will empower you with the necessary tools to think more clearly and confidently about important issues that affect all our lives.

INTRODUCTION

10 YEAR ANNIVERSARY EDITION

It was indeed an honor to learn from Prometheus Books that they would be releasing a second edition of this book to celebrate its 10th year anniversary. To help mark the occasion, I was asked to write a new Introduction considering why being a critical thinker and asking the right questions is now more important than ever. As I reflect upon the past decade, I find that there are many reasons for writing the book and giving it such a title. But now, as I consider the current state of the world compared to what it was like 10 years ago, there is clearly a more urgent need for such a book. What we are witnessing today is a manic demonstration not only of great progress both culturally and scientifically, but of an anti-scientific and anti-logic movement, occurring simultaneously. On the one hand, over the last ten years, we saw the first black US president elected for two terms; we witnessed the development of CRISPR Cas9 genetic interventions which will allow modern medicine to rapidly advance in the treatment of numerous diseases, including cancer and COVID-19; and we saw rockets take off and then re-land with absolutely remarkable precision and efficiency. And on the other hand, we saw the 45th President of the United States deliberately spread false information which appears to have led to a violent insurrection on the Capitol Building on January 6, 2021; we experienced a predictable global pandemic which shut down much of the world in many respects; and we witnessed for the first time in human history, a group of people devoted to Qanon—a conspiracy theory which has no actual basis in reality, and yet millions of people believe in it, including several Republican

13

congressional representatives and senators. In the last five years alone, we entered into a new age—the *age of post-truth* where "alternative facts" and personal feelings matter as much in the political and public arenas as actual facts. And the fact that I now have to make a distinction between "alternative facts" and actual facts ironically demonstrates the absurd level to which our means of communication have devolved; and that's a fact. Over the last several years, there has been a gradual but definite erosion of the relevance of facts, logic, critical thinking, self-reflection, accountability, and all other manner of values to which we ought to hold in high regard when discussing important issues.

With the ideological polarization of Democrats and Republicans in the United States, the divisiveness of political sovereignty in the UK leading to Brexit, the many new authoritarian political parties gaining momentum throughout Europe, South America, India, and countless numbers of disputes going on throughout the rest of the world, we are at a point in history where civility has been eroded to a point where the public has been scratching its collective head wondering how we got here. But here we are, nonetheless. The question that stands before us now is: what are we going to do about it? Much of the problem can be found in the way in which information is now distributed, interpreted, and acted upon—especially online. Unlike any other time in history, we are inundated with information from many sources of media. And we are racing to catch up to what is reliable, dependable, and true—all the while, feeling very powerful and emotional attachments to our personal understanding of various issues.

In the last ten years, we have continued to lose the capacity in dialogue for what can be referred to as the art of disagreement. We no longer know how to have intelligent discussions, disagree, and still be able to get along with one another. Sharply divided lines have been drawn both geographically and ideologically. We need to get back to a place of security, of universal acceptance for common rules of discourse, and dependability of information accuracy. That confidence will only be established and maintained when we recognize and accept the power and importance of the tools of critical thinking. Now, more than ever, is the time for critical thinking to be front and center in all of our educational institutions—from kindergarten to post-doctoral levels. If you're wondering why the world is the way it is today—where political polarization has created a far left woke generation and a far right post-truth-alternative-facts generation—you need look no further than the failing education systems that have lost the capacity to train their students with critical thinking skills. But it is not simply our education systems; we need to teach critical thinking skills to all politicians, civil servants, medical staff, legal staff, and throughout the entire business world. With a World population of over seven billion people, we cannot hope to get along unless and until we agree to abide by the most fundamental and universal of all laws of civil discussion and dialogue—and this involves a collective agreement to use the skill set of critical thinking.

And so, I consider this book to be a part of a Socratic mission, as it were, to bring greater clarity and agreement to the world through respectful dialogue that abides by the principles, rules, and laws of critical thinking. Although there are hundreds of books available that deal with ways to improve your thinking, I wanted to write a book that contained information that would stay with the reader years after they read it. This is why I have divided the book into three distinct but related parts.

The first part deals with the most important tools that comprise what we might call the critical thinking skill set. This set contains six individual tools that every person can learn, understand, and apply in their daily lives. I have distilled what I believe to be the six most important critical thinking tools which conveniently follow a handy mnemonic to make them easy to remember. Each tool follows the first six letters of the English alphabet. A is for argument. B is for bias. C is for context. D is for diagramming. E is for evidence. F is for fallacies. Each one of these tools provides the reader with the capacity to better understand why it is they believe what they do, how they came to believe what they do, and to question how their beliefs affect their actions. These critical thinking tools provide the skill set which empowers people to organize their thoughts better, more clearly, and more confidently, which in turn allows them to more effectively communicate their thoughts. In this way, the intentionality of one's ideas will be interpreted by others more clearly and accurately, which will greatly increase the likelihood of being understood. People may not always agree with your ideas—or you, with theirs. But if we can articulate and communicate our thoughts and ideas better and more effectively, this will go a long way towards the likelihood of civilized discussion.

The second part of the book examines some of the teachings of Socrates and the works of the Ancient Skeptics. It is important to remember how valuable such works were and continue to be in appreciating methods that we can all employ in an effort to hold those in power accountable for their beliefs and actions. For if we do not exercise these skills, then our leaders can easily take advantage of us. And in so doing, we may find ourselves living in societies that no longer value such things as facts, truth, knowledge, civility, dialogue, and compromise. Around the world, we see evidence of divided nations talking past one another and refusing to even entertain the possibility that their side could, in some way, be in error. These are indeed dangerous times. For there are too many countries in the world, today, run by leaders who have no intention of abiding by the commonly accepted rules of civilized discourse—grounded in the skill set of critical thinking—that were developed and nurtured by Socrates and the Ancient Skeptics for the purpose of holding people accountable for their beliefs. Through the Socratic Method and the Skeptical modes, we see two great historical examples of a classic embodiment of what it means to be a really good pain in the ass. It is predominantly because of Socrates and the Ancient Skeptics that the book is named what it is. Society today, more than ever, needs people trained in critical thinking so that they can become really good pains in the ass by asking the types of questions that hold people in power accountable. We cannot even begin to "speak truth to power" unless we collectively become familiar with, and practice, the skill set of critical thinking.

And finally, the third part of the book is devoted entirely to the ways in which we can answer what I call the Big Five. These are the five most important questions we can ask ourselves and others: What can I know? Why am I here? What am I? How should I behave? And what is to come of me? How we answer these questions tells us a great deal about ourselves and others. As well, much of the world's difficulties are directly or indirectly the result of the differing opinions that people have regarding answers to the Big Five. How humans have answered these questions over the past 5,000 years has led to the current state the world is in today. I sincerely believe that if all humans on this planet were able to discuss the manner in which they answer these questions, and we did so fairly in accordance to the critical thinking skill set, there would be a lot less hatred, anger, violence, and bloodshed throughout the world. This may seem like wishful thinking. But I believe we have a moral imperative to relearn how to have civilized and intelligent discussions no matter how emotionally attached to the issues we have become. To avoid this would be to do so at our own peril, which has become more evident as each day passes. If we are to survive as a species, and live in a world of ideological, political, moral, and religious differences, then we must have the intellectual maturity and respect to be able to discuss not only the Big Five, but all-important issues, candidly and honestly. And we must not be pressured by ideologies either from the left or the right in terms of what is sacrosanct and off the table for discussion. For if we know how to utilize the tools of our critical thinking skill set, then we should have no real concerns about how to have intelligent discussions in a civilized manner regarding any and all topics. It follows, then, that the practice of critical thinking skills is a cornerstone for both freedom of thought and freedom of speech.

It is for these reasons and more that we need to introduce critical thinking into all levels of education. If children are taught how to fairly engage in discussions and dialogue about important issues at a young age, this will stay with them for the rest of their lives and will undoubtedly lead to greater conflict resolutions, better decision-making, greater problem-solving, and overall, a more civilized world in which we need not fear discussing important issues but will be empowered to do so. Critical thinking is our greatest hope for the future of humankind. Unlike any other subject, we don't leave it in the classroom, or in the office, or in the home, or in any other place; it follows us out the door and permeates every aspect of our being. It is not like *Windows 95*, where it becomes obsolete and replaced by more evolved and developed forms of information technology. Instead, the skill set of critical thinking is permanent, universal, and unchanging. We can rely on critical thinking skills to lead us to the most responsible ways in which we can interpret, understand, and act on information. And we must never forget that critical thinking isn't simply something you do, it's what you live.

Christopher DiCarlo,
Guelph, ON

WHY BECOME A REALLY GOOD PAIN IN THE ASS?

Everyone will have his or her own reasons for wanting to become a really good pain in the ass. But since the subtitle of this book is *A Critical Thinker's Guide to Asking the Right Questions*, you probably have already guessed that you can accomplish this goal with the greatest success by asking the most important questions. This book revolves around asking and answering five very important questions. They are so important that I call them the Big Five:

1. What can I know?
2. Why am I here?
3. What am I?
4. How should I behave?
5. What is to come of me?

These are the Big Five because the way we answer them reflects significantly on how we answer many of life's other questions. They offer insights about ourselves and others. In fact, the way we have answered these questions throughout history is the reason the world is the way it is today. If you want to get to know someone, ask him or her any or all of these questions. You will very quickly see how views on politics, heathcare, law, education, and so on, are related and connected. So before we go any further, take the time to answer these questions to the best of your ability. That means you need to be completely honest. Please don't start your journey to becoming a really good pain in the ass by lying to yourself. We practice enough self-deception just to get through the day; we do not need to do it now. You know well enough how you would answer these questions, so please do so now. I should warn you, though, that by the time you have finished reading this book, you may not answer them in the same way. Go ahead and answer the Big Five on the worksheet that follows; I'll wait.

MY ANSWERS TO THE BIG FIVE

1. What can I know?

_____

_____

_____

2. Why am I here?

_____

_____

_____

3. What am I?

_____

_____

_____

4. How should I behave?

_____

_____

_____

5. What is to come of me?

_____

_____

_____

As mentioned, the way we answer these questions tells us a lot about ourselves and others. A social activity that has gained popularity in the past decade in clubs, in bars, and online is speed dating. In times ranging from one to fifteen minutes, strangers can meet and talk to other strangers to see if they are interested enough in each other to pursue a second date or develop a relationship. Whether it's speed dating or the more traditional form, or a blind date, or a casual relationship, I guarantee you that asking any or all of the Big Five questions to your partner will tell you a great deal about the person, how he or she thinks, what that individual values, and so on. As mentioned, many of the ways we respond to important questions about politics, law, labor and industry, art, healthcare, and so forth, are the direct result of how we answer the Big Five.

Some people who answer the Big Five will be unwilling to consider changing their views because they believe they have answered any or all of the five questions with absolute certainty. In other words, they believe they have insight into Reality: the actual way in which you and I, the world, and the universe are functioning, have functioned, and will function forever and for all time. Sound a bit much? Not to them. There are millions or perhaps billions of people who believe they are absolutely certain when answering the Big Five. Don't be surprised if they refuse to entertain the possibility that they could in some way be mistaken. They are quite comfortable with their beliefs and have no intention of investigating them any further. Socrates and the ancient Skeptics referred to such people as dogmatists. Such people think they know the absolute answers to the Big Five, but they are mistaken. They really don't. And the sad part is that they're not even aware they don't know what the absolute answers are to the Big Five. The tools in this book will allow you to demonstrate this to them and help them understand how they are lacking in this regard. This is how you will become a really good pain in the ass. And if we are humble enough to accept that we don't know all the answers to the Big Five, we may even appreciate that someone has gone through the trouble to clarify things for us.

This book is divided into three parts. So it can be read either as three separate smaller books or as one collective whole. In part 1, "The Tools of the Trade," you will learn the ABCs of critical thinking (as well as the DEFs). These tools will equip you to think more carefully about the Big Five and many of life's other related questions. If you just want the nuts and bolts of critical thinking, this section is for you.

In chapter 1, "A Is for Argument," we look at the structure of our views and how we can effectively communicate our ideas to others. Even though others may not always agree with you, nor you with them, stating your position clearly in the form of an argument will increase your chances of being understood. If others do the same, then you will have a greater chance of understanding what it is they believe or why they have a particular opinion about a topic. This type of clarity then increases your chances for more effective communication.

In chapter 2, "B Is for Biases," we consider many of the relevant factors that influence the ways in which we and others see and understand the world. We are sometimes unaware of our biases and how they influence the decisions and beliefs in our lives. But it is extremely important to put ourselves under the microscope in this respect, because biases are inescapable. It's not as though we can simply turn them off. From how we were raised to our ethnicity, to our religious or nonreligious beliefs, to whether we're male or female, there are both biological and cultural biases that we need to think about very carefully. The better we understand our biases, the more reflective we will be when discussing important issues that stem from how we answer the Big Five and many of life's other essential questions.

In chapter 3, "C Is for Context: Time, Place, and Circumstance," you will learn the importance of setting or the situation of events when discussing important issues. We need to understand the context in which issues take place. Otherwise, we may make decisions based on incomplete information. Without this information, we may find that we have made up our minds about an issue too quickly and, in so doing, have judged unfairly and perhaps acted too hastily. Many television sitcoms and movies depend on the notion of lack of context. A character is somehow mistaken about a bit information because it was taken out of context, and the entire episode revolves around how he or she eventually realizes the misinterpretation: "You mean that person was your sister and not another woman you were seeing? Oh, honey can you ever forgive me?" Understanding context allows us to better understand the reasons why someone might think and act in a particular way.

In chapter 4, "D Is for Diagramming," you will learn the basic fundamental skills for analyzing the structure of arguments, whether it involves your own or those of others. The skill of diagramming arguments allows us to literally see and understand how a person has (or hasn't) supported his or her view on a particular topic. You will learn how to distinguish between the conclusion (or what position a person has taken) and the premise (or reasons for maintaining the position). This skill allows you to see what a person believes and why. This leads to more pointed and productive discussions because it reduces the amount of time you would spend trying to second-guess or assume what it is he or she is trying to say.

Chapter 5, "E Is for Evidence," gives considerable attention to the different types of evidence that you can use to support your arguments. Carl Sagan said, "Extraordinary claims require extraordinary evidence." The larger or more grand the claim is, the greater the need for more compelling supporting evidence. So it follows that evidence comes not only in degrees but in different types as well. We will look at both aspects of evidence and consider the different types, such as anecdotal evidence (or personal experience), scientific evidence, legal testimony, and intuition. Since the strength of our arguments lives and dies according to our evidence, it is important to know if and when we have the right type and degree of evidence in support of our beliefs.

In chapter 6, "F Is for Fallacies," we will consider the various ways in which people commit logical errors in reasoning. These are the tools that will allow you to spot problems with arguments. As such, these tools, when used properly, will make you a really good pain in the ass. There are easily over one hundred formal and informal fallacies, but we will focus on the most common and most popular ones. From fallacies of consistency to relevance to adequacy and more, we will examine and learn how to spot various fallacies in the arguments of others and in our own reasoning.

In part 2, "The Best Damn Pains in the Ass in History," we briefly look at the methods of both Socrates and the ancient Skeptics in chapter 7. Each developed a technique for demonstrating the shortcomings of the ways in which people answered the Big Five. We examine these techniques and consider how they may be applied to questions in our own lives. We currently see use of the Socratic method by fake reporters on *The Daily Show with Jon Stewart* and *The Colbert Report* through their use of satirical comedy. This method involves an initial agreement with the person with whom you are having a discussion. Socrates referred to this as "feigning ignorance" or pretending you have no idea what the person wants you to believe but agreeing with the individual while he or she explains the position held. The next step is to ask questions that lead the person to violate criteria in reasoning and logic, thereby revealing contradictions or inconsistencies in his or her beliefs. By asking the right sorts of questions, you will be able to reveal problems inherent in the person's reasoning. In so doing, you will be able to walk people through their beliefs until they arrive at points of controversy, confrontation, conflict, frustration, ambivalence, and confusion. At this point, there is no turning back. They will either dig in their heels and abandon any rules of reason and argumentation and guard their beliefs in the face of inconsistency or contradiction, or they will recognize some of the shortcomings of their beliefs and appreciate the clarity you have brought to the conversation. Either way, by being a really good pain in the ass you will be empowered with the tools that can make you a more responsible and critical thinker.

In part 3, "Answering the Big Five," we will apply our critical-thinking tools as well as the Socratic and Skeptical methods as we examine the ways in which the Big Five can be answered. Generally, we can respond to these questions in any of four ways:

1. We can respond naturally (or through science and reason).
2. We can respond supernaturally (or through religion or spirituality and faith).
3. We can respond using a combination of natural and supernatural answers.
4. We can choose not to respond at all.

To demonstrate a good contrast, I present answers to the Big Five strictly from the natural and supernatural sides. In chapter 8, we consider the first question: "What can I know?" Based on our recently acquired critical-thinking tools, our first task in becoming a really good pain in the ass is to clean our own houses and make sure we are not guilty of the same types of claims as those we wish to constructively criticize. To do this, we start with an honest understanding of the limitations of what we can claim to know with absolute certainty. These tools of empowerment will reveal to you a clearer understanding of the types of beliefs people have. In this way, we can distinguish beliefs that refer to everyday matters—for example, "Does this dress make me look fat?" or "Do you think I'm a good lover?"—from beliefs that some claim to know with absolute certainty, like "Does God exist?" or "What is the meaning of life?" We need to apply our tools to seriously consider what counts as evidence or criteria for both natural and supernatural responses to the Big Five. For example, if I were to say, "I like the smell of carnations," you would expect to be given far less evidence for this claim than if I were to say something like this: "When you die, an immaterial part of you survives and is either eternally rewarded or punished in an afterlife." The two statements differ drastically in the way in which support can be provided and an appeal to specific criteria to measure their truth can be determined. All our beliefs about the Big Five require *assumptions* that the criteria we use to justify our beliefs are acceptable or warranted. So we need to look at ourselves and consider very carefully how we think about things. For this reason question 1—"What can I know?"—is the most important of the Big Five and needs to be considered first. It sets the groundwork for the other four. That question 1 is our foundation becomes evident when we realize that in answering questions 2 through 5 we are making claims to knowledge. And we need to be clear on what counts as knowledge before we can start providing answers to these four remaining questions. When you know what is behind a person's beliefs by understanding the criteria to which they appeal, you are in a better position to understand whether you should accept what he or she believes and how you can criticize these beliefs based on your tools of empowerment. So the criteria used for natural answers to the Big Five

Fig. 1.
Reality Measuring Stick.
Image created by
Sarah Sienna.

differ considerably from those at the supernatural level. As you will see, it is much more difficult to justify beliefs on the supernatural side because we cannot attain as much agreement regarding criteria to measure the truth of those beliefs. In other words, we do not possess a Reality Measuring Stick (see fig. 1). If we had such a device, there might be far less disagreement (and perhaps bloodshed) in the world.

So again, I must warn you, when you demonstrate the shortcomings of someone's beliefs, he or she may not like what you have to say. That person may think of you as a bit of a troublemaker, a gadfly, or a pain in the ass. Our first task then, is to clean house and make sure we are aware of what our shortcomings to knowledge are. This awareness will give us a better perspective on how all of us are equally humble in this regard. The main lesson in examining question 1 is to admit that we really don't possess absolute certainty about Reality. In this regard, Jack Nicholson's character in *A Few Good Men* was right: many people can't handle the truth—and they may be quite angry when you demonstrate this to them. So be forewarned.

In chapter 9, we consider the question "Why am I here?" Again, this can be answered in either a natural or a supernatural way. Some people believe that they are here because of a special creator. Others maintain that they are here due to accidental conditions that have led to the gradual development of life and the blind and apparently meaningless processes of evolution. No matter which way this question is answered, it will have a profound effect on how we may answer many questions in life, including the next question.

In chapter 10, we look at the nature of humanity. What defines us as human beings? Who are we? What are we? Some people believe us to be just another species of mammal. Others believe we are distinct and specially created. Some believe we possess souls or spirits that survive bodily death. So we need to ask the basis of belief of a person who maintains that we have been specially created, because the answer can lead to many different ways of understanding who apparently created us and what we are. In this chapter, we ask some questions that might make some readers uncomfortable. But this discomfort will be due to a lack of reflection and introspection on their part. Using the Skeptical and Socratic methods and applying the tools of the trade will reveal the shortcomings of those who make extraordinary claims without providing sufficient extraordinary evidence.

In chapter 11, when we consider the question "How should I behave?" we are talking about ethics. Just as we assume that there are better and worse ways for understanding ourselves and the universe, so too do we assume that there are better and worse ways of behaving toward ourselves, one another, and other species on this planet. If you answer this question on a supernatural level and believe that you are on Earth to do God's bidding, your behavior might be guided by a set of doctrines laid out in a particular religious or spiritual source. If you answer on the natural side, you may maintain that how we should behave is something we need to decide for ourselves; we have to come up with the rules for determining good and bad or right and wrong actions. Either way, the importance of how we answer this question cannot be overstated, as it clearly demonstrates the connection to how we answer the other four questions. If *what* we believe determines, in some significant ways, *how* we act, then we really need to understand how people can justify their behavior based on poor or specious reasoning and argumentation. In its worst form, some can feel justified in harming others in the name of their answers to the other four questions. We simply have to watch the evening news to see what a far-reaching effect this type of thinking can have on the lives of others.

In chapter 12, we tackle the final question of the Big Five: "What is to come of me?" How we answer this question depends on whether we interpret this to mean while one is living or after one has died. Some believe that what happens to us while alive depends on the choices we make and that our choices are simply the product of blind chance and luck. Others believe that a supernatural force (or forces) affects events in our lives through the use of miracles, divine intervention, and so on. In reference to the idea of an afterlife, obviously nobody knows for sure what happens after we die. But we are fairly certain that death is going to happen whether or not we like it. The majority of people on this planet believe in an afterlife. Some believe it so strongly that it affects the way in which they behave toward others. Numerous television series center around premises related to the afterlife: shows about so-called mediums talk to the deceased relatives and friends of audience members, ghost hunters who explore allegedly haunted buildings, angels sent through divine providence, and so on. Contemporary music and videos regularly reference the afterlife. And comments about the hereafter, filled with longing and hope, appear daily in obituaries. But what if there were no afterlife? How might this affect the way we answer the other four questions? We will take a very sobering look at this last question of the Big Five. And some may not like what they find.

I designed this book to equip you with some very powerful tools for reasoning and argumentation. You will also gain insight into two of the greatest methods for argumentative discourse, which stem from Socrates and the ancient Skeptics. Combined, this knowledge will provide the means by which to consider where you stand on answering the Big Five. From there, you will be empowered with the ability to understand your own beliefs and thoughts more clearly and to cross-examine those of others more effectively. Most of all, I am trying to accomplish what may not be possible: I want to be fair in presenting both the natural and supernatural responses to the Big Five. But what happens more often than not is that the more fair you try to be, the less your efforts will be appreciated by those who neither value nor play by the rules of fairness. And this is because some of us, for reasons we will examine shortly, can handle only so much fairness.

I hope you enjoy the book.

CdC
Guelph, ON

PART 1

THE TOOLS OF THE TRADE

THE ABCs (AND DEFs) OF CRITICAL THINKING

CHAPTER 1

A IS FOR ARGUMENT

What comes to mind when you think of the word *argument*? Do you think about images or sounds of people arguing or angrily yelling at one another? Does the term conjure up images of individuals embroiled in heated screaming matches? Or do you think of Monty Python sketches? In a now-famous skit shown in an episode of *Monty Python's Flying Circus*, Michael Palin looks through the doorway of an office and asks John Cleese the question: "Is this the right room for an argument?" Cleese responds, "I've told you once." Palin says, "No, you haven't." Cleese: "Yes, I have." Palin: "When?" Cleese: "Just now." Palin: "No, you didn't." Cleese: "Yes, I did." And so on. If we came across such people, we might think they were arguing or engaged in a dispute and could not come to an agreement. But neither is presenting an argument at all. In fact, all they are doing is disagreeing by contradicting each other's assertions without putting forth reasons that support either side— something Palin points out during their bickering, to which, of course, Cleese simply responds: "Yes, I did."

When it comes to critical thinking, an argument is actually a good thing. An argument is the way you put together or structure your ideas, opinions, or beliefs so that people will better understand what it is you're trying to say. People may not agree with what you have to say, but if you phrase your ideas in the form of arguments, you will stand a far greater chance of being understood. If others do the same, you will have a greater likelihood of understanding why they believe or think or have a certain opinion about a particular topic. So when you hear the term *argument* in critical thinking, think about the *structure* of your ideas. You will learn to structure your ideas so that they are in the form of arguments, and you will stand a far greater likelihood of being understood.

So what is an argument? An argument is made up of two things: the point you believe and the reasons why you believe it. Therefore, any and all arguments must have a main point and reasons that support it. In informal logic, critical thinking, and reasoning and argumentation, these two parts of an argument are called: the *conclusion* and the *premises*. To have an argument, you need at least one premise and one conclusion:

$$\text{Premise(s) + Conclusion = Argument}$$

Your conclusion is the point you wish to make, for example, George W. Bush was the greatest president in US history; the New York Yankees are the greatest team in all of baseball; abortion should be legal; capital punishment should be abolished, and so on. Whatever your opinions, beliefs, ideas, or understandings, you need to realize that unless you can formulate them into arguments, you have nothing more than unjustified opinions. Avoid being caught in such a circumstance because it demonstrates weakness in your ability to focus your thoughts and articulate or discuss your ideas in an intelligent manner.

WHY AN ARGUMENT IS LIKE A HOUSE

When it comes to arguments, you need to think of a house (see fig. 1.1). A house is generally made up of three basic parts: the roof, the walls, and the foundation. This is similar to the structure of all arguments. For all arguments have a roof (the conclusion), walls (your premises), and a foundation (your assumptions).

For your roof to be secured safely over your head, you need to make sure your walls are sturdy; and for your walls to be sturdy, your foundation must be solid. The same is true for your ideas when you place them into the form of arguments. The stronger your foundation or assumptions, the

Fig. 1.1. Argument as House.
Image created by Sarah Sienna.

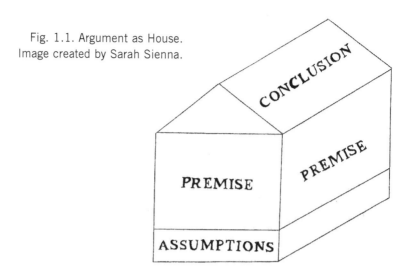

greater the support provided to your walls or premises/reasons to help maintain your roof or conclusion. The stronger your house is, the more difficult it is to knock down and the better it can weather an attack and stand against the tremors of criticism to which all arguments are prone. You want to make sure that your arguments are sound and strong, and I'm going to show you how to do this in a number of easy-to-follow steps. Let's look at the following example:

Suppose John says, "I think Lady Gaga is a great performer because she attended NYU's Tisch School of the Arts, she pushes the boundaries of societal norms, and she brings vitality to the pop music scene."

What is the overall point that John is trying to make? It can be found in the first sentence: Lady Gaga is a great performer (see fig. 1.2).

When considering the structure of John's argument, whether you agree or disagree with his conclusion is beside the point. How is John's argument like a house? We now know what John's roof is. But why does he believe this? John has provided three reasons or premises that act as supports to his conclusion:

Fig. 1.2. Lady Gaga.
Image created by
Vanessa Tignanelli.

1. Lady Gaga attended NYU's Tisch School of the Arts.
2. She pushes the boundaries of societal norms.
3. She brings vitality to the pop music scene.

Each one of these premises has underlying foundations or assumptions. To what degree these assumptions support the premises requires us to do some homework. What does the first premise, that she attended NYU's Tisch School of the Arts, assume? It assumes that the school is highly regarded or recognized and that those who attend it are fairly talented individuals who wish to become more accomplished actors, dancers, musicians, producers, and so forth. We are to accept, then, that Stefani Germanotta, years before she took her stage name, Lady Gaga, was talented enough in a number of areas that deal with musical and theatrical performance art to be accepted into a fairly prestigious university. Such a history means that the school will be more exclusive and difficult to get into; its programs will be more demanding, with highly specialized and qualified instructors; and it has gained a reputation for producing talented individuals. These assumptions are implied as being good criteria by which to measure the talent of individuals who attend such a school. This in no way guarantees that one will like the music of Lady Gaga; it is merely one premise that states a reason why John believes she is a good performer. The second wall, or premise, that supports John's conclusion is that Lady Gaga pushes the boundaries of societal norms. Is this a satisfactory criterion for measuring the greatness of a performer? Sometimes yes, sometimes no. What are the assumptions behind John's premise? John believes pushing societal norms does, in some ways, contribute to making a person a great performer. In and of itself, pushing societal norms does not guarantee this. For example, I could push societal norms by torturing kittens or walking naked in public. But such acts are simply cruel and unappealing and in no way guarantee that my performance would be great. So pushing societal norms, by itself, is not enough to guarantee that one is a great performer. In terms of Lady Gaga's pushing of societal norms, however, her elaborate costumes, original lyrics, and unpredictable on- and off-stage behavior may add to her status as a pop icon. But by itself, pushing societal norms is not a strong premise to support John's conclusion. His third premise, that Lady Gaga brings vitality to the pop music scene is apparently true. But this would depend to some degree on what John means by "vitality." John's underlying assumption here is that bringing vitality to the pop music scene is a good thing. For the most part, we could agree. After all, Lady Gaga does turn heads with her on- and off-stage antics and behavior. So John's first premise seems to be strong; his second premise is his weakest but could become stronger with further support; and his third premise could be considered acceptable. This is a fairly simple argument. That means that the premises are fairly straightforward and lead directly to the conclusion. However, once we ask John about his underlying assumptions, we will see a much more complex argument with many more premises (or walls) added, which will help support his overall conclusion. Remember, we do not have to agree with a person's argument for it to be sound and well structured. Simple disagreement does not, by itself, bring down an argument. (Cleese: "Yes, it does." Palin:

"Oh, shut up!") To dismantle an argument requires careful consideration and critical analysis.

A is for Argument. And when you need to put your ideas into a coherent format, think of a house.

DEDUCTIVE AND INDUCTIVE REASONING

In everyday reasoning and discussion, we generally use two types of argumentation: *deductive* and *inductive*. These forms of reasoning give us two unique types of arguments. Your first experience with deductive reasoning may have come from reading Sherlock Holmes novels, watching *CSI*, *Law & Order*, or *House*, or even playing a classic board game like *Clue* (see fig. 1.3).

Deductive reasoning involves coming to conclusions after looking at information or evidence in a certain way and seeing specific patterns within the evidence that lead inevitably to a conclusion ("Colonel Mustard did it with a lead pipe in the library!"). If you have ever played *Clue*,

Fig. 1.3. Sherlock Holmes.
Image created by Vanessa Tignanelli.

you know that once the murder has been solved, it cannot be otherwise. So it's not as though it was Colonel Mustard, but it really didn't take place in the library, and the victim actually slipped and hit his head. When the murder is solved, it *has* to be a specific character, *with* a particular object, *in* a particular room. In fact, it *cannot* be otherwise. This is because the conclusion (in this case, the murderer) is *guaranteed* by the premises (or evidence) that led to it. Deductive reasoning guarantees the conclusion of an argument. In other words, the conclusion must necessarily follow from the premises. Using this type of reasoning is a very powerful tool because it is impossible for the conclusion *not* to follow from the premises. The conclusion is a lock, a done deal, a slam dunk, if you will. Consider the following example:

> At a city meeting, the master of ceremonies, Father Flanagan, was informed that the guest of honor, Senator Robert Jones, would be arriving late. To kill time, so to speak, the good father began telling a story of how, when he became a priest, his very first confession was from a man who confessed to murdering his wife for the insurance money and making it look like an accident. Father Flanagan admitted that he was somewhat overwhelmed by the magnitude of this, his first confession. Shortly thereafter, Senator Jones arrived and, after apologizing for his tardiness, decided to lighten things up a bit by letting the crowd in on a little secret: "Father Flanagan does not know this," said Senator Jones, "but I was his very first confession."

What conclusion can be drawn from these premises? Is it that Senator Jones killed his wife and made it look like an accident? We just saw how, in deductive reasoning, if the premises of an argument are true, the conclusion must be true as well. This is called *logical validity*. What we know about Father Flanagan and Senator Jones is that *if* what the priest says is true and *if* what the senator says is true, *then* we *must* conclude that Robert Jones murdered his wife. The conclusion is *guaranteed* by the truth of the premises. There could be exceptions to this, of course. Senator Jones may have been lying in the confessional in order to give the priest a difficult first confession. Or Father Flanagan may have misremembered the day's events, and the murderer was actually his third confession. But if we do some investigating and find out that, indeed, Senator Jones's wife died at some time before the confession, and Senator Jones did receive a large settlement from his insurance company, the physical evidence could support the logical evidence given by both Father Flanagan and Senator Jones—and witnessed by a room full of people. We can see how deductive reasoning works so well in this example because of a man who devoted much of his life to developing proper forms of deductive arguments: Aristotle.

A BIT OF HISTORY ON DEDUCTION

Back in the days of the ancient Greek philosophers (around 2,300 years ago), Aristotle was concerned with the way in which people were arguing about various ideas (see fig. 1.4).

Some people—the Sophists—would brag that they could make the worse case sound the better using tricks of rhetoric, argumentation, and reasoning to bamboozle, confuse, or otherwise hoodwink people into

Fig. 1.4. Aristotle.
Image created by Vanessa Tignanelli.

believing what they had to say. Today, we call such people lawyers or politicians. I'm just kidding. Or maybe I'm not.

In any case, Aristotle decided it was time to develop a rigorous methodology to logic so that people would be able to empower themselves with these tools, and then they would know when others were trying to mislead them. So he set out a number of argumentative structures that are called *syllogisms*. These syllogisms are universal patterns of deductive logic, and any argument that fits into one of these patterns will possess a conclusion guaranteed by the premises which precede or support it. We will look at some of these patterns set forth by Aristotle and others because they are very important to the way in which we put together our ideas and talk about important issues in the world.

Deductive reasoning allows us to know that a conclusion *must* follow from the premises. As in the game of *Clue*, it's not as though the conclusion might or could or possibly will follow from the premises. In deductive arguments, the conclusion definitely, absolutely follows from the premises. This is where things get interesting, because Aristotle's treatment of deductive logic is based on the very structure of the argument itself. So at this point, content is secondary. Usually, when we have discussions with people, it is the content we are most interested in, for example, whether we are for or against abortion, capital punishment, or same-sex marriage. Aristotle begins instead with the structure of an argument and is interested with the formal or structural relationships between the premises and the conclusion. So we're going to look at a number of the structures or forms of arguments that Aristotle developed. Any argument or part of an argument that can be put into one of these forms is considered acceptable because it satisfies specific conditions that guarantee logical validity—meaning that the conclusion *must* follow from the preceding premises.

We have been tossing around the idea of the conclusion being guaranteed by the premises, but what does this really mean? Generally speaking, it's very similar to arithmetic or mathematics. If you multiply the number 7 by the number 5, you will correctly arrive at the answer: 35. But this is true only if you know what 7 means, if you know what 5 means, if you know the principles behind multiplication, and if you know what "=" means. If you do, then you will realize that all these symbols taken together produce the inevitable conclusion 35. In logic, deductive reasoning guarantees the conclusion from the premises in much the same way as the answer in a mathematical equation is guaranteed.

FORMS OF DEDUCTIVE ARGUMENTS (VALID)

You may not always be able to structure your arguments into these types of forms, but if various parts of your arguments take on these forms, then at least you will know that your arguments (or parts of them) are deductively valid. The *content* of arguments is something we consider later on when we look at evidence and fallacies. But for right now, let's stay focused on the *structure* of arguments.

Modus Ponens (Affirming the Antecedent)

(1) If A, then B.	(1) If you build it, he will come.
(2) A.	(2) You build it.
Therefore, B.	Therefore, he will come.

This argument pattern takes on the form of a conditional, that is, "if, then." In other words, if A is going to occur, then B is going to occur. A just occurred. So the conclusion can be made that B is going to occur. And this is because the first premise comes in the form of a conditional statement where the first part of the conditional (A) is called the *antecedent* (think antipasto before the meal, ante up before betting in cards); the Latin term *ante* just means "before." So the end of the conditional (B) is called the *consequent*. In the case of *modus ponens*, once we know the conditional (If A, then B) and we *affirm the antecedent* (A), it follows that the conclusion (B) must be the consequent. When the structure is valid and the premises are true, we classify an argument as being *sound*. This argument is sound both because it is logically valid and because the content happens to be true. This is the highest praise an argument can achieve. I am at a loss to understand why the term has yet to be picked up by the rap and hip-hop communities as a term that could represent high praise: "That guy is sound!" or "Did you check out that ride? Sound!" So sound reasoning is the highest praise any argument can receive. The interesting thing about logical validity is that you can still have a valid argument with false components. For example, let's look at our modus ponens form:

(1) If A, then B.
(2) A.
      Therefore B.

We can substitute anything in place of A and B and, as long as the argument has this form, it is logically valid:

(1) If I am a man, then I am a woman.
(2) I am a man.
      Therefore, I am a woman.

In terms of content, this argument is absurd. However, it is *logically* valid. Logical validity alone does not guarantee that we should accept a person's argument. It guarantees only that the structure of the argument is acceptable. In the absurd example just provided, the conclusion would have to follow the two prior premises; there is no other alternative but to arrive at this conclusion. The conclusion cannot be otherwise because the very structure of the argument itself guarantees it. But the content is lacking considerably and therefore it cannot be considered a sound argument. Remember, deductive arguments deal only with the form of an argument. Let's take a look at a few more.

Modus Tollens (Denying the Consequent)

(1) If A, then B.	(1) If you ate peanuts, you would have trouble breathing.
(2) Not-B.	(2) You are not having trouble breathing.
Therefore, not-A.	Therefore, you must not have eaten peanuts.

In this example, the consequent, B, is being denied after the conditional "If A, then B." In this example, we were told that if A occurs, B will occur. But we learn that B did not occur. So it follows that A could not have occurred. Now, imagine you're waiting at a bus stop and someone says, "If the bus is on time, it should be here in two minutes." When five minutes has gone by and the bus has not arrived (denying the consequent), you can now validly claim that the bus is not on time. This is just one example of how we use deductive reasoning in everyday situations.

Disjunctive Argument

(1) Either A or B.	(1) Either I should watch *Ellen* or I should watch *The View*.
(2) Not-A.	(2) I am not going to watch *Ellen*.
Therefore, B.	Therefore, I'm going to watch *The View*.

In this case, we are presented with two and only two choices. When presented in this way, when one of the choices is no longer an option, the other becomes the choice. The choice could have just as easily been not-B (not watch *The View*), in which case A (watching *Ellen*) would have been the conclusion. Remember, the reason these forms are deductively valid is because the conclusion must follow from the preceding premises. The form of these arguments guarantees that the conclusion must follow from the premises. Keep in mind that this form of deductive argument works only when there are two—*and only two*—choices. This is known as a genuine disjunct or genuine dichotomy. There are times in life when only two options are available, for example, you have an operation or you don't; you can afford to go on a cruise or you cannot; you are pregnant or you are not; when you die a part of you continues to exist in some way or it does not.

However, it is often the case that people will argue in such a way as to make you believe there are only two options when in fact there are more. If you can imagine a third, fourth, or tenth option, then you know that the disjunct is really a false dichotomy. We examine this fallacy more closely later on, but you see this verbal maneuver often in the speech of politicians: "Either you are with us or you are with the terrorists," "Either we raise taxes or we cut social spending," and so on. Clearly, I can be neither with you nor with the terrorists (a third option); and we could both raise taxes and cut social spending, or we could do neither (third and fourth options).

Hypothetical Argument

(1) If A, then B.	(1) If I pay now, then I'll save.
(2) If B, then C.	(2) If I'll save, then I'll have money later.
Therefore, if A, then C.	Therefore, if I pay now, then I'll have money later.

The way in which this argument structure works is by association. If A occurs, then B will occur; and if B occurs, then C will occur. So it follows that once A occurs, C is eventually going to follow. You could see how often this might apply in everyday situations. One example is in the use of tobacco products, for example, if you continue to smoke, you will have reduced lung capacity. If you have reduced lung capacity, you won't be able to compete as an athlete at a high level. So if you continue to smoke, you won't be able to compete as an athlete at a high level. Or if you are out of an item, you will have to go to the grocery store; and if you have to go to the grocery store, you will need to use the car. So if you are out of an item, you will need to use the car (to get to the grocery store).

Predicate Instantiation

(1) All P_1's are P_2's.   (1) All politicians are liars.
(2) m is a P_1.   (2) Jones is a politician.

Therefore, m is a P_2.   Therefore, Jones is a liar.

In this last valid argument form, we see a reference to two classes of things and acknowledge that if an individual has the property of one class, then it follows that he or she has the property of the other class. This form can be used in so many different ways, and there are plenty of ways in which the content could disagree with the form of the argument. For example, it is generally true that all students who study hard eventually show improvement. But you could study very hard and still not show improvement. But this would not make the claim any less valid; it would simply make it untrue in your case. Never forget that logical validity in deductive arguments deals only with the form of the argument. And the form guarantees that *if* the premises are true, then the conclusion must be true as well. And sometimes, that's an awfully big *if*.

FORMS OF DEDUCTIVE ARGUMENTS (INVALID)

Here are two argument patterns that demonstrate when an argument's form is invalid.

Fallacy of Affirming the Consequent

(1) If A, then B.   (1) If it rains, then I will get wet.
(2) B.   (2) I am wet.

Therefore, A.   Therefore, it rained.

We can see how this structure is invalid because, in our example, we can easily imagine that there are other ways to become wet aside from rain. In this instance, we cannot conclude that just because a person is wet, it was rain that caused it. This is putting the cart before the horse. Remember, the conditional stated that *if* A occurs, *then* B will occur. Just because B happens to have occurred does not mean it was A that caused it. A dozen different things could have caused B to occur. Notice how this structure seems similar to modus ponens. But instead of affirming the antecedent (A), it affirms the consequent (B). In so doing, it "jumps the gun," so to speak. It assumes wrongly that A must be the *only* cause of B, when in fact it may be one of many causes for B.

Fallacy of Denying the Antecedent

(1) If A, then B.	(1) If it is sunny, then I will get tanned.
(2) Not-A.	(2) It is not sunny.
Therefore, not-B.	Therefore, I do not get tanned.

We can see why this is an invalid argument by realizing, as we did in the previous example, that there are other ways achieving the consequent—in this case, there are other ways of getting tanned than having the sun cause it. I could use a tanning bed or one of the wonderful spray-on techniques so commonly used nowadays, and so forth. Remember, the conditional stated: *If A, then* B, which means that *if* A occurs, *then* B will follow. The conditional did not say anything about what would happen if A does not occur. The antecedent (A) is merely one cause for the consequent (B); it's not necessarily the only cause. In denying it, we are not guaranteed that the conclusion (not-B) will follow. The consequent (B) could still occur through other causes.

Keep in mind that the power of deductive reasoning and argumentation lies in the form the arguments take. Any arguments that violate the forms of the five valid arguments listed in this chapter demonstrate errors in reasoning. Aristotle provided us with the means by which to demonstrate these errors to others. To become a really good pain in the ass, you need to know some of the important rules of reasoning and how to apply them. We can show people where and how their reasoning may be flawed by demonstrating how they have violated these formal structures. Deductive reasoning is a powerful tool because, when used properly, you know the conclusion must be guaranteed. Lawyers use this type of reasoning; doctors use it; forensic scientists use it; and so do we use it in our everyday lives.

VALIDITY/INVALIDITY AND INTUITIVE INSIGHT

Although there are formal methods for determining the validity of specific arguments, we are not going to examine them here because you will probably never use them. Instead, we are going to use an informal method. To use this method properly, you must develop the capacity to intuitively "see" how the conclusions must either deductively follow from the premises or not. As we saw earlier, like arithmetic, once you understand what the symbols 12, 144, ×, and = are, you can then "see" that $12 \times 12 = 144$. The same structure holds in deductive argument patterns as well. However, the means by which to check formal validity do differ somewhat from mathematics. In determining validity/invalidity we must remember that to be valid it is impossible for an argument to have true premises and a false conclusion, so we can try to construct scenarios in which there are particular circumstances whereby *if* the premises were true, the conclusion *could* be false. And if we can establish such a case or scenario, then we can conclude that the argument is not valid.

INDUCTIVE REASONING

Unlike deductive reasoning, with inductive reasoning we find that our conclusions are not logically or necessarily valid. They are not a lock or a slam dunk. So instead of having the conclusion guaranteed by the supposed truth of the premises and the very structure of the argument, in inductive reasoning, our conclusions are considered to be "warranted" or "more likely" or "more probable." Like deductive reasoning, we use inductive reasoning every day of our lives. It is also the hallmark of scientific reasoning because it is based on what are called *statistical generalizations*. Induction allows us to make generalizations that we can see in the following example: Let's say you read a government poll that claims 85 percent of people in Lincoln, Nebraska, over the age of twenty-five possess a valid driver's license. Shortly thereafter, you meet Tom, who is a thirty-eight-year-old male living in Lincoln, Nebraska. If the source of your information were reliable and accurate, you would then be warranted in your belief that Tom *likely* or *probably* has a valid driver's license. Your inference or conclusion that Tom has a valid driver's license is not certain but is likely. The premises do not guarantee that Tom has a valid driver's license because there is a 15 percent chance that he does not. But if you were to bet on whether Tom did have a valid driver's license, you would probably put your money on the belief that he does indeed possess one. With inductive reasoning, we generalize using statistical probability. In science, as in everyday life, we make observations of behavioral patterns. When those patterns of behavior have a significantly high level of frequency—that is, they occur over and over again—we can make generalizations about them. Here's an example I use often with my students: Take a set of keys and hold them between your thumb and index finger (see fig. 1.5). Hold that hand over a table, and ask someone what will happen when you release the keys from your fingers.

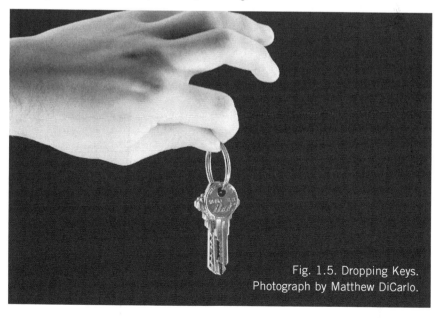

Fig. 1.5. Dropping Keys.
Photograph by Matthew DiCarlo.

More than likely, he or she will say that the keys will fall downward toward the tabletop. It would be odd for someone to say that the keys will hover in midair or that they will rise up in the air. To do so would violate our expectations. We expect the keys to fall because that is the way they have always acted in the past. This frequency of behavioral pattern becomes ingrained in our thinking and allows us to make better sense of the world. In class, I ask individual students what will happen to the keys when I release them from my grip. On most occasions, students say the same thing: they will fall to the podium or desk. Every now and again, though, a student wants to be clever and claims that the keys will not fall downward. To such claims, my response is always the same: "Would you like to make a bet?" For effect, I often wager my house against anything he or she may have of equal or greater value. I never get any takers. And the reason is obvious: though there could be a possibility in which the keys will not behave as we predict, we generally expect them to behave according to previously observed patterns of behavior. The interesting thing about this particular example is that even though it does not provide absolute certainty—for the laws of physics might change in the next ten minutes or so or other factors could cause the keys to behave differently—we can establish universal agreement on the likelihood of the predicted behavioral pattern of the keys. That is, every student in my classes agrees that the keys will drop and would be extremely surprised if they did not. This is one of the reasons why magic shows can be so much fun: Magicians violate our expectations. We know people don't disappear, levitate, reappear, and so on. To do so would be, well, magical. Instead, we know magicians perform sleight-of-hand acts sometimes involving elaborate tricks, optical illusions, and other means for our entertainment. Half the fun of magic shows is trying to figure out exactly how a trick was done. And if you are Internet savvy, you can now find out how most of these tricks are done.[1]

The effect of gravity on keys is a good example to demonstrate why identifying statistical frequency through inductive reasoning has become such a powerful tool in human reasoning. We use it by recognizing a repetition of patterns of behavior. We then generalize that future episodes will be similar. For example, instead of keys, you could generalize and say that the same behavioral pattern will occur when I release a pen or a spoon or any other normally weighted object from my grip. So inductive reasoning works by making specific observations that lead to a generalization. This generalization can then be applied to future similar instances. It does not mean that our conclusions are guaranteed, but that's not really a problem. Understanding the probability of events has served our own and other species very well in the past, and it is likely to continue to do so well into the future. Using inductive reasoning in science allows us to make predictions about future occurrences with considerable accuracy.

A is for Argument. And it is important to remember that an argument takes the form of a house with its conclusion as the roof, its premises as walls, and its assumptions as foundation. We have considered two types of reasoning used in argumentation: deduction and induction. Deductive arguments are the type you would use in solving a murder in the board game *Clue*. Through a series of logical inferences, you arrive at a conclusion that cannot be otherwise. We examined a number of specific forms of valid and invalid arguments. When checking the components or overall structure of our arguments or those of others, it is important to be able to determine if they abide by or fail to follow the structure of some of the syllogisms of Aristotle.

When we considered inductive arguments, we learned that the conclusions are not guaranteed by the premises, but they are warranted. Instead of knowing for sure that a conclusion must necessarily follow from its premises, inductive reasoning provides us with probability or likelihood. It is important to understand the differences between deductive and inductive reasoning because we use both of them every day as tools that provide understanding and stability to our world. Knowing the ways in which these types of reasoning are used empowers us with the ability to identify them as they apply to important issues discussed by us and by others.

CHAPTER 2

B IS FOR BIASES

One of the most important reasons to answer the Big Five in the introduction is that your answers will reveal what you are thinking in terms of these very important questions. How you answered the Big Five can tell you a lot about yourself. You now need to become intimately familiar with your *biases*. A bias is a way in which a person is influenced in order to understand and act on particular types of information. Biases are why we don't allow members of the clergy or parents to testify in court for family members, and with good reason. No matter how violent an offender is, clergy may see a sinner who is ready to repent, and parents may see their children as the charming and darling infants or toddlers they once were. I cannot imagine anyone viewing a young child in a baby carriage and suggesting that he may be cute now but will one day grow up to become a despised serial killer. It is often difficult for parents to give up this image of innocence regardless of how their children turn out. And so it can be very difficult for us to recognize and overcome our biases.

There are several reasons why we need to familiarize ourselves with our biases and to understand their influence on how we see the world, think about it, and act in it. One may argue that a central purpose of psychological counseling is to get us to recognize our own biases as underlying causes for our behaviors. How we eventually come to acquire, revise, and retain opinions, beliefs, and attitudes about issues is the result of a long process of development. From before the time we are born, there are factors that influence the way we see and understand the world. We need to become familiar with these factors to better understand why we now believe the things we do. To illustrate this, take a moment to think about this question: How did the universe begin?

Some readers believe the universe came into existence with a Big Bang (see fig. 2.1). Others will maintain that a supernatural being (a god or gods) created the universe. Some might say that it has always existed and never had a beginning. Still others will not care to answer or even think about this question. Whatever your views are, and no matter how you answer this question (or choose not to), you cannot escape your own biases. Like your answers to the Big Five, how you answer this question will show great insight into your personal biases. For example, were I to respond to this question in my childhood (during the late 1960s and a good part of the 1970s), I most assuredly would have said that God (the Abrahamic or Judeo-Christian God of Catholicism) created the entire universe in six days and rested on the seventh, as stated in the Book of Genesis from the Old Testament, taught in grade school, preached at church, supported by family members, and depicted in various forms of art and literature, as well on television and at the movies. But when I think about this question today, my response is quite different. Upon some simple reflection, I can easily come to recognize what my biases were as a child and what they are now. As a child, I was educated as a Roman Catholic by my par-

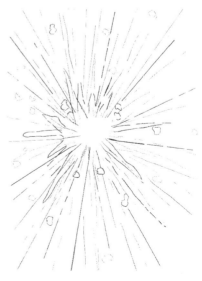

Fig 2.1. The Big Bang.
Image created by Sarah Sienna.

ents, siblings, school, community, and church. I was baptized, had my first communion, was confirmed, and served as an altar boy for five years. I even briefly considered a vocation in the priesthood. It never occurred to me that others might disagree with my view of the origins of the universe. For I knew I was right. Why else would my parents and everyone else I knew or cared about believe the same thing? So it becomes fairly obvious that my Catholic upbringing—presented to me through my family, my education, the media, and my friends—deeply biased my views about the universe's origins. As a child, I had little or no reason to question these views because I trusted my parents, church, school, and community. Upon reaching adolescence and young adulthood, however, I had reason to question some of the ideas behind my religious upbringing. Other influences, including friends, education, the media, and so on, contributed to changes in my views of universal causation.[1]

In this chapter, we will carefully examine the many different types of biases that contribute to how we see and understand the world. Generally speaking, there are two main contributors to bias: biology and culture—or, in other words, nature and nurture. We shall see how these two very important influential factors work not in isolation but in conjunction.

BIASES FROM BIOLOGICAL INFLUENCES

Genetic Influences

From the structure of DNA, cells in our bodies are given instructions on how to produce proteins in order to grow and function in specific ways. If the instructions are interrupted or interfered with, or mutated, then cells may function in unexpected ways that may be harmful or, on rare occasions, beneficial to an organism. In some cases, all it takes is one single gene to alter the health and behavior of an individual. For example, both color blindness and Tay-Sachs disease are caused by single gene mutations. Other gene-related behavioral factors are more complex and difficult to determine but still provide insight into the ways in which biology contributes to our biases. For example, consider attention deficit/hyperactivity disorder (ADHD) and homosexuality. Both seem to have contributing genetic factors, but scientists have not yet identified all the genes that contribute to these behaviors. However, it is currently maintained that although extremely complex, there are indeed at least some underlying genetic components to both ADHD[2] and homosexuality.[3] If this is the case, then we have opened an extremely important window into understanding these aspects of human behavior. Let's consider a couple hypothetical scenarios.

Attention Deficit/ Hyperactive Disorder

Imagine a young boy named Timmy in midwestern America in the 1950s. Now, let's say Timmy has ADHD and that such a genetic propensity causes his behavior to become disruptive in grade school. During the 1950s in the Midwest, Timmy's behavior may well have been viewed as the result of poor parenting, or perhaps Timmy himself would receive the brunt of the blame because he would simply be considered a brat. We can imagine in this scenario attempts by his parents, his teachers, and others to change Timmy's behavior. While at school, he may have been sent to the corner, ridiculed, ostra-

Fig. 2.2. DNA. Image created by Sarah Sienna.

cized, forced to wear a "dunce cap," strapped, given detention, and so on. His parents may have been blamed for his behavior and may also have used similar means of behavior modification in an effort to control him. If Timmy attended a religion-based school, it's possible his behavior would have been considered a result of his inability to follow the rules of his religion. There have been documented cases of exorcism as treatment for ADHD in some children.[4] Although his elders of the time were unaware of it, Timmy's so-called bad behavior may have been in large part influenced by his genes, in conjunction with several other causal factors. Should his behavior have worsened, he may have found himself expelled from school. Should his parents have lost patience with him, he may have found himself less wanted and less appreciated at home. Since Francis Crick and James Watson did not publish the double-helical model of DNA until 1953, it is likely that Timmy's behavior would have been diagnosed as a social problem rather than as a biological condition.[5] But what we need to understand is that Timmy's body has been in some ways hardwired or predisposed to behave in a particular way. It may be very difficult for him to overcome this condition regardless of the moral or cultural incentives for doing so.

The Gay Gene?

History cannot account for the number of homosexuals who suffered horrible atrocities throughout the millennia simply for being gay. Compelling evidence currently suggests that a strong genetic component instills a propensity for homosexuality. No longer considered a "life choice," homosexuality may be as genetically based as heterosexuality. If this is the case, we need to seriously reflect on the capacity for choice that any person has in his or her sexual preference. This would make matters of sexuality amoral—that is, morality simply does not enter into the discussion. If some people believe homosexuals should choose heterosexual activities, it implies that they *can* do so. But if the hardwiring predispositions for human behavior make such choices impossible, do we not have to reevaluate how we view free choice and morality in this regard? There is at least some reason to believe that such a biological understanding of some aspects of human behavior scares the heck out of a lot of people. For example, homophobes *want* to be able to morally blame homosexuals for their choices. But it just may be the case that choice does not enter into the debate. Did I choose to be heterosexual? No. I just am. It's not as though as an adolescent boy I considered my options: "Let's see. There are women, men, goats, sheep, and various inanimate objects.... I'll choose women!" Current biological evidence indicates that sexual preference is not really a matter of morality or choice at all. The same is true for ADHD and many other genetic propensities to which we humans are prone.

Having said this, it is important to remember that genes do not simply work in isolation when it comes to human behavior. A complex interaction takes place between any given set of genes (referred to as a *genotype*) and the way in which they produce an organism (referred to as a *phenotype*) and the interplay each has with a given environment. The exciting new field of epigenetics is examining the complex interplay between gene suppression and activation within an environmental context. In some cases, having a single gene will produce a specific effect regardless of the environmental constraints (e.g., cystic fibrosis, Huntington's disease, muscular dystrophy). However, there are cases where the influences of environmental conditions affect genetic behavior. As Matt Ridley says,

> Genes are not puppet masters or blueprints. Nor are they just the carriers of heredity. They are active during life; they switch each other on and off; they respond to the environment. They may direct the construction of the body and brain in the womb, but then they set about dismantling and rebuilding what they have made almost at once—in response to experience. They are both cause and consequence of our actions.[6]

So it is important to keep in mind the complex interplay of component parts that makes up our particular species and influences the ways in which information is attained, revised, and acted upon. We looked at only two genetic predispositions—ADHD and homosexuality—which commonly bias the behavior of millions of people every day. But scientists are uncovering dozens of genetic pathways and epigenetic processes that give us good reason to consider how much influence these biological factors have in terms of our current biases. We shall consider in greater detail some of the aspects and influences of epigenetics later on in part 3.

Neuropsychological Influences

It would be an oversight if we did not consider in what ways brain chemistry (or neuropsychology) plays a part in how we see the world. Brain science is still very much in its infancy. But what neurologists, psychologists, and cognitive scientists do know comes usually, but not always, from a series of studies of people with brain disorders. From time to time, we read in a newspaper, see on television, or hear on the radio a report about someone who jumps from a bridge or a building or jumps in front of a subway train with a child in his or her arms.[7] After one of these events, I can recall hearing numerous listeners who had phoned in to comment on a radio talk show: The majority of callers morally blamed these adults for taking their children's lives. Psychological disorders such as depression, schizophrenia, and bipolar disorder can have devastating effects on individuals and their families. To what extent do we find people afflicted with such illnesses morally accountable for taking their own lives, along with those of their children? What makes someone decide to commit suicide with a child in his or her arms? It's not the type of thing one simply does on a whim. I think we can state with considerable confidence that the minds of those who suffer from mental illness are biased in ways that make specific actions beyond their control.

But at what point does someone lose control over the ability to think rationally? When does sanity slip away to the point where an individual is no longer to be considered morally and legally responsible for his or her actions? And how would we make such a determination? The Court of Appeal for Ontario is currently reconsidering the plea of infanticide by mothers who kill their infant children. *Infanticide* is defined as an act of homicide in which a woman willfully kills her newborn child when her mind is disturbed as a result of childbirth or lactation. The maximum sentence for such a crime is five years, but for first-degree murder it is twenty-five years. In one case, a woman in my hometown of Guelph, Ontario, killed two of her own children four years apart—the first when she was sixteen and the second when she was twenty. The prosecution believes both cases should be considered murder and not infanticide because the woman was not suffering from postpartum depression, nor did she demonstrate any other signs of mental illness.[8] There seems to be a very fine line in terms of when we are in control of our neuropsychological biases and when they are in control of us.

There are also less drastic but still compelling examples of the ways our neurochemistry biases how we understand and act in the world. For example, if someone happens to possess a gene that diminishes the amount of the neurotransmitter serotonin in the brain, he or she may act extremely impulsively under certain conditions.[9] Still others have the misfortune of possessing genes that increase neural chemistry reactions, which foster a greater likelihood for addiction.[10] So for me to walk into a bar and order an orange juice (because I don't like the taste of alcohol and never have) shows little restraint and moral value in comparison to any alcoholic who does the same thing. We are biologically biased quite differently. The alcoholic will have a great desire to consume alcohol, while I do not. He has a much more difficult time controlling his desires and urges for alcohol than I ever will. My abstinence is hardly an act worthy of moral praise, especially in comparison to his.

This does not mean that we can never modify our behavior. All is not so bleak or grim. Recent studies in neuroplasticity indicate that the brain has the capacity to rewire itself so the neural signals do not continue to follow the same patterns that cause human behavior to follow similar patterns. People like Norman Doidge have commented that those who suffer from obsessive-compulsive disorder (OCD) can alter the ways their brains are accustomed to working.[11] Instead of seeing the brain as fixed and static, Doidge and many others now see the brain as plastic or somewhat more flexible. Through specific training techniques, people have been able to overcome post-traumatic stress disorder (PTSD) and OCD, and there has even been some success in the treatment of schizophrenia using neural recircuitry techniques. These represent only a few of the many ways in which we can learn how such neuropsychological factors can deeply bias, influence, and affect our beliefs and actions.

Emotions

I cannot stress how important it is for us to realize the crucial role emotions have played and continue to play in our lives in biasing our beliefs and actions. Broadly defined, emotions are affective states that can motivate human behavior. There are basic human emotional states, such as fear, anger, sorrow, joy, disgust, anticipation, surprise, and acceptance.[12] But there are more subtle variations of these, such as terror or phobia, rage, sadness, grief, depression, happiness, gladness, gratitude, and so on.[13] These states are cross-culturally universal. That is, regardless of where we find ourselves in the world, we can all recognize when someone is happy, sad, angry, afraid, surprised, and so forth. But what causes emotional states? And why are we humans so much at the mercy of them? For example, there have been numerous cases of jealous rage ending in bitter hatred, stalking, pain, suffering, and even death. The perpetrators are sometimes calm, levelheaded, highly educated people. What is actually going on in our bodies when emotional states interfere with rational states?

Antonio Damasio, a neurologist and director of USC's Brain and Creativity Institute, has demonstrated how important emotions are to decision-making situations. In one experiment, two groups of individuals were asked to participate in a gambling task where the objective was to maximize profit on a loan of play money. Each participant was asked to select one hundred cards, one at a time, from four different decks. Two of the decks provided larger payoffs (e.g., $100), and two provided smaller payoffs (e.g., $50). The deck that provided larger payoffs also provided larger penalties at unpredictable intervals. Those subjects who chose from the higher-reward decks lost, on average, $250, with every ten cards chosen, while those choosing cards from the lower-reward decks gained an average of $250 with every ten cards chosen. One of the groups participating in the experiment had lesions to the ventromedial prefrontal cortex of the brain. Such people have normal intellectual function but lack the ability to use emotions in making decisions. The other group consisted of so-called normal people—those whose brains were unaffected by any such legions. Since there was no way for any of the participants to accurately calculate which decks were riskier during the experiment, they had to rely on their "gut" feelings in order to avoid losing money. The brain-lesion group could not use emotions in their decision making and subsequently lost significantly more money than the normal group.

Looked at this way, it would appear that human emotions are a product of millions of years of evolution during which our ancestors were placed in situations requiring them to behave and react in specific ways. At times, human emotions provide us with useful feedback, for example, fear induces in us avoidance of unfamiliar territory that could be harmful. So it is in our best interest to avoid or stay away from such situations. At other times, human emotions get in the way of more levelheaded thinking, for example, voting for a candidate because the person has the same first name as your mother or father. The interactions between our thinking or rational selves and our emotional selves generate conflicting beliefs, attitudes, and behavior. We need to be attentive to the fact that we are a highly emotional species.

Discussing issues that we find emotionally charged creates an environment in which controlling our biases becomes extremely difficult. If you are passionate about a particular topic—say, pro-life or pro-choice in the abortion debate—it may become very difficult to consider what the other side has to say. But it is very important to look in a mirror and consider why you are so passionate about this particular issue (see fig. 2.3). What has led you to become so convinced of your view, and why are you less willing or even unwilling to consider what the other side has to say? You can see this type of bias play out clearly at sporting events. When fans[14] are cheering for their team, and a player from the other side makes a great play, it is often very difficult for the opposing team's fans to acknowledge this feat. I have witnessed generally mild-mannered friends who will abandon reason, fairness, and sportsmanship in an effort to win at a particular recreational sport. Many of us have witnessed those moms

Fig. 2.3. Self-Reflection.
Photograph by Matthew DiCarlo.

and dads who become quite emotionally absorbed when watching their kids play sports. The values of fun, sportsmanship, and teamwork often become eclipsed by the desire to be better and win a competition.

Never forget that we were emotional beings long before we became so-called rational beings. Emotions deal with specific areas within the brain that often override our abilities to think rationally. For example, consider the concept of the fight-or-flight response—a psychological and physiological reaction to a perceived threat that causes a stressful reaction in us. Robert Sapolsky has done considerable work in the study of stress in humans and other primates.[15] He has found that in an instant, the emotional center or limbic part of the brain will transfer information interpreted as a perceived threat to send out messages to the endocrine system. Our heart rate and blood pressure increase significantly, pumping more oxygen into our lungs; our glucose blood levels will rise; and our bodies will start converting sugar to energy. The flow of our blood will be more heavily concentrated in our digestive tract and muscles. In the language of hockey, this is called "dropping the gloves" (see fig. 2.4). And thanks to the long-running television series *Seinfeld*, this reaction is also referred to as "go time."

Our nervous system (sympathetic) will quickly produce a chemical called epinephrine (the same chemical found in the EpiPen® tool that adults and kids with severe allergies use to control an attack), which will, in turn, activate our adrenal glands, causing an adrenaline rush. All these reactions occur within a split second. They prepare our bodies to challenge a perceived threat or to flee from it. When we come into contact with information that triggers a fearlike response, such as a phobia, there

Fig. 2.4. Hockey Fight: Dropping the Gloves.
Image created by Vanessa Tignanelli.

will be an almost immediate response within us to try to deal with it; this usually brings about a fight-or-flight response. An example I sometimes use in class to demonstrate how quickly this reaction occurs is telling my students that I brought a show-and-tell item with me: my son's pet tarantula, Harry. Given that my classes can be quite large, I know ahead of time that the odds of several students being arachnophobic (having a fear of spiders) is going to be fairly high. I pretend to reach into my briefcase for a jar containing Harry. Of course, there is no actual spider (my son, Matthew, also has a considerable fear of them), and I quickly let them know; but before letting them in on this I sometimes pretend that Harry has escaped from my briefcase. Simply by mentioning the spider and offering to hand him around to the class is enough to cause arachnophobes to squirm in their seats (see fig. 2.5).

Of course, I play this game with my students for only a very short time. Because regardless of how intelligent we may be, a phobia can reduce us to irrational, illogical people whose behaviors are modified considerably by this fear. Emotional fears demonstrate very quickly how our

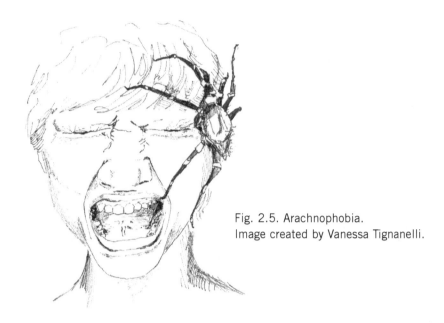

Fig. 2.5. Arachnophobia.
Image created by Vanessa Tignanelli.

rational brains can be bypassed in ways beyond our control. Of course, there are ways in which we can overcome our irrational fears, but this requires a considerable amount of commitment and time. The point to note here is how powerful our emotions can be in terms of biasing our thoughts and actions—and phobias are an excellent illustration of this.

Sex, Health, and Biological Equilibrium

Much of the literature on sexuality defines us humans on a spectrum from male to female. For the most part, when speaking of averages in biology—including human biology—most of our species are definitively male or female. But there are those who are less clearly defined in this regard. There are transgendered people who defy such strict categorization. Many of these people unfortunately can face serious identity problems and social backlash due to ignorance and misunderstanding. To be clear, in this section, I concentrate my treatment of sexual biases predominantly on either ends of the spectrum of male and female.

At the risk of receiving complaints of being sexist, I will say that males and females are biased differently in how they perceive and understand the world. This does not suggest that one is better in any regard; nor does it mean that either sex should be treated any differently in terms of societal rights and freedoms. It means simply that noticeable differences reveal variations in the way each sex is biologically biased. Some researchers have found that gender differences appear shortly after birth and are mostly a product of innate predispositions.[16] Anne Moir and David Jessel have found that, on average, males possess far greater efficiency in spatial ability, whereas females are far more efficient than males in speech. Female brains are considerably larger (18 to 20 percent) in Broca's and Wernicke's regions—each being a central locale for speech. Researchers at Johns Hopkins University have found that the part of the brain called the inferiorparietal lobule (IPL) is significantly larger on the left side in male brains, but with females, the IPL is significantly larger on their right side.[17] It is this area that anatomists have found to be excessively large in Albert Einstein's brain, as well as in the brains of other mathematicians and physicists. This indicates a strong correlation for IPL size in males and mathematical abilities. Findings have shown that the right IPL is more actively involved in understanding spatial relationships and the perception of our own feelings. The left IPL is involved more with the perception of time and speed, and one's capacity for rotating three-dimensional figures. The role of hormones in males and females also contributes to differences in development. Studies have found that girls who were exposed to higher levels of testosterone (because their mothers had congenital adrenal hyperplasia) demonstrated better spatial awareness than other girls and exhibited signs of malelike aggressive behavior.[18]

What these studies indicate is not a superiority of one sex over the other. That is neither their intention nor their findings. Instead, studies into the physiological, hormonal, and neural differences between males and females provide important information in the treatment of sex-specific diseases, the function of medications, different procedures for surgeries, and so forth. Although males and females differ only by a single chromosome, the sexes differ considerably in so many ways that we must realize these differences will bias the way in which both sexes interpret, revise, retain, and act upon information.[19]

Biological Equilibrium

Now that we have some understanding of the biological constraints on belief acquisition, revision, and retention, we need to recognize that all organisms on this planet—including us—attempt to attain and maintain a balance within our various ecological (and social) niches. This balance between what we eat, how our cells are operating, whether we are sedentary or active, and so forth, produces in all of us a balance of health or what is called *biological equilibrium.* This balance allows us to comparatively recognize when we are feeling "normal" and when something may be afflicting us. It should come as little surprise, then, that the majority of our evolutionary past has been spent as an arms race between us and various other organisms in our ecological niches. But since the extinction of large predators and with the advent of technology, the species humans fear most today are predominantly microorganisms like bacteria and viruses. For example, every year, the World Health Organization (WHO) attempts to anticipate which flu viruses will afflict the world. In so doing, they prepare vaccines for specific strains in an effort to thwart pandemics in the upcoming flu season. Those most susceptible to flu viruses are the very young and the elderly. The purpose of such vaccines is to keep us healthy while combating specific organisms in our ecological niches. If you believe that vaccines are not helpful in this regard, consider your premises that support this view. When we come to chapter 5, "E Is for Evidence," you will find that when it comes to our health, fewer things are more important. So it is equally as important to try to get our facts straight and to refer to the proper type of evidence when it comes to extremely important issues like our health. Therefore, the idea that vaccines are dangerous simply because a particular celebrity says they are should never by itself be enough evidence to convince anyone. As we saw in chapter 1, an argument lives and dies by its premises, assumptions, and the evidence in support of it. The endorsement of an argument by a famous person with no authority in the field does not change the acceptability of the argument in any way. In fact, it has no effect on the argument at all. We need to bear this in mind when we read about or see celebrity endorsements of products and ideas. An argument gains in strength only if the endorsement comes from a person who is a respected authority in his or her field of study. Celebrity endorsements could never match this level of credibility. Let's get back to talking about biological balance.

If we remain healthy, we maintain a certain balance or biological equilibrium. When we become sick or injured, our equilibrium may be disrupted. Such equilibria are different for each person and may shift and change throughout one's life. So one's biological equilibrium at age sixteen may be drastically different from one's biological equilibrium at age sixty. Nonetheless, we still have a sense of what it means to maintain a healthful balance. Even more important, we are quite capable of recognizing when all is not well.

Emotions play a large role in governing our biological equilibrium. If I am expecting one of my children to return from school at 3:30 p.m. and the time is 4:15 p.m. and there is still no sign of him, my concern for his well-being may lead to worry and concern. This increased level of stress may reduce my appetite, increase blood pressure, elevate adrenaline, and so on. In this way, my regulated biological equilibrium becomes disrupted, and my physical responses are entirely due to emotional attachments to my offspring. The same is true at sporting events, operas, the movies, rock concerts, and so forth. And as we age, become injured, or get sick, we tend to see the world differently than when we are feeling healthy. Someone who is terminally ill will understand and discuss issues differently than those who are not. For the majority of us, we have no idea when our lives are going to end. So we have the luxury of deceiving ourselves in this regard. As such, it means that we will be biased differently than those who are terminally ill. Should we be lucky enough to age through the years, we will find that we see the world quite differently at different stages of maturity and development. If you read the same book several times at different ages, you will probably get something different out of it each time you read it. This is because the way in which you see the world at those different times greatly influences or biases the manner in which you experience that particular book. As a young boy, I greatly enjoyed Bugs Bunny cartoons. As I matured through adolescence and into adulthood, I began to understand humorous references to jokes and gags that I did not understand when I was younger. And even now, in the early throes of middle age, I enjoy these cartoons from an older frame of mind. I remember how delighted I was with myself as an older boy for suddenly getting the context of a joke that I hadn't understood in my youth. It seemed like an unusual right of passage, but I felt quite proud of myself. My sons have had similar experiences in watching *Family Guy* and *South Park*. So passing from an age of innocence to one of experience is another very important aspect of our lives that will have a profound effect on how we understand the world around us.

These represent some of the most influential biological aspects that can bias the ways we perceive, interpret, revise, retain, and act on information. Ask yourself how these factors have contributed to influencing you in your own life. When you have discussions and present arguments to others, it will give you greater insight into understanding some of the biological factors that contribute to why it is they might be thinking and acting the way they do.

CULTURAL INFLUENCES

Memes

According to archaeological data, about forty thousand years ago it appears that the necessary conditions for consciousness and language in our ancestors reached a critical point.[20] Instead of blindly functioning within various ecological environments, over hundreds of thousands of years our ancestors developed the conscious ability to better understand cause-and-effect relationships within their environments. Becoming more aware of what was going on in their worlds, our ancestors developed many specialized tools, ideas, and procedures that affected their lives in significant ways. A cultural explosion ensued. A helpful word to describe such cultural artifacts comes from Richard Dawkins. He coined the term *meme* to refer to tunes, ideas, catch-phrases, clothes, fashions, ways of making pots or of building arches. Just as genes propagate themselves in the gene pool by leaping from body to body via sperms and eggs, so memes propagate themselves in the meme pool by leaping from brain to brain via a process which, in the broad sense, can be called imitation.[21]

Memes include any cultural artifact imaginable. Memes also include one's beliefs, habits, and customs. The way you answered the Big Five represents some of your most important sets of memes. Not surprisingly, over the last forty thousand years, the quantity of our memes has increased exponentially. For the majority of our evolutionary past, our ancestors were relatively few in number, and they were nomadic—they moved in and around and out of Africa, foraging, scavenging, and hunting for sustenance. Then, around ten thousand years ago, something rather remarkable happened: Agriculture was invented and developed rapidly. Moving from a predominantly nomadic lifestyle to an agrarian lifestyle changed the world forever. For it was now possible to produce surpluses and develop commerce. This cultural change led to specialization in trades and services. And this new specialization led to the origin and development of economies.

Memetic Equilibrium

In the same manner that we try to establish and maintain a *biological equilibrium*, we also try to maintain a balance among all our cultural artifacts as well. From the way you brush your teeth to how you pay your taxes to your answers to the Big Five, every aspect of your life that relates to objects or ideas of culture creates an equilibrium of memes. After the discovery and development of agriculture around ten thousand years ago, cultures began to grow and flourish quite rapidly. Most world population growth charts reveal a fairly consistent pattern that looks something like the graph shown in figure 2.6.

About ten thousand years ago, there were only around five million people living on this entire planet. Think about that for a moment: Just ten thousand years ago, the population of the greater Toronto area occu-

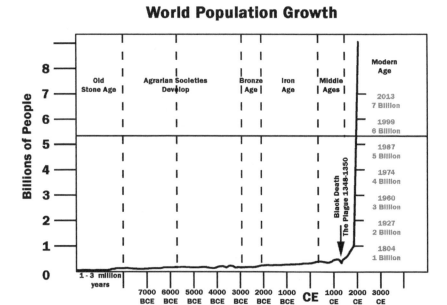

Fig. 2.6. World Population Growth. Graph courtesy of Robert Loucks.

pied this entire planet. By year 1, there were around two hundred fifty million people. By 1800 CE, there were an estimated one billion people on Earth. And just two hundred years later, the population rose to over six billion. It's projected that before the end of 2011, the global population will top seven billion. This dramatic increase means that there are vast amounts of cultural memes throughout the world. Wherever we live in the world, we gravitate toward an equilibrium with these various memes. Sometimes our memes clash with others—especially when they involve the Big Five. How one group defines itself and lives according to its memetic equilibrium may be exclusive to other groups that define themselves differently by living according to a different memetic equilibrium. We have seen throughout history major clashes over memes: from African, Asian, and Aboriginal wars, to the Crusades, to world wars, to unspeakable acts of inhumanity and atrocities. Groups have fought over what each believed to be a better memetic system. And there is no shortage of such clashing today. Even Dr. Seuss captured this well in his commentary on the Cold War in *The Butter Battle Book*. Based on two hostile cultures called the Yooks and the Zooks, each culture lives on opposite sides of a wall. The Yooks are clad in blue clothes; the Zooks prefer to wear orange. The Yooks eat their bread with the butter-side up, while the Zooks eat theirs butter-side down. This difference leads to an escalation of hatred, and an arms race ensues—with each side making bigger and more powerful weapons until they reach a level of mutually assured destruction (MAD).

The memes we find most important define us all in what we believe to be highly significant ways. This has led and will continue to lead to what is called in-group/out-group identities. The in-group of Yooks in Dr. Seuss's book believe their meme of eating bread butter-side up is the "proper" way to consume buttered bread, while the out-group of Zooks disagree and eat their bread butter-side down. Seuss used this irrelevant aspect of two imaginary cultures to paint a very vivid picture of our memetic differences. How we come to define ourselves and establish our identities is the result of culture and what are called *social biases*. Just as we are all biased by specific biological factors, so too are we biased by cultural or social influences. We now need to consider how these biases affect the ways we understand the world in which we live and act.

Social Biases

As mentioned previously, several biological factors have considerable influence over what we believe and how we act. Culture, however, is just as important because we have evolved as beings with hundreds of developed cultures and millions of memes. It should come as little surprise that social biases influence the way we see, understand, and interact in the world. The following sections describe just a few of some of the most predominant forms of social biases.

Ethnic Background

The topic of immigration seems to be a perennial problem in the United States and elsewhere in the world. Those within one country become despondent over the amount of so-called foreigners invading and taking jobs away from its citizens. This type of hatred is a complex issue, but it does tend to center around differences in ethnicity. How we define ourselves ethnically can play a crucial role in how we understand issues.

The values, customs, habits, and rituals of various ethnicities can present barriers of understanding and incite a *Butter Battle Book* type of dislike for others simply because they do not belong to the same group. For the most part, we generally tolerate and even celebrate the ethnic differences we find in our multicultural communities. But we still find that the memes of one ethnic group often clash with those of another. We have seen this type of ethnic hatred carried out in much more horrific forms today with warring in the Middle East, the Congo, Darfur, India/Pakistan, and so forth. Before you can become a really good pain in the ass, you need to consider to what extent your ethnic values and attachment to ethnic memes influences the ways in which you see the world and consider any issue.

Family Upbringing

How and by whom we were raised will have an obvious effect on our development through important stages of our lives. Did you come from a single-parent home? A home with a mother and father? One with two moms or two dads? Were you raised by grandparents or siblings or other relatives? Or wolves? Our home life greatly influences how we come to see and understand the world. How strict your caregivers or parents were in terms of allowing you to experience different activities will have a profound impact on you. For example, were you given a curfew to be home at a given time? Did you have to eat everything on your plate before leaving the table? Did you have to do chores? Were you allowed to date anyone you liked? If you are gay, how was this dealt with in the home?

Families develop entire sets of memes around how things get done in a day. Who takes out the trash, does the dishes, cuts the lawn, takes care of the shopping, decides which television programs and Internet sites are suitable for viewing, and so forth—all are aspects of home life that generate a family memetic equilibrium. Violating the rules of the family household can be very upsetting to this equilibrium.

Epigenetic factors can also influence behavior later in life based on the ways we were treated in our early developmental years. For example, recent studies indicate that a deficit in the amount of nurturing received from our mothers is linked to an increased risk for mood, anxiety, impulse control, and substance disorders.[22] Individuals who experience what is called early-life neglect seem to exhibit these types of behaviors more frequently. Recently, neurological researchers have found a link between the language development of a child and the manner in which and extent that the child's mother spoke to him or her since birth. In collaboration with an entire team of researchers, Maryse Lassonde of the University of Montreal's Department of Psychology carried out the following procedure:[23]

> We applied electrodes to the heads of 16 babies while they were sleeping . . . and we asked the mother to make the short "A" vowel sound—like in the French word "allô." We then repeated the exercise with the female nurse who brought the baby to the lab. When the mother spoke, the scans very clearly show reactions in the left-hemisphere of the brain, and in particular the language processing and motor skills circuit. Conversely, when the stranger spoke, the right-hemisphere of the brain reacted. The right-hemisphere is associated with voice recognition.[24]

This experiment tests "motherese," or the higher-pitched manner in which mothers tend to speak to their newborns. Lassonde believes "this research confirms that the mother is the primary initiator of language and suggests that there is a neurobiological link between prenatal language acquisition and motor skills involved in speech."[25] So there appears to be a strong indication that the way in which we develop is linked to how we were nurtured by our mothers at a very young age. Consider your behavior right now and think for a moment about how much of your current day-to-day life is regulated by family patterns of behavior developed from the time you were born.

Religion

It is unquestionable that religion has had a huge influence on human behavior for thousands of years and still does today. If you are religious, ask yourself how you came to develop your current metaphysical beliefs. The usual path of religious indoctrination comes to us from our parents. But there are many cases in which, as adults, we choose a particular religion for various reasons. Some may find the way that a particular religion answers the Big Five is appealing and informative. Others may favor the communal sense of support that is often found when like-minded individuals gather for a common purpose (see fig. 2.7).

Whatever the reasons, religions provide an outlook on life that greatly influences how one thinks about various aspects of life. For example, many devout or orthodox religions do not accept homosexuality as a biological fact of life but instead see it as a life choice that is in direct viola-

Fig. 2.7. Religion.
Image created by Sarah Sienna.

tion of their god's wishes. To be a homosexual, then, is to act in ways that are in direct opposition to how God wants us to behave. If a devout couple of faith happen to have a close relation—like a son or a daughter—who happens to be gay, how will they reconcile their love of their child with the will of their god? For many, this is not an easy reconciliation. In fact, numerous students have told me stories of how, due to the family's religious beliefs, their parents stopped talking to them after they came out as gay. Religion is an obvious cultural influence that can generate social biases regarding many societal issues.

Geographic Location

Simply living in a particular part of the world will have an influence on how you interpret and act on information (see fig. 2.8). How someone in the United States will understand the Israeli–Palestinian conflict will be different from those who live in Middle Eastern countries. There are even geographic and regional identities and differences between provinces in Canada, states in the United States, regions of England, and so forth. Rivalries can develop even between neighboring cities.

The sense of municipal community that develops in a given part of the world contributes considerably to and can become thoroughly

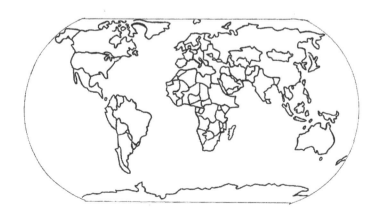

Fig. 2.8. Geography. Image created by Sarah Sienna.

ingrained in our lives. This can give us a comparative ability to view differing customs, actions, and attitudes in a way that might make us think, "That's not how we do things around here." So even regional geography can bias us according to our preferred in-group ways of doing things.

Education

The idea of education is defined in a very broad sense that can range from information transferred at home to formal settings such as primary, middle, secondary, and postsecondary institutions. It does not take much imagination to consider the differences in education the average citizen in the United States has access to in comparison to that of, for example, young Taliban-educated boys in Pakistan. In the United States, all children generally have access to various school systems that teach boys and girls equally. The Taliban, however, teaches boys only; and the main learning text is the Koran. For mathematics skills, textbooks teach the boys to count with AK-47s—and to learn subtraction by killing members of rival groups.[26] Where and how you were educated will contribute greatly to how you interpret, revise, retain, and act on information (see fig. 2.9).

Consider how likely it would be for a Taliban-educated boy to study some of the ideas found in the Torah or Talmud. Conversely, what would be the reaction of a Hassidic child reading the words of the Koran? One

Fig. 2.9. Education.
Image created by Sarah Sienna.

of the central ideas behind education is to open the minds of those who seek knowledge and to impart upon them important, interesting, and helpful information. But education can also be used to indoctrinate specific beliefs, thereby stifling free thinking, introspection, and the thirst for knowledge. Think for a moment about how you were educated and the ways in which it influenced you in your abilities to think critically.

Friends

The influence our friends have on us and how we understand and act in the world goes much further than we imagine. From the time when we are very young, we are actively involved in making friends and becoming connected to an intricate connection of influences. One of the first times in our young lives that we most acutely feel the influence of friends comes at that most difficult developmental stage in life: adolescence. With our brains awash in a bath of hormonal changes and our bodies adjusting to bigger and different parts, we also begin to see ourselves independently from parental guidance and control. Peer and group pressure contribute considerably to how we view ideas and issues, and sometimes conformity is much easier than independence. In a recent book, *Connected: The Surprising Power of Social Networks and How They Change Our Lives*, authors Nicholas Christakis and James Fowler put forth the idea that social networks influence our ideas, emotions, health, relationships, behavior, politics, and other aspects of our lives. In their studies, they were able to observe how powerful friendship influences can be from even three degrees of separation. For example, in one study they were able to show that if your friend's friend's friend becomes obese, it increases the likelihood that you will become obese. The same is true for other behaviors like smoking, drinking, exercise, and so forth. If you are happier, wealthier, and more fit than others, it is largely due to the friends with whom you associate within a network. The same can be said for bad behavior. It is virtually impossible for any of us to live in total isolation and remain unaffected by others. The friendship associations we make—whether close, casual, or remote—will embed us into the fabric of a network in which the influence and effects are tangible. Keep in mind these questions: How influential are you on your network of friends and how influential are they on you? To what degree can you have meaningful discussions with your friends? Do you always tend to agree? Or can you accept that you will have differences of opinions? Our social biases can run deep with alliances between friends. We need to be on our guard in recognizing this very strong and far-reaching bias.

Media

The various forms of media (the Internet, television, movies, music, news-papers, magazines, art, etc.) and the way in which various people and events are depicted has a strong impact on how we see and understand the world. Understanding the nature of media and empowering yourself with media literacy is a necessary tool in becoming a really good pain in the ass (see fig. 2.10).

Ask yourself where you get your information. Is it mostly from online sources? Television? Newspapers? Magazines? On your campus? From your neighbor? You must realize that all information—no matter the type—comes to you already biased (including this very book). There is no such thing as bias-neutral information. Whether you watch *The O'Reilly*

Fig. 2.10. Media.
Image created by Sarah Sienna.

Factor or *The Daily Show with Jon Stewart*, turn on Fox News, MSNBC, or Al Jazeera, the information you receive will have a slant to it. Understanding the political ideologies behind the media you use will empower you with the ability to recognize how the source wants you to interpret the information. Everyone has an agenda—from your local crossing guard to Rupert Murdoch. It is very difficult for humans to play fairly, especially when it comes to discussing perceived important matters. This is because our agendas often get in the way and limit us in this regard.

Biases Are Filters of Information

Think of your biases as a series of filters through which information must pass in order to be considered. When it comes to experiencing new information, one generally has three options: acceptance, rejection, or suspension of judgment. When one accepts new information, this has a cognitive relationship to other ideas, concepts, or beliefs concerning similar events, activities, functions, and so on. At times, the new information is simply acquired and added into the repertoire of beliefs. At other times—as is the case of belief revision—it may be necessary to surrender or abandon previously held beliefs regarding specific information in order to account for the new information or evidence. For instance, I now have few specific beliefs concerning the operation of diesel engines, but that is not to say that I cannot acquire more information about them. Any future information I acquire about such engines gets screened through the biases of my accumulated current belief system. This screening process may have many false or partially false beliefs that, in some ways, may impede my learning. But gradually I will add new information to my belief database.

As noted, our biases create a series of filters that develop and evolve as new experiences and information is acquired (see fig. 2.11).

These bias filters are also intimately related to our biological and memetic equilibrium. In fact, they're inseparable. For one's emotional and physical well-being is heavily influenced by one's meme set. Disruption to the memetic equilibrium often—though not always—leads to biological disequilibria. For example, if your best friend owns a dog and someone

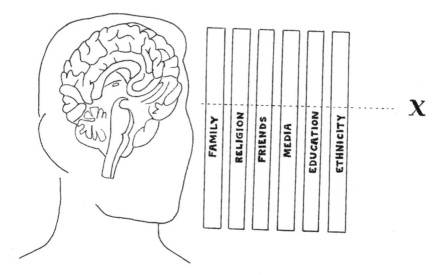

Fig. 2.11. Biases. Image created by Sarah Sienna.

tells him it was just struck by a car, your immediate reaction to this information might be highly emotionally charged. We can quite easily *sympathize* and in some cases *empathize* with another person's situations based
on our own biases. Using the following worksheet, take some time to
write down what you perceive to be your most influential biases.

FILTERS OF INFORMATION: MY LIST OF BIASES

Biological Biases

  1. Genetic:

  _____

  _____

  _____

2. Neuropsychological:

_____

_____

_____

3. Emotional:

_____

_____

_____

4. Sex, Health, and Biological Equilibrium:

_____

_____

_____

Social Biases

1. Ethnicity:

_____

_____

_____

2. Family:

_____

_____

_____

3. Religion:

_____

_____

_____

4. Geography:

_____

_____

_____

5. Education:

_____

_____

_____

6. Friends:

_____

_____

_____

7. Media:

_____

_____

_____

Once you have made a list of your biases, you will be in a better position to understand why it is you believe what you do and act the way you do. In so doing, you will be better equipped to recognize biases in others. The danger of *social biases* is particularly strong in areas where we have vested interests, in other words, in cases where we stand to benefit from things being seen in a particular way. For example, if you own a substantial number of shares in a company that is making you quite wealthy, and the company is accused of wrongdoing, for example, violating workers' safety codes, which will cost the company and you a significant amount of money, you may be biased toward the reported findings. As with the media, it is often difficult to diminish one's biases and vested interests to objectively report the facts. You must learn to recognize social biases, both in others and in yourself, because they can distort sound reasoning, which leads to unwarranted conclusions. It is difficult to see clearly through our own biases, especially when we are emotionally connected to a particular issue. But to argue clearly and present our ideas in a precise, consistent manner, we must learn to recognize and compensate for our biases, which is not easy. Thus critical thinking is both an art and a science and has led us to realize the following:

> The most difficult part of becoming a good critical thinker (or a good pain in the ass) is to acknowledge any biases in yourself that may distort your reasoning.

Biases and Fairness

And now we come to the most difficult part of the book: playing fair. This is one of the first rules instilled in kids when they are sent off to play with other children, yet it is a rule we often abandon as we age. The reason this lesson is forgotten or forsaken is because much that happens in the world is perceived to be unfair. There is precious little justice in life. "It's a dog-eat-dog world out there, and I'm wearing Milk-Bone® underwear."[27] We are often victims of unfairness, sometimes to the point of cruelty, despair, and ruin. For me to say that we must resolve to play fair may sound like advice you would just as soon skip. But as an ideal, fairness always wins out over deception and cheating.

It's not easy to be fair. We like to win. We all have egos, drives for status and resources, and ambitions (some of us more than others). It is no wonder that we like to be right when it comes to making a point or taking a position. When confronted with an opposing view, the most difficult thing to do is accept it as a good argument, even if you disagree with it. Good professors and teachers should be able to read student assignments without their own personal political/philosophical biases tainting their grading process. Good bosses should acknowledge when an employee makes a good point that is counter to his or her own. As well, good politicians should admit to their biases (and mistakes) and acknowledge good ideas from opposing party members. A well-written paper that makes a good case deserves a good mark irrespective of personal philosophy. The same approach must be taken in the consideration of opposing views and arguments.

B is for Biases. Now that we have seen what an argument is and how biases contribute to the ways in which we interpret, understand, revise, and act on information, we turn our attention toward context. Understanding the context in which information arises is just as important as the information itself.

CHAPTER 3

C IS FOR CONTEXT:
TIME, PLACE, AND CIRCUMSTANCE

When you think of context, think of time, place, surroundings, and circumstances. These factors, along with other factual forms of background information, will allow you to more fairly assess information. In the old crime series *Dragnet*, the main detective, Sergeant Joe Friday (played by Jack Webb), would often pull out his notepad and take down information about a crime from witnesses.[1] On several occasions, people would sometimes ramble or editorialize; in such cases, Friday would say, "Just the facts, Ma'am/Sir." In determining the context of information, you need to know enough facts to more completely appreciate the context in which they are presented. For example, if you were at a social gathering in a large building and you overheard someone say that "the roof is on fire," what would be your reaction? Until you knew more information, your first inclination might be toward safety and survival. But if you were to find out that this particular person was talking about a song called "The Roof Is on Fire," your feelings of threat and danger would be diminished (see fig. 3.1).

So once the additional facts are understood—that the person was referring to a song and not a real fire—the context is better understood and you are in a better position to judge and react. All too often people—especially on daytime talk shows—react far too quickly and emotionally over information without establishing context. It is so important for us to identify context related to arguments or information because if we fail to do so, we may judge and react unfairly and too quickly. Then, once we determine the proper context, we may have to backpedal and apologize

Fig. 3.1. "The Roof Is on Fire." Image created by Sarah Sienna.

for our rash judgment and response. When anyone is presenting ideas, you cannot simply isolate the ideas as being separate and removed from a specific context. All of language is embroiled within a context in which we try to convey not only what it is we're thinking but also how we're feeling and what the setting is in which these interactions are taking place. To ignore context is to ignore a very important aspect and dynamic of critical thinking and reasoning and argumentation. Context allows us to better understand the reasons why someone might think and act in a particular way. For example, I live in Ontario, Canada, and when I watch the news on any given evening, I see images of atrocities occurring in the Congo, Sudan, the Middle East, and elsewhere. It is a luxury for me to live in a country where I can wonder why these people cannot simply get along—why they can't just understand that life would be better for both sides if they could limit their hatred and violence and cooperatively strive together for better living conditions. My privileged view of trying to understand what is happening in other parts of the world has limited contextual background. Since I am removed from their world, and I experience it through the filtered and biased views of television news editors (as well through the filters of my own biases), I may not be getting the complete story and may find myself divorced from some of the contextual nature of the activities that are taking place. This is not to say that I am not justified in wanting the violence and bloodshed to stop. On the contrary, most people have the same desire. However, the perpetuation of violence is often the result of aspects that may be hidden from us due to the limited news perspectives we are subject to through mainstream media. I have not lived in such conditions, so it is perhaps unfair of me to judge too quickly about a matter from which I am contextually so far removed. Too little information is available to make sense of a situation that is so horrifically different from my day-to-day life.

We need to be careful when interpreting information to make sure we have established enough background information to be able to acknowledge the context in which the information is being presented. In this way, when context is sufficient, we can more fairly interpret what is being presented and why the information is being presented in the way it is. Without full context, we may interpret information in such a way that our own biases creep in and unfairly influence us. We make quick judgments because we have been blinded to the context in which the information has been presented. Remember that it is usually prudent to wait until you more clearly understand the context of a situation, issue, or action before you make a judgment.

This may seem a bit gruesome, but consider whether you could, at this very moment, consume human remains. I'm not testing to see whether you're a zombie but because it will reveal another important aspect of context. In all likelihood, you may not be far from available food sources. And so you do not need to consider whether you wish to consume human body parts. But if the context of your current situation were to suddenly change, you might think and act quite differently. For example, imagine yourself surviving a devastating plane crash. Imagine there is no available food and rescue is not coming for weeks. To survive, the only available food source is the remains of the other passengers who did not survive the crash. Now that the context of your usual, everyday life has changed, you seem to have only two options: eat or choose not to eat human remains. It would be difficult to answer this question without having lived through the experience. And there have been quite a few people who have had to survive by consuming human remains.[2] As horrific as it may sound to some, if eating human flesh is what stands between your living and dying, you may have no other choice.

Ask yourself how many times you have heard or read this phrase: "That was taken out of context." This refers to an unfair interpretation of an issue due to either a lack of factual information or a misunderstanding of the surroundings or circumstances in which the information was situated. Consider a fairly recent event in US politics: In mid-July 2010, Andrew Breitbart, a white, male Tea Party activist, released an edited clip of a video in which Georgia State Director of Rural Development for the US Department of Agriculture (USDA) Shirley Sherrod, a black woman, was claiming to have discriminated against a white farmer when she was working for a nonprofit organization twenty-four years prior. She claimed that she hadn't used the "full force" of her abilities to help the farmer avoid foreclosure because he was white. She claimed to have been torn in terms of helping him because there were so many black farmers who were also facing foreclosure of their farms. So she decided to help him "just enough" and took him to a white lawyer. Soon after Breitbart's release of the video clip, Benjamin Jealous, the national president of the National Association for the Advancement of Colored People (NAACP), came out with the following statement: "According to her remarks, she mistreated a white farmer in need of assistance because of his race. We are appalled by her actions . . . her actions were shameful."[3] Tom Vilsack, US Secretary of Agriculture, responded: "There is zero tolerance for discrimination at USDA and we strongly condemn any active discrimination against any person."[4]

President Obama was briefed on the issue and supported Vilsack's statement. Sherrod resigned from her position. What no one fully understood at the time was the *context* in which the speech was being given. When you watch the entire video you can see how Sherrod was using the example to illustrate change, in other words, that she may have been racist and biased against white farmers twenty-four years ago because she felt that black farmers were in equal need as or greater need than white farmers.[5] Soon after the context of Sherrod's speech was revealed, Jealous and the NAACP released the following statement:

> The NAACP also has long championed and embraced transformation by people who have moved beyond racial bias. Most notably, we have done so for late Alabama Governor George Wallace and late US Senator Robert Byrd—each a man who had associated with and supported white supremacists and their cause before embracing civil rights for all. With regard to the initial media coverage of the resignation of USDA Official Shirley Sherrod, we have come to the conclusion we were snookered by Fox News and Tea Party Activist Andrew Breitbart into believing she had harmed white farmers because of racial bias.
>
> Having reviewed the full tape, spoken to Ms. Sherrod, and most importantly heard the testimony of the white farmers mentioned in this story, we now believe the organization that edited the documents did so with the intention of deceiving millions of Americans.[6]

Shirley Sherrod claimed that, working for the nonprofit those twenty-four years ago, she came to realize her mistake in judging people according to skin color or ethnicity and found a common denominator between all people who were in similar situations: harm as the result of poverty. The idea that people suffer equally regardless of irrelevant characteristics like skin color (one might also add: gender, ability, age, etc.) would seem to be an important observation of the human condition. Harm is harm, pain is pain, and hardship is hardship. And when it happens, it is equally as bad regardless of who is experiencing it. The point that Mr. Jealous, Mr. Vilsack, President Obama, and others missed from this speech was that Shirley Sherrod learned from her own biased and discriminatory views and came to realize why she had been mistaken. Her speech, when viewed in full, was actually about confessing that she had committed an act of racism but had since come to recognize the unfairness of her actions. The main point Sherrod seemed to be making was to demonstrate growth and understanding, tolerance and reason. Once we appreciate the context, we have reason to think just the opposite of what was presented in Andrew Breitbart's edited video clip. This is exactly what the White House did when it issued Ms. Sherrod a formal apology and offered her a new position in the USDA—which she declined.

Of course, there may still be further information yet to be revealed that gives us reason to revise our current understanding of the situation. For this reason, we must always be ready to adjust our views based on new or unknown information or evidence. This leads us to consider our next very important questions: When is enough information and context really enough? What is the litmus test for determining this? And is there ever a time when we have *enough* information to really develop a reasonable stance on a particular issue? In many circumstances, the answer would simply be yes because there are many cases where there is very limited information. For example, Mary hears a crash in the kitchen. She rushes in to find young Evan standing on a chair that's been positioned so he can reach above the refrigerator. Smashed on the floor is the cookie jar, which is kept on top of the fridge. What is Mary to infer? The most obvious conclusion is that Evan caused the jar to crash as he was reaching in it to get a cookie. Of course, we can imagine scenarios in which Evan could be completely innocent. For example, he may have been chasing the family cat, which jumped up on top of the fridge. Evan might have then attempted to pet the cat or rescue it from on top of the fridge. In the process, the cat knocked over the cookie jar. If there is no cat in sight—or if Evan's family doesn't have a cat—Mary would be more justified in believing that Evan had knocked over the cookie jar. But Mary must always be prepared to change her view should new information (or evidence) arise. That is what happened in Shirley Sherrod's case. The lesson of this chapter is that we should always keep our minds open to the possibility of accepting new evidence or information as it arises. We must always try to attain sufficient information and appreciate the context in which that information was determined prior to taking a stand on any issue. Determining the facts, the context in which those facts take place and unfold, and recognizing our biases will go a long way in making us more responsible critical thinkers. This will lead to greater fairness when acting on the information. Believe it or not, *fairness* is a principle best shared equally among all—including rivals. We must realize that there are going to be times when we think too rashly or quickly. We need to have guidelines and criteria in place to allow us to be self-correcting and, when necessary, apologetic. Context and enough relevant information is dependent upon the conditional that one believes to be in possession of enough relevant information and the context in which that information is found. The conditional can be stated in various forms, as shown in the list that follows, but they all mean the same thing:

1. "Based on the information I have before me and the context in which it is placed, . . ."
2. "All things considered, . . ."
3. "Given what I now know, . . ."

The conclusion to these statements would be, "I believe X," where X refers to your views or beliefs on various issues—whatever they may happen to be. All our reactions toward information will always take this conditional form. And this is because we simply cannot know everything. Nobody can. So we must establish criteria to help us better understand the value of ideas. These criteria can help determine to some degree how some views may be considered more relevant and better argued than others. You are learning these very rules as you progress through this book. And this is due to the accuracy and relevance of facts along with properly acknowledging the context in which they are housed.

CONTEXT, BIAS, AND FAIRNESS

Consider the following example: On October 15, 1998, the 2010 Republican senator hopeful from Delaware, Christine O'Donnell, said on Bill Maher's television show, *Politically Incorrect*, that evolutionary theory was a myth. It's likely that she felt she had enough information—both factual and contextual—in order to make this claim. I would be willing to bet my house that she did not have enough information or she would never have made such a naive claim. One of her main premises in support of her conclusion is that monkeys are not still evolving into humans. Because she does not see any evidence of this happening today, she feels justified in doubting the truth of evolutionary theory. But there are many reasons why neither she nor anyone else sees this happening today. First, evolutionists maintain that humans separated from a common ancestor to the chimpanzee some seven million years ago. All other lines of humans—of which there were over a dozen that have so far been identified—became extinct, and *Homo sapiens* was the only species that survived. Around thirty thousand years ago, scientists claim that there were three other distinct species of humans alive on this planet: *Homo neanderthalis*, *Homo florensiensis*, and *Homo erectus*. Second, chimps are apes, as are we, not monkeys. So I wouldn't count on any species of monkey achieving spontaneous speciation into a human anytime soon. Third, without artificial selection or genetic tinkering, macroevolution can take a very long time. It took me over seven million years to write this book. Did Ms. O'Donnell expect to see such changes occurring on a given Tuesday afternoon? Fourth, chimps and other apes went their way on the evolutionary tree, and we went ours. Different genetic and environmental pressures caused our line of descent to evolve differently than those of the other ape species. To what extent any organism evolves is dependent upon a complex number of variables and constraints, of which I have named only a few. It appears that Ms. O'Donnell doesn't know much about basic evolutionary theory, because evolutionary theory is very well supported by enormous amounts of data and evidence, thereby making its house extremely well built and supported.[7] I have stated only a few premises listed by evolutionists. As you may have expected, there is a school of thought that directly opposes this theory and disputes much of its evidence. Ms. O'Donnell appears to be from this camp. This is something we will look at more closely in part 3 of this book when we consider both natural and supernatural answers to the Big Five. But for right now, let's return to the concept of fairness.

Overall, Ms. O'Donnell is not being fair in her treatment of evolutionary theory for a number of reasons. First, her views are biased by her belief in a world created by a Christian God who created all species at one time and created humans in his own image. So claiming that we evolved from apes is information that will not pass through Ms. O'Donnell's bias filters because, in her mind, this lowers us to the same level as feces-throwing "monkeys." Ms. O'Donnell has no intention of losing her divinely created exalted status to coexist alongside such primitive creatures. Second, Ms. O'Donnell's knowledge of evolutionary theory is lacking. It is possible to imagine that if she had more information, she might not have made such a naive statement about monkeys not evolving into humans today. However, plenty of people have read evolutionary theory and understand it and still choose to disbelieve or reject it based on supernatural biases. So fairness is directly tied into the amount of information determined and the context in which it is found in light of the way it is understood according to specific biases. So why should we "play fair"? The rest of the world doesn't. Wouldn't doing so make us suckers or chumps? No, not really. Because playing fair and cooperating is the only way we can truly keep order and respect in a world where there are so many cheaters. When everyone plays fairly, the majority gets more of what it wants. When some play unfairly, some will gain more at the cost of others. So the rules of playing fair will always be the same.

THE RULES OF FAIR PLAY FOR CRITICAL THINKING

1. Acknowledge your existing biases and determine how they filter the way in which you see and act in the world.
2. Make every effort to attain enough facts before formulating a position on a particular issue.
3. Make every effort to acknowledge the context in which the facts occur before formulating a position on a particular issue. Use a conditional: "All things considered, this is what I now believe."

4. Acknowledge that, due to the way in which so many people are biased differently, there are going to be disagreements on many issues.
5. Be open to the possibility of revising your position.

C is for Context: Time, Place, and Circumstance. Within the bounds of context lie the rules for fair play in critical thinking. These rules are simple enough to state but are sometimes extremely difficult to follow due to the complex ways in which we are biased. By understanding how our biases affect our judgments—and considering the amount of information we have attained along with the context in which it is presented—we can go a long way toward increasing the likelihood of a fair account, which will ultimately lead to more effective communication for all parties.

CHAPTER 4
D IS FOR DIAGRAMMING

We have come to the point where we can actively take part in drawing the structure of arguments—not only our own but also those of others. In critical thinking, this is known as *diagramming*. This tool allows us to represent and visually identify the structure of an argument from the overall conclusion (roof) to the supporting premises (walls) to the underlying assumptions (foundation). Once you do this, you will be able to literally see what a person's argument looks like on paper, and you will be empowered with the ability to gain clarity regarding what his or her intentions are. The structure of an argument is important to determine because whenever anyone states his or her views, there is always *intention* and *interpretation*. Of course, this is a two-way street. When you wish to be understood and present an argument, you too will have a specific intention in mind that you want to have interpreted by others in a fair manner (see fig. 4.1). The same is true for anyone who desires to be understood when presenting an argument. The central reason behind this is fairness.

If you willingly or subconsciously misinterpret a person's intentions in an argument, you are not playing fairly. Playing fairly is one of the first rules we learn in life, and it applies just as well in critical thinking. Diagramming arguments brings about clarity and fairness in interpreting meaning and intention. It also allows us to better organize our thoughts so that what might appear to be overwhelmingly complex can actually be drawn in a visually coherent manner. Diagramming allows us to identify a number of key components of an argument:

1. The conclusion: The overall, main point
2. The premises: The reasons that support the main point
3. The assumptions: The underlying criteria that anchor the premises
4. Noise: Factors that may or may not provide context

When you are presented with an argument, you first need to determine the conclusion. Ask yourself what the overall point is that an argument's presenter wants you to believe. Whether you are listening to someone speak or reading what he or she has to say, it's important to establish the argument's conclusion first. What will remain are the other components. For example, consider the following fictional argument that is reflective of the sentiment of many shrimp fishermen interviewed after the BP oil spill:

Fig. 4.1. Intention/Interpretation. Image created by Vanessa Tignanelli.

Big oil companies need to stop drilling wells thousands of feet below the ocean floor. In the Gulf of Mexico, this practice has led to catastrophic devastation of plant life and wildlife. It is unsafe to the workers who operate these wells. And it has cost my family shrimp business thousands of dollars in lost revenue. (Bob Smith, Louisiana)

Here we see that Mr. Smith's overall conclusion is that oil companies should stop using deepwater drilling. Why he believes this can be seen in his three premises: it devastates plants and wildlife; it is unsafe to its workers; and it cost his business a lot of money. Once we see what his conclusion is, it becomes easier to identify his premises. No noise is present here, but the main underlying assumption of Mr. Smith is that he thinks it is unfair and wrong for people to harm humans, animals, and plant life through specific actions—in this case, it was business, in other words, for the purpose of making money. It may not be that Mr. Smith objects to drilling or to companies making lots of money; it's just that people should not do it if it will *harm* other forms of life (including his own livelihood). The so-called no-harm principle runs through much of human reasoning and behavior, and we shall consider it in more detail in chapter 11.

Before we go any further, let's take a minute to become familiar with some abbreviations that stand for the various parts of an argument. This may seem a little boring at first, but I assure you it is absolutely necessary for you to be able to understand and use this diagramming tool if you want to become a really good pain in the ass.

All premises are abbreviated as P. The conclusion is abbreviated as C. For example, consider the argument:

It is a beautiful day today. The birds are chirping, the sun is shining, and there isn't a cloud in the sky.

In this example, the three premises support the conclusion. To diagram this argument, you would do the following:

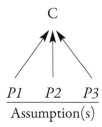

So the three basic premises, P1, P2, and P3, are the supports for the conclusion, C, just as the walls support the roof. The foundational assumption here is that such features as chirping birds, clear skies, and sunshine are the types of things that make a day beautiful. How acceptable these premises and assumptions are will be discussed in the next section of this chapter. For now, it is important to understand how arguments are structured like houses.

The second type of premises are called main premises and are appropriately abbreviated MP. As just noted, a premise (P) is a support for a conclusion (C), but it can also support a main premise (MP). Consider the following example:

> I like lemons, limes, and oranges. These are all citrus fruits that provide me with the essential vitamin C that my body needs every day in order to remain healthy. (Marge Henderson, Cedar Rapids, Michigan)

The bottom line here is that Marge wants to remain healthy. This is her conclusion (C). Consuming citrus fruits that contain vitamin C will ensure this. This is her main premise (MP1). The various citrus fruits she consumes include lemons (P1), limes (P2), and oranges (P3), which are premises that support her main premise. So if we were to diagram this argument, it would look something like this:

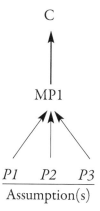

So Marge's argument resembles a house with her roof (C) as her desire to remain healthy, and her main support being food containing vitamin C (MP1), and the individual supports being lemons (P1), limes (P2), and oranges (P3). Her underlying assumption is that consuming fruits containing vitamin C will contribute to her continuing good health. She may have heard or read this somewhere, and it is now her firm belief.

As we can see from this example, conclusions are abbreviated as C. There are two types of conclusions: C and HC. The conclusion can either be stated (C) or hidden (HC). As we saw in Marge's example, when a conclusion is stated, it becomes labeled as C. But when it is unstated and we have to figure it out for ourselves, it is hidden and becomes labeled as HC. The most common arguments that have hidden conclusions are advertisements. The conclusion to every advertisement is generally the same: "Buy this product." But such a conclusion is rarely stated in any ad. Instead, advertisements use other techniques in their arguments to try to convince you to buy their products. If they convince you, you may buy their products and they will make money. In lieu of money, in the case of, say, public service announcements, they can responsibly inform the public. Many of you encountered advertisements like the following either through spam in your e-mail or as a generic letter in the mail. I once received an ad in the mail for penis-lengthening pills that claimed to really work (MP1) as proven by their scientists in the lab. (I wonder who the test subjects were?) The ad told me that for women, penis size really does matter (P1). (I was so naive to have thought otherwise.) Aside from the obvious omission of marketing to gay males, the ad also said that I could be a better lover to a woman if I had a larger penis (P2). So the diagram of this argument would look something like this:

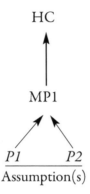

So with these three premises, I am to be convinced that I should buy this product (HC) because it "really works" (MP1) to allow me to add three more inches to the length of my penis, because size really does matter (P1) in order to please my wife sexually as a better lover (P2). Pretty impressive promises. The assumptions include the idea that unless I add three inches to the overall length of my penis, I will not be a good enough lover. In other words, the advertisement assumes that three additional inches is sufficient to make me a better lover regardless of all other factors. To what extent do these premises really support the conclusion in convincing me that I should purchase this product? This will be discussed in detail in the next section. But for now, we can determine that we would need to be shown some *very* convincing evidence for us to believe such claims.

Now that we have literally seen how the structure of arguments can be drawn, we need to broaden the process a bit. For all arguments, we need to determine and separate the conclusion from the premises. In all arguments—written and verbal—we are sometimes given clues as to where these are. These come in the form of what are called *indicator words*. As their name suggests, they *indicate* to us where the premises and conclusions are. Here is a partial list of both types:

Premise Indicators

since	the reason(s) is (are)
as indicated by	*for*
if	*as*
because	given that

Conclusion Indicators

therefore	we may infer that
hence	*I conclude that*
thus	which shows/reveals that
so	*which means that*
ergo	*establishes*
then	implies
consequently	proves
as a result	justifies
follows	supports

Those indicators in italics are the most commonly used in everyday language. It should be noted that not every argument will contain these terms because they can be used in ways that do not indicate either premises or conclusions. However, it is often the case that they do indicate the specific parts of an argument. Learning this distinction simply takes time and practice. If you are reading an argument, begin by circling words that show where the conclusion is and where the premises are. Once you have located the conclusion, underline it. What remains will be the supporting premises and noise. At this point, simply place brackets around what you believe to be individual premises. Then determine if they are basic premises (P) or a main premise (MP), and number them accordingly: P1, P2, MP1, and so forth. For example, Marge Henderson's argument expressing her love of citrus fruits would look like this:

P1[I like lemons], P2[limes], and P3[oranges]. MP1[These are all citrus fruits that provide me with the essential vitamin C that my body needs every day] in order to remain healthy.

Now you are ready to make a legend. For example, in this argument, the components would be set in the following manner:

P1 = I like lemons
P2 = I like limes
P3 = I like oranges
MP1 = These are all citrus fruits that provide me with the essential vitamin C that my body needs every day
C = In order to remain healthy

Creating a legend allows you to faithfully and accurately represent what you believe to be the intention of the person making the argument. Sometimes it will be necessary to apply the principle of charity with some of their premises. In other words, if a person uses slang or jargon, you need to present what you honestly believe he or she intended to mean in the legend. For example, if someone states within a premise that the boss must be "out of his mind," this needs to be translated to read that the boss is "misguided" or "not thinking straight." In the legend, we must clean up things like double-negatives (for example, "ain't got no"), slang, personal assaults, and so forth, in order to reflect the person's argument in its best possible light. By doing so you are *playing fair* by interpreting and representing his or her intention as accurately as possible.

After we have completed a legend of the argument, we can depict its structure. And as we saw with Marge's argument, it can be diagrammed in the following way:

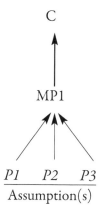

So let's review. D is for Diagramming, and the best way to assure that you understand another person's argument is to mentally or physically draw out its structure. To do so, follow this checklist:

1. Determine the conclusion or overall point that the person is trying to make. If it is a written argument, underline the conclusion. If the overall point is not clearly stated, it is probably hidden.
2. Consider whether or not the person is using indicator words. If any are present, circle them.
3. Put brackets around and number the various basic or main premises.
4. Create a legend, and adjust the wording of the premises, if necessary.
5. Build a house with the conclusion on top, premises beneath, and assumptions on the bottom.
6. Consider the underlying assumption(s).

Please keep in mind that the examples we have considered so far involve what are called *simple* arguments. Most arguments presented in real life are much longer and far more *complex*. This is why it is so important to understand them in terms of their structure. Consider this example:

We have got to get US troops out of Afghanistan. First of all, the costs to the United States are staggeringly high. One report estimates as much as one trillion dollars has been spent on this war by US taxpayers. At this rate, we will never recover our costs. Second, the death toll of our soldiers is too great. With the use of IED [improvised explosive device] strategies, our soldiers have no warning. And because of the increased use of suicide bombers, our infantry have no idea who is a local and who is a member of the Taliban until it is too late. And there have been far too many deaths caused by so-called friendly fire from allies not recognizing our soldiers on the ground. And then there is the fact that it is largely an unwinnable war. Russia tried to conquer Afghanistan and failed miserably. So did several countries before Russia. Afghanistan is surrounded by mountains, which act as a perfect barrier against enemies. The Taliban too easily can pass through mountain trails from Pakistan into Afghanistan to renew the insurgency. And finally, US morale is at an all-time low. This is now the longest war in US history. The news media don't help morale much either; they keep showing images of how often the Taliban reoccupies territories near Kandahar. (Fred Truscott, Santa Fey, New Mexico)

To diagram this argument will take a little more time and patience. But we will use the same techniques as were used in the simpler arguments. Just follow the checklist. In this argument, Mr. Truscott wants to convince us that the US government should pull its troops out of Afghanistan. When we ask ourselves why he would want us to believe this, we can see a number of basic and main premises offered. The first main premise is the costs to US taxpayers. He supports this with some basic premises stating how much it is costing the US taxpayers and the unlikelihood of recovering the costs. His second main premise is that the death toll of soldiers is too high. His basic premises to support this include IED strategies, suicide bombers, and deaths caused by friendly fire from allies. His third main premise is that the United States is engaged in an unwinnable war. Russia, along with several other countries, failed to conquer Afghanistan. Due to Afghanistan's geography, the mountainous regions present a barrier against enemies, which allows the Taliban to move from Pakistan into

Afghanistan and renew the insurgency. Mr. Truscott's final main premise is that the war has taken its toll on the morale of the US people. He supports this by stating that it has gone on too long and the media are partly responsible for adding to the decline in morale.

At this point, you do not need to focus on whether you agree, disagree, or suspend judgment on some or all of Mr. Truscott's premises. Right now, your concern is with the structure of his argument. When we analyze his argument, it looks something like this:

<u>We have got to get the US troops out of Afghanistan.</u> (First of all) MP1[the costs to the United States are staggeringly high].

(One report estimates) P1[as much as one trillion dollars has been spent on this war by US taxpayers]. P2[At this rate, we will never recover our costs]. (Second,) MP2[the death toll of our soldiers is too great]. P3[With the use of IED strategies, our soldiers have no warning]. P4[And because of the increased use of suicide bombers, our infantry have no idea who is a local and who is a member of the Taliban until it is too late]. P5[And there have been far too many deaths caused by so-called friendly fire from allies not recognizing our soldiers on the ground]. And then there is (the fact that) MP3[it is largely an unwinnable war]. P6[Russia tried to conquer Afghanistan and failed miserably]. P7[So did several countries before Russia]. P8[Afghanistan is surrounded by mountains, which act as a perfect barrier against enemies]. P9[The Taliban too easily can pass through mountain trails from

Pakistan into Afghanistan to renew the insurgency]. And finally,

MP4[US morale is at an all-time low]. P10[This is now the longest war in

US history]. P11[The news media don't help morale much either; they

keep showing images of how often the Taliban reoccupies territories

near Kandahar].

Legend:

C = The US government should pull its troops out of Afghanistan.

MP1 = The dollar costs of the Afghanistan war to the United States
are too high.

P1 = As much as one trillion dollars has been spent on this war by US
taxpayers.

P2 = The United States will never recover the costs of the war.

MP2 = The death toll of US soldiers is too great.

P3 = With the use of IED strategies, soldiers have no warning.

P4 = Because of the increased use of suicide bombers, our infantry
have no idea who is a local and who is a member of the Taliban
until it is too late.

P5 = There have been far too many deaths caused by so-called
friendly fire from allies not recognizing our soldiers on the
ground.

MP3 = The Afghanistan war is unwinnable.

P6 = Russia tried to conquer Afghanistan and failed miserably.

P7 = Several countries before Russia tried to conquer Afghanistan
and also failed.

P8 = Afghanistan is surrounded by mountains, which act as a perfect
barrier against enemies.

P9 = The Taliban too easily can pass through mountain trails from
Pakistan into Afghanistan to renew the insurgency.

MP4 = US morale is at an all-time low.

P10 = The Afghanistan war is now the longest war in US history.

P11 = The news media don't help US morale because they transmit images of how often the Taliban reoccupies territories near Kandahar.

Diagram:

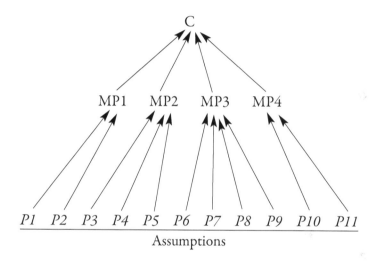

As you can see, Mr. Truscott's argument is rather complex. But he stated it in a way that is very easy for us to follow and understand. We can make a fair estimate that his underlying assumptions include the criteria that any war that costs so many lives, so much money, and so much time is not justified. Some arguments are much more complex than this and would require a significant amount of time and energy to decipher. Some arguments are much simpler. For now, the best practice for diagramming is found online on blogs or in local newspaper letters to the editor. Usually, short letters and blogs about various issues provide plenty of information that will allow you to practice your diagramming techniques. If you want to know if you are using these techniques properly, please feel free to check with my blog at www.CriticalDonkey.com.

D is for Diagramming. All arguments can be diagrammed in this way. Some are simple, but many are very complex. Every argument can be diagrammed if we take the time and patience to consider its structure. Now that we have covered the ways in which we can see the structure of a person's argument, it is time to consider the evidence within his or her premises.

CHAPTER 5
E IS FOR EVIDENCE

In the movie *Schindler's List*, the commandant of the prisoner-of-war camp, Amon Goeth (pronounced "Girt"), had a fondness for a Jewish female prisoner of war, Helen Hirsch. He selected this woman to be his maid in order to be close to her. Commandant Goeth faced an obvious moral conflict between his Nazi beliefs of hating Jews and his passion for this Jewish woman. To resolve the conflict, he would, on occasion, beat her. When she asked, "Why are you beating me?" he responded, "The reason I beat you now is because you ask why I beat you." There is no sound reasoning here. The beating initiated the question—not the other way around. Goeth's response to the question violates a basic rule of reasoning: consistency. His response is inconsistent with her question. As the audience, you and I can hypothesize why the commandant resolves his moral dilemma in such a manner.[1] But his answer is insufficient—in fact, it is absurd because the premise he uses to justify his actions does not provide adequate reasoning or evidence. What possible rational recourse is there if someone decides to play by entirely illogical and irrational rules? There is none. We must establish some ground rules upon which we can agree in our attempt to create a level playing field for reasoning. Otherwise, people can simply say and do whatever they want without recourse. I don't believe that's the type of world in which we want to live.

We have already looked at the structure of arguments and the types of reasoning that can be used; we have considered how biases can influence our thinking and actions, examined context, and learned how to diagram arguments. Now we need to carefully consider what counts as good evi-

Fig. 5.1. Carl Sagan.
Image created by Vanessa Tignanelli.

dence in the support of our premises. In other words, what gives our walls their strength? There are many different types of claims that we and others make every day. Some of these claims require very little evidence to convince someone of our views. Other claims, however, require considerably more evidence. Remember Carl Sagan's statement: "Extraordinary claims require extraordinary evidence."[2] We might refer to this as the Sagan principle for evidence (see fig. 5.1).

As we shall see in part 3 of this book, any of the responses to the Big Five are going to require evidence in some form—and they will require considerably more convincing and powerful evidence if the responses are extraordinary. But why is evidence so important? A nineteenth-century British mathematician named William Kingdon Clifford summed it up well:

> It is wrong always, everywhere, and for any one, to believe anything upon insufficient evidence. If a man, holding a belief which he was taught in childhood or persuaded of afterwards, keeps down and pushes away any doubts which arise about it in his mind, purposely avoids reading of books and the company of men that call in question or discuss it, and regards as impious those questions which cannot easily be asked without disturbing it—the life of that man is one long sin against mankind.[3]

Fig. 5.2. William Kingdon Clifford.
Image created by Vanessa Tignanelli.

We might refer to Clifford as an *evidentialist*—that is, one who maintains it is morally binding to accept information for which one has satisfactory evidence (see fig. 5.2).

This is simply being responsible and fair. And to paraphrase David Hume, wise people proportion themselves to the evidence. But we may now rightly ask: what counts as "evidence"? To determine the answer, we must first try to better comprehend the limits and constraints on human knowledge.

INFORMATION CONSTRAINTS

If you were asked to state three things you now know with absolute certainty, what would you say? And what would your evidence be in support of such information? Try it. Use the space provided here to make a list. Then check it carefully.

Things I Know for Sure

1.

_____

_____

_____

2.

_____

_____

_____

3.

_____

_____

_____

You will find there is, in fact, very little information that you (or anyone else) can claim with absolute certainty because you can never be sure you are not being deceived in some way of what Reality actually is. Like the recent series of Old Spice® commercials, what you think you're seeing might not be real at all. The same can be said about our claims to knowledge; if we are truly certain, that would mean we cannot possibly be wrong. How many things can we be so sure of? Some of the responses I get from first- and second-year students include the following:

> "I know I love my boyfriend/girlfriend (and that he/she loves me too)."
> "I know that God exists and He loves me."
> "I know the sun will rise tomorrow."
> "I know the sky is blue."
> "I know I am now breathing."
> "I know that 1 + 1 = 2."
> "I know that I am not feeling well."

"I know how to ride a bike."
"I know that I exist."

Each of these statements or assertions is called a *proposition*. A proposition has special status as a statement because it possesses something that other statements do not: contextual information content. For example, the statements "*Le ciel est bleu*" and "The sky is blue" declare the same information content given the context in which they were spoken; that is, we can imagine that both speakers may have been situated in the context of standing on planet Earth and looking up at the sky during the daytime on a cloudless day. Whether spoken in French or in English, the speakers are referring to the same thing: that the color of the sky (at that time) is blue. So another characteristic of propositions is that they can be confirmed or denied or considered true or false. They express judgments or opinions. So when people have beliefs or doubts, or when they reject or claim to know things, it is propositions to which they refer.[4]

Many of these assertions or propositions are common to us. Some of us might agree that these can be known with absolute certainty. How, for example, could I not know that I now exist? Or that $1 + 1 = 2$? These seem so obvious that their denial would lead to contradictions and absurdities. Yet if we think carefully for a moment, we realize that all these propositions assume or, to use a philosophical term, *presuppose* information, which requires evidence to accept such statements. Some of the things we presuppose include the notions that we are sensing, thinking, physical beings who use an underlying logic, language, and context to make sense of the world. But how can we determine whether our assumptions are certain? What would prove this to us? Wouldn't we now need to prove that what underlies our assumptions is certain? The regression appears infinite. At some point in our search for certainty we simply must accept that there is some basis for justification that we assume will lead us in the direction of truth. It is seemingly impossible to make an assertion about some aspect of the world and not make an assumption. Go ahead and try it. You may come to the following conclusion: No assertion without assumption.[5] This simply means that you cannot make an assertion about any aspect of the world without making assumptions regarding it. We saw this when diagramming arguments. For example, if you believe that 1 + 1 = 2, then you assume that 1 and 2 are numbers, that the symbols + and = have meaning, and that there is a relationship between the numbers and symbols. We assume that if all these aspects are accepted, then we can claim that 1 + 1 = 2 is true. But we have nothing to tell us if our assumptions are true. The same is the case for statements about the physical world. For example, if I claim that boiling water evaporates, then I assume that water is composed of specific elements (like hydrogen and oxygen) and that thermal activity causes water to reach a temperature at which the process of boiling converts liquid to gas. Every assertion I make presupposes some underlying information that I assume to be true. But this doesn't mean that we must become paralyzed with inactivity. On the contrary. These types of assertions and assumptions have allowed us to manipulate the world in extremely novel ways, like putting people on the moon, curing diseases, and so on. And this is because we don't really need certainty. As we shall see in greater detail in part 2, certainty is so elusive that we have learned to get by just fine without it. For the moment, let's concern ourselves with information that may be far from certain but is nonetheless very important to us.

Whenever we make a claim or state an argument, our premises act as supports to our conclusion. Our underlying assumptions toward criteria that we believe to be the foundations upon which our premises rest often require various forms of evidence. If you make any claim, then the *burden of proof* lies with you to support that claim. You must provide evidence to try to convince somebody why it is you believe something to be true. The stronger the claim, the greater the burden of proof, the more convincing the evidence is going to have to be. Varying types of evidence can be supplied, and criteria are used to measure the effectiveness of those types of evidence.

PERSONAL EXPERIENCE
AS ANECDOTAL EVIDENCE

There are different ways in which people support their conclusions through their premises. For example, some people will state they have had personal experiences of a given type and that is why they believe what they do. For example, Judy says, "I never eat at Joe's Diner anymore because the last time I did, I was sick for days." For this reason, Judy has made an association that the food at Joe's Diner caused her sickness and not some other bacterium or virus contracted in another venue or through human contact (see fig. 5.3).

Without knowing for sure what the cause of her illness was, Judy believes that simply because her illness arose *after* eating at Joe's Diner, it must have been caused by the food *at* Joe's Diner. She believes this because even though Judy ate at several other restaurants prior to eating at Joe's Diner, she became ill only after her meal at Joe's Diner. Based on this before-and-after experience, she came to the conclusion that it was the fault of the food at Joe's Diner. Judy may not realize that some forms of bacteria take days to incubate before a person becomes sick. So it is possible that she became sick from the food at Joe's Diner, but we would need more evidence than simply the fact that it was the last restaurant she ate at prior to becoming ill. If tests identify the specific bacterium that was making Judy sick, we would have more evidence to go on. For example,

Fig. 5.3. Joe's Diner. Image created by Sarah Sienna.

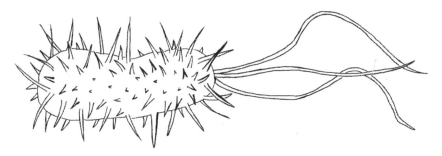

Fig. 5.4. General Bacterium. Image created by Sarah Sienna.

Campylobacter bacteria in chicken has an incubation period of two to five days (see fig. 5.4).

If *Campylobacter* is the cause of Judy's sickness, then it is almost assured that it could not have been the food from Joe's Diner but something she ate two to five days earlier. It is also possible that Judy had a bout of gastroenteritis (i.e., a stomach/intestinal virus), which was not a food-borne pathogen at all but contracted from perhaps a handshake or use of a public washroom. For Judy, her personal experience of getting sick right after eating at Joe's Diner may be enough evidence to convince her it was Joe's food that caused her sickness. But the burden of proof lies with Judy, who is making this claim. Her argument is supported by a single premise: she became sick shortly after eating at Joe's Diner. We may rightly demand of her (after she's feeling better, of course) to present more convincing evidence. So we need to be wary of personal testimonials. These can be powerful indicators of evidence, but they can also be misguided and often require more sufficient evidence to become convincing. If Judy were able to determine that a number of people with whom she had lunch at Joe's Diner also became sick with similar symptoms, then she may have some evidence to make such a claim. If we were to learn that only those people who ate the same dish as Judy became sick, while those who did not never became sick, we would have even more evidence in support of Judy's claim. Judy's evidence would now possess what's called *statistical signifi-*

cance. It is no longer just Judy's individual personal experience, which in science is referred to as *anecdotal* evidence. Her claim would now have much more solid and convincing evidence to support her conclusion. Anecdotal evidence usually involves individual personal experience, which often involves cause-and-effect relationships. It can lead to stronger forms of evidence (e.g., scientific evidence), because it often begins as a correlation between two events—in Judy's case, her illness shortly following a meal at Joe's Diner.

LEGAL TESTIMONY

In terms of the various types of evidence that can be provided in support of our premises, we have seen personal testimony or experience as well as anecdotal evidence. There are also *legal testimonials*, which are presented in courts of law from the municipal to the federal levels. In legal testimonials, witnesses in a court of law swear under oath that the information they are providing is true. Sometimes eyewitness accounts are given. At other times, so-called expert witnesses are brought in to support either the prosecution or the defense. In most cases, lawyers try to demonstrate why testimonials for their side should be considered as valuable evidence, while testimonials from the other side should not. Keep in mind that the basis of legal testimony rests on the *assumption* that a person providing information or evidence has agreed to swear an oath that the information he or she is providing is "the truth, the whole truth, and nothing but the truth." Sometimes the statement "so help me God" is added at the end. This means that for those who are religious, they are being watched and recorded not only by the members of the court but by God as well. If they lie under oath and are caught lying, they can be charged with perjury and sentenced to serve time in prison. If they are religious, should they lie under oath, even if we do not know they are lying, their god apparently will know. They believe this will somehow affect their lives in some way—possibly through punishment during this current life, or perhaps in another life or an afterlife.

INTUITION

There are also *intuitive* approaches to providing evidence, for example, "I didn't walk down that dark alley because I felt as though it might be dangerous" or "I didn't purchase the car from that salesman even though it seemed like a great buy because there was something suspicious about him." These intuitive approaches to evidence come from personal feelings about specific situations that are triggered by cues or behavioral patterns that elicit emotional responses in us. They are sometimes referred to as *hunches*. They are sometimes right but often wrong. There is no way to personally regulate these feelings. What you intuitively "feel" might be the opposite of what I'm intuitively feeling. Who's right? How could we possibly measure this type of evidence? It should come as little surprise then that intuitive evidence is the least justifiable because of its very nature; we cannot measure hunches.

SCIENTIFIC EVIDENCE

Scientific evidence includes claims involving our understanding of the natural world that require that we present physical, empirical evidence to show we are on the right track in terms of understanding natural properties and mechanisms (see fig. 5.5).

As we saw in chapter 1, *induction*, as a form of reasoning, is the hallmark of scientific investigation. We look at some behavior in the world, observe that it repeatedly occurs the same way under the same circumstances, and then conclude it is likely to behave the same way in the future. For example, Earth rotates as it revolves around the sun and has done so every day since I can remember, so it will likely do the same thing tomorrow morning as well.

Although there are no guarantees with this type of inductive generalizing, it has so far served our species extremely well. So inductive reasoning moves from particular observations of phenomena to general claims about how it, and similar phenomena, will behave. As well, it also moves from the

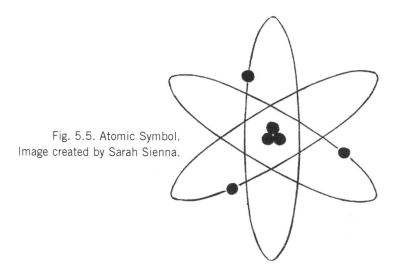

Fig. 5.5. Atomic Symbol.
Image created by Sarah Sienna.

general to account for a particular instance. Overall, induction gives us good reason to accept the conclusion, given the premises. It is not as airtight and certain as deduction, but so what? It has put men on the moon, given us electric light, and helped us create and develop thousands of other forms of technology and human achievements.

THE SCIENTIFIC METHOD IN SIX EASY STEPS

The scientific method for acquiring evidence generally follows this type of pattern:

1. We often first make an observation of something that has happened.
2. We then consider what caused this thing to happen by posing educated guesses (or hypotheses).
3. We can then make predictions about what we should expect to see if our hypotheses are correct.
4. If necessary, experimentation and data collection may be conducted.

5. Further observation is necessary, which will lead to three possible outcomes:
   a. If we observe that our data positively support our prediction, then we have hypothesis confirmation (at least for now, or tentatively).
   b. If we observe that our data do not support our prediction, then we have hypothesis falsification, and we may be forced to either give up or modify our hypothesis.
   c. If there are simply not enough data to decide either way, then we suspend judgment.
6. Finally, we need to consider whether there are any other competing hypotheses that provide an equally plausible or likely explanation of our observation. If there are, then we need to ask ourselves which seems more reasonable. If there are no others, then we may decide to tentatively accept the hypothesis based on the currently available information.

This form of reasoning is actually used by us every day. Here's an example. Let's say you go to your kitchen one day, put bread in the toaster, and turn on the device so it will toast the bread (see fig. 5.6).

After a short time, you expect, when you return to your toaster, to retrieve your golden-brown toast. To your surprise, when you get to the toaster the bread is—well, it's still bread. Oh, the humanity! Why isn't it toast? Now begins the process of scientific inquiry.

Step 1: Observe something that has happened: No toast!
Step 2: Formulate educated guesses:
   a. Toaster not plugged in.
   b. No electricity supplied to outlet.
   c. Toaster is broken.

These three educated guesses attempt to explain why you don't have toast. How do we know which, if any, is the correct explanation?

Fig. 5.6. Toaster with Bread. Photograph by Matthew DiCarlo.

Step 3: Make predictions in the form of *if/then* statements.
   a. If the toaster is not plugged in, then we will observe this fact.
   b. If no electricity has been supplied to the outlet, then no other electrical appliances should work in the same outlet.
   c. If electricity is supplied to the outlet *and* other appliances work, then something is wrong with the toaster itself.

Step 4: Collect data next.
   a. Use your eyes and determine whether the bloody thing is plugged in.
   b. If the toaster is plugged in, unplug it and plug another appliance into the same outlet.
   c. If electricity is working, troubleshoot possible problems with your toaster.

Step 5: Three possible outcomes will arise. For each of the educated guesses, you will have any variety of possible outcomes. The simplest outcome occurs if the toaster was simply unplugged. If power has been cut, you will need to determine if it is a problem with the supply of energy to your outlet (e.g. a tripped circuit breaker) or if there is no power at all to the entire building. If the problem lies with your toaster, you will have to use the scientific method again to determine what the specific problem might be.

Step 6: If you have confirmed any of your three educated guesses and have resolved the problem, you can happily move on to enjoying some wonderful toast. If not, you may need to consider other possible explanations for why you are still without this golden wonder.

For the most part, this is how scientific reasoning proceeds. It is so ingrained into our everyday thinking that we probably don't even think about it while we're using it. It has become our most powerful tool in understanding cause-and-effect relationships in the natural world, and the evidence it provides gives the greatest strength to our premises in support of our explanations.

SCIENTIFIC STUDIES: ASKING THE RIGHT QUESTIONS

It is often the case that whenever people want to add credence to their arguments, they quote statistics from studies or polls. For example, four out of five dentists recommend that you should brush twice a day with Colgest toothpaste. Since dentists are an obvious authority on what is good and bad for your teeth, and four out of five of them recommend Colgest, you would be justified in using such a product. Whenever you come across scientific studies or polls, you need to ask the right questions. Otherwise, anyone can sound intelligent and convincing by using big words and weak correlations. Remember what Mark Twain once said: "There are three types of lies: lies, damn lies, and statistics."[6] Likewise, as the old joke goes: 67.52 percent of all statistics are made up on the spot. The results of polls and statistics can be accurate or misleading. Much of the information is dependent upon how the polls or studies were conducted and how the information from them has been interpreted. Whenever you quote studies or polls as evidence to support your premises, you need to consider a number of factors and ask yourself the right questions. Here are some examples of important questions to ask:

1. Who conducted the study?
2. What was the motivation for the study—in other words, why was it conducted in the first place?
3. Who funded the study?
4. What was the methodology of the study, or how was the study carried out? (Remember to consider sample size and representation.)
5. Is the study repeatable? That is, would any other scientists, under similar conditions, arrive at the same findings?

Asking these questions will empower you with the ability to cut through any references to studies as evidence for premises in any given argument. If an annoying loudmouth who's had too much to drink at the annual holiday party starts telling you why the death penalty should be federally legislated because studies indicate that it deters crime, you first of all ask him for the names of the studies, where he read them, and where you can find them. Should he be able to provide any information regarding these so-called studies, ask him any or all of the questions just listed. If he hasn't simply made up his reference to studies and can actually provide one, you will be able to determine fairly quickly how reliable his source was.

EVIDENCE AND CRITERIA

We have seen a variety of different types of evidence that can be supplied as providing strength to our premises. From personal and legal testimonials to anecdotal evidence and intuitive approaches to scientific accounts, many types of evidence can be applied. Each must conform to our underlying assumptions regarding what counts as good evidence.

Fig. 5.7. Consistency. Image created by Sarah Sienna.

We assume that the evidence we provide to support our conclusions is acceptable. But we need to be aware of the fact that evidence itself is dependent upon criteria. We assume that the *criteria* justify our evidence, which gives strength to our premises, which in turn support our conclusion. But what are criteria, specifically, and how do we distinguish between good and bad assumptions about them? First of all, in critical thinking, *criteria* are really just standards of judgment we use for evaluating or testing our claims and those of others. The mother of all criteria in logic, science, and critical thinking is *consistency* (see fig. 5.7).

Consistency as a criterion determines the level of agreement, compatibility, or coherence among our claims. You may now be asking how I can make such a bold claim. Would I not need to use an argument to support this claim? Would I not simply be making assumptions about the very criterion that I said was so important to support our arguments? Well, yes, I would. As we saw previously, it seems impossible to escape the fact that we must always make assumptions at some level. Remember that there is no assertion without assumption. If I believe X, and the reasons for my belief in X are because of a, b, and c; and the reason I believe a, b, and c support my belief in X is because I believe they do not commit any logical errors in reasoning and are consistent; then I must admit that, ultimately, I have no certain knowledge of my assumptions that my criteria guarantee absolute truth. I simply have to accept the fact that it makes more sense for an argument to be consistent than inconsistent. If we can come to some agreement about the criteria used to support the evidence of our premises, then we can all speak to one another on a fairly level playing field. And at this particular point in history, this is about as good as it gets. Plus, have you ever come away from hearing a lecture or reading a passage and thought to yourself how much you were impressed by the inconsistency of the message? Consistency is so important to critical thinking that it has been called the guiding principle of rational behavior.[7] One of the quickest ways to spot inconsistency is to identify contradictions. As we will see in part 2, Socrates and the ancient Skeptics were extremely good at demonstrating contradictions in the arguments of others. Socrates was so good at this, he was put to death—basically, for being such a good pain in the ass. So how does consistency work as a criterion for evidence? Suppose someone said to you, "I always take a walk after dinner because it improves digestion, I don't like sitting around feeling full, and I like to take in the night air." But in the past, when you dined with this person on several occasions, you noticed that he did not go for a walk after dinner. These episodes contradict his statement of *always* going for walks after dinner and demonstrate that his argument lacks consistency. You would not be disputing the value of his walks or the length of his walks, simply that he made the universal claim that he *always* does so. Whenever anyone makes a *universal claim*—whether affirmative (e.g., "I always do X") or negative (e.g., "I never do X"), you can demonstrate inconsistency in his or her claims by providing just one counterfactual incident. We need to be careful in making such grand claims because they can be shown to be false by a single counterexample. To better understand some of the underlying rules of consistency and to understand why this criterion is so important to reasoning and argumentation, we need to look at some classical laws of thought.

THE THREE LAWS OF THOUGHT

Much of our understanding of consistency comes from ideas developed by Aristotle and other classic Greek philosophers. In classical logic, philosophers discussed three laws of thought that some believe to be so necessary to the way we think that we could not reason without them. They are called the law of identity, the law of noncontradiction, and the law of excluded middle. Each law is *comparative* in nature, and all three are at the heart of many of our assumptions regarding consistency. Each law distinguishes things or states of being from other things or states of being. They are sometimes referred to as the most basic cornerstones of reasoning and are so fundamental that other species rely on them as well. These laws are considered to be axiomatic, in other words, they require no further proof to indicate their soundness. They are basic, assumed self-evident principles by which reasoning must abide, and many of us have abided by them all our lives without even realizing it. We should keep in mind, though, that there are times when nature does not abide by these laws. This occurs at the quantum level—that realm at which nothing is something, energy and matter are both waves and particles, and there is a built-in uncertainty regarding the determination of a particle's position and momentum. But humans do not interact at this very tiny level of being. So for us, these laws work just fine.

THE LAW OF IDENTITY

The law of identity is the most basic law and states simply that "X is X," where X refers in both cases to the same thing at the same time and in the same respect. The truth of this principle should be immediately apparent when we consider that it makes no sense to make such claims as: "A gun is not a gun." When one violates the law of identity, it often involves an equivocation on the meaning of the first and second X in the statement "X is X." Explicit statements of the law of identity are indeed rare because they are so obvious that we commonly assume them. A few examples follow:

> Everyone has flaws. = No one is flawless.
> The price is 50 cents. = That will be half a buck.
> Their country is at peace. = There is an absence of war.

This law not only identifies the properties of anything but also allows us to distinguish and better categorize everything. We can therefore come to understand what things are by what defines them, but we can also better understand them by what distinguishes them from everything else. This law helps provide order and consistency in our world. For example, imagine a toaster and what it does. Consider the properties that identify such a household appliance. Now imagine a world in which things like toasters randomly changed properties. For example, if you put bread in your toaster and on some occasions it produced toast but on other occasions it produced butterflies and on still other occasions it produced bananas, you would never be able to predict and exercise any type of control over the natural world. It is a good thing we have the law of identity to help us identify the properties of things in the world.

THE LAW OF NONCONTRADICTION

The law of noncontradition says that a statement or state of being and its negation cannot both be true. We can also say that a statement cannot both be true and be false simultaneously. It is impossible—both logically and physically—for an object to be entirely red and entirely green at the same time and in the same respect. It is impossible for me to be both hop-

Fig. 5.8. Cake and Noncake. Photograph by Matthew DiCarlo.

ping on one leg and not hopping on one leg at the same time and in the same respect. And it is impossible for you to be reading this sentence and not reading this sentence at the same time and in the same respect. The idea that both these statements (or states of being) could be true at the same time would be obviously (i.e., self-evidently) contradictory. It's sort of like saying, "You can't eat your cake and have it too" (see fig. 5.8).

THE LAW OF EXCLUDED MIDDLE

This law states that any meaningful claims are either true or false. In other words, there is no middle ground between these two truth values or states of being. It must be either true or false that you can run a two-minute mile. And there's no such thing as being a little bit pregnant. Now we all know that there sometimes appears to be cases where things seem a little "fuzzy." That is, it is neither the case that something either is in one state or is in another. This is sometimes referred to as multivalued or "fuzzy logic." I do not wish to enter into a debate at this point regarding the different valued logics that currently exist. What I wish to emphasize is that the three laws of thought are used in everyday, commonsense discussions as well as in the most detailed and complex arguments. And they contribute greatly to our understanding of the importance of consistency as a criterion to which evidence and premises should adhere.

So, to review, consistency is possibly the most important criterion that we assume as a standard of judgment for evaluating or testing our claims and those of others. The three classical laws of thought represent examples of how consistency is used as such a standard of judgment. The law of identity deals with identifying what things are and what they are not. It is perhaps the most basic law of thought because it affirms what is and is not the case about things and states of affairs. A pen is used for writing and not as a parachute; my desk is brown and black, is large, and has four drawers; our pet Giggles was a rat and not a camel. There are billions of such examples because there are billions of things in the universe to which we refer. This is why Alzheimer's disease can be so devastating:

people gradually begin to lose the capacity to identify people, places, and things. For the law of noncontradiction, we see a negation of what cannot possibly be the case. It is physically and logically impossible for two opposing states of being (e.g., an animal being entirely a cat and entirely a dog) to exist at the same time. It is also impossible for two propositions, statements, or assertions (e.g., the sky is blue) to be true and false at the same time. And for the law of excluded middle, we know that in many cases there is no middle ground between states of being or propositions (e.g., you are either pregnant or not; it is either true or false that Barack Obama was born in the United States; OJ Simpson is a murderer or he is not). There is literally no middle ground. A quick and easy way to remember these rules is to categorize them as shown here:

Law of Identity: One and the same: $X = X$
Law of Noncontradiction: Never both: Cannot be X and not-X at the same time
Law of Excluded Middle: One or the other: X or not-X

Aside from consistency, there are several other very important criteria to which we assume our evidence should adhere in helping us to state convincing arguments. These include *simplicity, reliability, relevance, sufficiency,* and the *avoidance of common logical fallacies*. We shall deal with fallacies in the next section, but we will consider the others at this point.

Simplicity is assumed to be a valuable criterion for evidence because we believe that a less complicated and more precise manner for providing evidence for a conclusion is better than a drawn-out and complicated one. This is to echo what is called Occam's razor. William of Occam was a fourteenth-century Franciscan friar and scholastic philosopher who specialized in topics like logic, physics, and theology. He is perhaps best known for his idea of explanatory simplicity, which goes something like this: "Don't multiply entities beyond necessity." In other words, if a simpler explanation will do, stick with it. Don't complicate things. It is found even in the derogatory KISS principle ("Keep It Simple, Stupid"). One of the reasons why Einstein's equation $E = mc^2$ is so wonderful is because of its simplicity and elegance. It says a great deal about the equivalence of matter and energy in a very concise and simple manner.[8] We feel the same way about arguments and evidence. If a simpler explanation or proof will do, then there is no further need to complicate things. This is not to say, however, that *all* arguments should be simple. Many arguments are complicated because that is the only way in which they can be expressed. Sometimes aspects of life are very complicated and require complex means by which to express and understand them. However, whenever and wherever possible, we should aim for the KISS principle in critical thinking and abide by the criterion of simplicity. So the point of Occam's razor is to use enough evidence and the right type of evidence to support your conclusion.

Another criterion to consider is reliability. This refers to the manner in which the evidence used to support one's premises was gathered. There are more and less reliable means by which one can gather information. If I told you that you should bet as much money as you could muster on the fifth horse in the sixth race at Churchill Downs on February 14 because my daughter had a dream about a pony with the number five on it that she was riding to a Valentine's Day party, and six is my lucky number, you might be a little suspicious about the reliability of my information. Reliability is really like a proven and successful record. If information is produced from a reliable source, a standard becomes established which informs us in the future that we can depend on it as a source of useful information. Reliable sources can come in different forms. For example, a certified licensed garage mechanic will be more reliable in telling you information about your car than an unqualified athlete; an ultrasound will provide more reliable information about the development of a fetus than a psychic could; and a qualified physician will be more reliable in being able to tell you about the importance of vaccinations than a famous model/actress.

We now need to turn our attention to the criterion of relevance. It seems obvious that premises should satisfy this criterion. Yet there are many ways in which people can introduce irrelevant premises into an argument in the guise of presenting relevant points. Remember, a conclusion should follow from the premises supplied, and if they are relevant, they will provide the conclusion with greater support. In the next section, we consider a number of fallacies of relevance that indicate when we should call specific premises into question and sometimes reject them outright because of their lack of or questionable evidence.

The next criterion to consider is sufficiency. We all have some conception of what it means for something to be sufficient. We all have some notion that sufficiency requires at least a certain amount of x in order to satisfy specific conditions, wants, goals, and so forth. If I am hoping to get a Ferrari Spider for my sixteenth birthday but, more important, I want a car in which to drive to school, then a Dodge Neon will be adequate. In critical thinking, we often talk of premises providing the conclusion with *enough* evidence for support. But how much is enough? When are the premises sufficient in providing enough evidence to convince someone of your conclusion? As we saw with the Sagan principle, "extraordinary claims require extraordinary evidence." The larger or more substantial your conclusion is, the more sufficiently convincing will the evidence need to be to support it.

Consider the following example: For days, I have traveled aboard an alien spaceship that landed in France. A twenty-five-thousand-year-old alien named Yahweh educated me about the origins of all world religions. He told me that humans in the past mistook the aliens for gods and angels, but they were really alien scientists. Yahweh gave scientific explanations of the creators, the Elohim, who created the Garden of Eden as a laboratory that was based on an artificially constructed continent. He told me Noah's Ark was really a spaceship that preserved DNA, which was used to reanimate animals through cloning, and the biblical reference of the Tower of Babel was really a rocket that was supposed to reach the planet of the creators. As well, he told me that the Great Flood was really just a by-product of a nuclear missile explosion that was sent by the creators, the Elohim. The tidal waves resulted from the Great Flood that was caused by the nuclear missile explosion, then scattered the Israelites and caused them to speak the language of other tribes. These claims are very grand. They require extraordinary evidence to convince anyone of their truth. They sound absurd and unbelievable. Yet they are the basis of the Raelian Movement to which up to fifty thousand people belong. The reasons I, personally, am not convinced of the truth of such claims is because they are not *sufficiently* supported by evidence. For example, the man who received such information from the alien, Yahweh, is named Claude Vorilhon, a former French auto racing journalist. He claims to have visited a spacecraft shaped like a flattened bell that landed inside Puy de Lassolas, a volcano near the capital city of Auvergne, France. Yet in all his experiences with Yahweh and the spacecraft, he never took a single picture. How odd. He does not account for why he was chosen as the communicator of such a magnificent event. If such aliens want to be among humans when they have reached a state of peace (another condition of the aliens), why wouldn't they speak directly to heads of state instead of to some obscure individual like Claude Vorilhon? Why wouldn't Mr. Vorilhon have asked for just one piece of alien artifact to demonstrate the truthfulness of his claims? One piece of an alien tool, clothing, recreational device, weapon, and so on, would have easily convinced even the most skeptical of us that there must be something to his story. Yet he did not manage to do this. As for his biblical references, these are clearly falsifiable—that is to say, we can test them scientifically. If, for example, the Great Flood was caused by a nuclear explosion, we can make a fairly safe prediction that when we search in the area in which this was supposed to have taken place, radiometric testing would confirm or deny this. In other words, there should be evidence that we can predictably locate to support Mr. Vorilhon's claims. Yet none has been found. So what are we to believe? Well, until he provides more—much more—evidence for his claims, the most responsible thing to do is recognize his claims as highly unlikely and keep the burden of proof squarely where it belongs— with the one who is making such extraordinary claims.

E is for Evidence. The criteria behind the consistency of evidence have become benchmarks for determining what counts as acceptable and as unacceptable in reasoning and argumentation. Criteria such as simplicity, reliability, relevance, sufficiency, and the avoidance of common logical fallacies are the main benchmarks that guide anyone who puts forward arguments. These criteria are generally universally accepted as indicators for sound reasoning and strong arguments. Violation of such criteria often results in what are called *fallacies*. It is to these errors in reasoning and argumentation that we now turn our attention.

CHAPTER 6
F IS FOR FALLACIES

A fallacy is an error in reasoning. It can occur in either deductive or inductive reasoning. Any search online will reveal that there are more than one hundred different types of informal fallacies available.[1] To become a really good pain in the ass, you need to become very familiar with some of the more common and popular fallacies and how people commit them.

As discussed in chapter 5, the main thing we strive to avoid in critical thinking is inconsistency. This is because when our thinking about and communication of our ideas is inconsistent, it means our arguments and ideas become less convincing. This type of inconsistency can manifest itself in a number of ways. One way occurs when one premise is inconsistent with one or several other premises, and we sometimes see contradictory reasons being stated for a particular position. For example, in my sons' *Star Wars* video games, the Jedi knights are often told, to "Listen to and trust their feelings." They are also told, "Don't let your feelings cloud your judgment." Well, which is it? Can a Jedi both trust his feelings and at the same time prevent them from clouding his judgment? Wouldn't his trust in his feelings mean that they *don't* cloud his judement? Neither statement by itself poses an inconsistency. However, when combined, they obviously are inconsistent because they violate the law of noncontradiction. Most inconsistent premises are not this obvious but are contained within a larger argument. It takes a sharp mind to weed out the inconsistencies of a complex argument, but the ability comes with practice. Remember, in so doing, don't let your feelings cloud your judgment.

Inconsistencies also become obvious when someone defies in action what he or she claims to believe—in other words, *hypocrisy*. Do you remember when President Bill Clinton lied to the world about his sexual relations with "that woman," Monica Lewinski?

> I want to say one thing to the American people: I want you to listen to me. I'm gonna say this again. I did not have sexual relations with that woman, Miss Lewinski. I never told anybody to lie, not a single time, never. And I need to go back to work for the American people. Thank you.[2]

Here we saw a man who spoke highly of "family values" who said that "with God's will" he would do the right thing (see fig. 6.1).

We can rightly ask, then, *which* family values include having oral sex with an intern in the Oval Office and *which* god supports lying to the entire world? It is vitally important at this point that you realize that I am not morally judging Bill Clinton's actions. I am pointing out an inconsis-

Fig. 6.1. Bill Clinton.
Image created by Vanessa Tignanelli.

Fig. 6.2. George W. Bush.
Image created by Vanessa Tignanelli.

tency between what he said and what he did. I could care less if he had orgies in the Oval Office; that is between him and his wife. But to swing things over to the Republican side for a moment, in case you didn't already know, George W. Bush admitted to doing some pretty heavy drinking, pot smoking, and cocaine using during an extended phase of his "youthful indiscretions," all before he found Jesus (see fig. 6.2).

As governor of Texas he saw many a man go to jail for trafficking various narcotics. We might label such actions as committing the "pot calling the kettle black fallacy." This type of hypocrisy presents itself when one person points out a perceived flaw in another only to be guilty of the same perceived flaw. For example:

> BOB: Frank, I can't believe you cheated on your taxes this year!
> FRANK: Bob, are you kidding me? You've cheated on your taxes every year for the last ten years. And you showed me how to do it!

These types of hypocrisies remind me of my childhood days when, on occasion, one of my parents would say, "Do as I say, not as I do."[3] It's not easy to get away from this type of hypocrisy. And in the interest of fairness, we could admit that we are all hypocrites. We just vary by degree. The important thing is to attempt to come to terms with our hypocrisies and limit the inconsistencies between what we think or say and how we behave. This can prove enormously difficult for the majority of us. We like to think we're right. But if we value consistency as a central criterion for acceptable arguments, then we need to acknowledge when anyone (including ourselves) is being inconsistent whether in word, action, or both.

A third way our arguments and ideas become inconsistent occurs when we commit specific fallacies. It's not easy to avoid these informal errors because we sometimes allow our emotions to get the better of us. But if we are aware of these fallacies in advance, then perhaps we too can be like Jedi knights and not let our feelings cloud our judgment. Here, in alphabetical order, are some of the most popular fallacies to consider in the analysis of your own arguments and those of others.

AD HOC RESCUE

The term *ad hoc* is Latin and literally means "for this purpose." It involves the addition of more premises in the attempt to save a particular belief or position. By itself, adding more propositions is not fallacious. It becomes fallacious, however, when one's new propositions do not possess convincing evidence but merely reflect a person's biased ties to the cherished belief or position. For example, imagine the following dialogue between Betty and Joe:

> BETTY: If you take this herbal medicine for fourteen days, it will cure your migraine headaches.
> JOE: I took your advice, Betty, but I still had several migraines in the past two weeks.
> BETTY: Did you take it exactly as prescribed?
> JOE: Yes, I did.
> BETTY: Well, then, it must have been expired.

JOE: No, it says on the box that it doesn't expire for another two years.
BETTY: Okay. Then, I suppose you picked the wrong brand name.
JOE: But this is the brand you told me to buy.
BETTY: Ah, then perhaps the company produced a low-dosage batch by mistake; that must be it.

It would seem that no matter what evidence counters or falsifies Betty's suggested migraine cure, in holding on to her cherished belief in the effectiveness of this medicine, she is determined to believe what she wants to and will come up with as many additional premises as it takes to do so.

AD HOMINEM

This fallacy can also be known as the "sticks and stones fallacy." The term *ad hominem* means "against the man." An abusive *ad hominem* occurs when we lose focus in our analysis and, instead of directing our attack against a person's argument, focus on irrelevant qualities or characteristics of a person. For example: Why on earth should we read anything written by Plato since it is clear that he was a homosexual (see fig. 6.3)?

Such an argument implies that a person's sexual orientation somehow affects the value of his or her work. Have you ever read a newspaper story about a killer and then looked at his picture and said, "This guy *looks* like a killer!" It is quite natural for us to have these preconceptions. However, like the Jedi knights, we should not let our feelings cloud our judgments when it comes to addressing someone's arguments. For I'm sure many of us have had the same reaction when reading about and then looking at pictures of wrongfully accused prisoners on television or in newspapers.[4] Resist the temptation to let your baser feelings stand in the way of the evidence itself. Lawyers tend to use the abusive *ad hominem* religiously in character assassinations. The worse they can make someone look, the more unlikely the individual's testimony will be seriously considered. This is quite a method in a profession whose symbol of justice is a blindfolded woman holding scales to represent unbiased accounts of evidence and fairness.

Fig. 6.3. Plato. Image created by Vanessa Tignanelli.

Be aware that once a person begins using *ad hominem* attacks in an argument, he or she has pretty much admitted defeat. Use of this type of attack reveals a level of desperation and a lack of depth in analyzing and dealing with the content of the argument and instead focuses on irrelevant aspects of a person's character through insults. I can recall one of the most famous cases of an *ad hominem* attack in Canadian politics. In the 1993 federal election, prime minister candidate Jean Chrétien (Liberal Party) was attacked by the Progres-

Fig. 6.4. Jean Chrétien. Image created by Vanessa Tignanelli.

sive Conservative Party in an advertisement because of the way he looked (see fig. 6.4).

The advertisement featured pictures of Chrétien's face edited with comments by actors posing as regular Canadians.[5] One person asks, "Is this a prime minister?" while other voices question his political accomplishments. Toward the end of the ad, one person says, "I would be very embarrassed if he became prime minister of Canada." The backlash was extreme. Chrétien, who suffered from a neurological condition known as Bell's palsy, commented the next day on the ad stating, "Last night, the Conservative Party reached a new low. . . . They tried to make fun of the way I look. . . . It's true I speak on the one side of my mouth. I'm not a Tory [Conservative]; I don't speak out of both sides of my mouth."[6] The Liberal Party won a landslide majority, taking 177 of the 295 seats in the 35th Canadian Parliament. Jean Chrétien was voted in as prime minister of Canada and remained in office until 2003. The Progressive Conservative Party, on the other hand, did not do so well. They won a total of two seats and lost official party status, as well as the parliamentary entitlement and federal funding that accompanies it. So remember, *ad hominem* attacks are, as my mother would often say, never in good taste. Focus on the premises, not on the person.

One last word on the *ad hominem* fallacy. In the past couple decades, it has become quite fashionable for political pundits and various members of the media in the United States to use attacks against people in an effort to demonstrate the severity of their views. What we might call the Nazi or Hitler *ad hominem* occurs whenever any public or private figure is compared to any aspect of the Nazi military regime. George W. Bush has been likened to Hitler; Barack Obama's administration has been cited as displaying "Nazi-like" fascism. You will, on occasion, hear or read about people making such comparisons in everyday usage. The problem with this reference is that it trivializes the devastating effects of the Holocaust. A US lawyer named Mike Godwin has come up with a "law" that humorously states, "As an online discussion grows longer, the probability of a comparison involving Nazis or Hitler approaches 1."[7] In other words, the longer two or more people discuss a particular issue, the greater the likelihood that someone involved in the discussion will inappropriately make an *ad hominem* reference comparing one of the discussion's ideas to those of Hitler or the Nazis or having similar fascistic effects on a person or group. This is not to say that we should never use comparisons to Hitler or Nazis. It's just that many references seem quite common and disproportionately used in ways to generate unfair analogies or comparisons. As comedian Jon Stewart once quipped, "You know who is like Hitler? Hitler!"

AD IGNORANTIAM

The *ad ignorantiam* fallacy is also referred to as the "argument to ignorance" but could also be called the "burden of proof fallacy" or the "for all you know fallacy." When this fallacy is committed it is because someone has taken the position that "I'm not absolutely sure it's false, so it must be true" or "I'm not absolutely sure it's true, so it must be false." Such arguments take our inability to establish the truth of a proposition as evidence for its falsity or, conversely, our inability to establish its falsity as evidence for its truth. Examples of this type of argument follow.

(P1) We can find no evidence for the truth of X.
(C) Therefore, X is false.

(P1) We can find no evidence for the falsity of X.
(C) Therefore, X is true.

If we assume that ghosts or UFOs or psychic abilities exist because it has not been completely proven that they do not exist, we are fallaciously appealing to this kind of reasoning. Now, there are good and bad forms of this type of appeal to ignorance. In law, for example, we assume that a person is innocent until proven guilty. In science, we propose theories and hypotheses that may eventually be rejected if no confirming evidence can be found. The key to a good argument to ignorance is a responsible attempt to establish evidence that either confirms or falsifies the claim in question. A good argument to ignorance is one in which we make a responsible attempt to establish evidence that a particular claim is true or false. Only after we have made a reasonable attempt and taken the necessary steps for a thorough investigation can we then make a tentative conclusion.

(P1) There is no supporting evidence for the existence of fairies or gnomes.

(P2) We have taken responsible steps to determine whether there are fairies or gnomes and have found no compelling evidence to convince us of their existence.

(C) There are no fairies or gnomes.

Some of you will remember the story of the Cottingley Fairies, which came to light in 1917 in the town of Cottingley, England (see fig. 6.5).

Two young cousins, Elsie Wright and Frances Griffiths, took some

Fig. 6.5. The Cottingley Fairies. Image created by Vanessa Tignanelli.

pictures of themselves with cut-out images of winged fairies. This drew international attention that such things as fairies really did exist. It even fooled Sir Arthur Conan Doyle, the esteemed author of the Sherlock Holmes stories. Doyle, a confirmed spiritualist, believed in such things as fairies and considered the pictures to be definitive proof of their existence. Elsie later stated that the pictures were of "the figments of her imagination," which led some to believe that Frances was able to take pictures of Elsie's thoughts—a bit too literal of an interpretation. In the 1970s, several experts, including James Randi (magician and skeptic), concluded that the pictures were fakes.[8] It was not until 1985 that the girls confessed their trickery. Elsie finally admitted that she and Frances were too embarrassed to say how they actually concocted the illusion, especially after Edward Gardner, a leading member of the Bradford Theosophical Society, and Sir Arthur Conan Doyle had endorsed them as real. Elsie's comments suggest a trick that had gone too far: "Two village kids and a brilliant man like Conan Doyle—well, we could only keep quiet."[9] In the same interview, Frances commented on exactly what was happening in the psyches of the believers: "I never even thought of it as being a fraud—it was just Elsie and I having a bit of fun and I can't understand to this day why they were taken in—they wanted to be taken in."[10] They wanted to be taken in, indeed. Why people persist in believing in such things is the central subject for many scholarly papers and other fine books.[11] What we generally see in such cases are two things:

1. A clear example of *confirmation bias*, in other words, people who want to believe in supernatural things will find ways to justify their views (defined in more detail later in this chapter).
2. An appeal to ignorance, in other words, since we don't know for sure that X is false, it may very well be true.

People could not initially explain why the figures appeared in the pictures. So they hastily decided to accept the pictures as empirical evidence supporting the conclusion that fairies actually exist. This seems like the simpler explanation and abides by Occam's razor, but it is actually complex because it raises far more questions than it answers. For example, are the fairies miniature humans? What are they made of? Do they have a respiratory system? Can they fly? How long have they existed? Do the principles of biology apply to them at all? Do they reproduce? Do they go through labor? Do young fairies experience adolescence? Can they die? So many questions to ask and to understand about this newly discovered supernatural species. The simpler explanation is that some kids were having a bit of fun with some pictures and wire at the expense of some adults with very strong confirmation biases.

There will also be those who commit the fallacy of appealing to ignorance in an attempt to add credence to or bolster their positions. For example, this fallacy is used prodigiously by many who do not believe that all biological life on Earth arose from simpler chemical origins. Because the various sciences connected to the biochemical origins of life have yet to replicate the creation of cellular organisms from inanimate matter, the conclusion is not only that this is impossible but that there must have been an intervening agent (i.e., God) that kick-started life. Many things in the past could not be demonstrated by science that have since been demonstrated, for example, floods, fires, locusts, disease, walking on water, parting of seas, and a round Earth revolving around the sun. And many of these will be discussed in part 3. The point to note is that just because science has not yet been able to explain a natural occurrence, this does not necessarily mean that there must be a supernatural explanation for it. This is another way of saying that gaps in natural explanations do not necessarily need to be filled with god(s). Given enough time, we will see what science has to say about such matters. It is premature to say that because science has yet to explain something, it will never be accomplished, and, in the meanwhile, we might as well incorporate a supernatural explanation. Remember, absence of evidence is not the same as evidence of absence. There are times when we have an obligation to continue to look for evidence, and there are times when we have continuously looked and found none. The origin of life is a case for the former, while the search for fairies fits the latter.

APPEAL TO AUTHORITY

This could also be called the "because I said so! fallacy." As a kid, I would often engage in discussions that would cover such cerebral topics as who would win in a fight between Batman and Spiderman or, as I matured into adolescence, which of the girls from *The Brady Bunch* one would most like to bed.[12] During my preadolescent days, arguments would escalate to the point of one of us saying, "Nuh-uh!" to which the other would adroitly respond, "Uh-huh!" This would go back and forth for some time until one of us would ask, "Says who?" It was at this point that the gauntlet of proof had been dropped and the challenge to back up one's claim rested on the authority appeals process. In many cases, the ultimate authoritative response would be, "Says Dad!" or "Says Mom!" Alas, who could have more authority than one's parents? (I'm being rhetorical here. The answer is: no one could.) Of course, for further confirmation, we might actually seek out said authority to confirm or falsify such a claim (or, when parents were unavailable, simply defer to an older kid in the neighborhood). The are many so-called authorities to whom we refer in support of our views. Sometimes these references are justified and sometimes they are not. But how do we determine which are justified and which are not?

It is often the case when making an argument that we appeal to the beliefs of various individuals in specific positions as support for our side. For example, if you believe violent demonstration and terrorism is the only way to bring about political change, you may quote from the early speeches and writings of Malcolm X. Whereas if you believe political change can be brought about much more effectively through passive, non-violent civil disobedience, you may quote from the works and speeches of Mohandas Gandhi. In both cases, we would be appealing to authorities whose words and deeds we believe give credence to and further justification for our side. What we must understand is that any appeal to authority is always *secondary* to the premises provided, which should be based purely on sound reasoning. So in our previous example, each side would have to demonstrate the feasibility and practicality of its claim. A nonviolent approach may have worked against Great Britain in India, but would it have worked against someone like Adolph Hitler? Against the Malcolm X supporter, one could say that violence only begets violence. So you overthrow a political power violently, and now a new violent regime has taken the place of an old one.

We must be careful about whom we choose as an authority in our appeals. But to help us in making such determinations, there are specific characteristics that authority figures possess. Aristotle called these *virtues*. How do we know who is virtuous? Simple: by assessing the consistency of their beliefs and actions. What then makes a person virtuous and worthy of the title "authority"?

1. First of all, we would hope the authority in question has the education or experience (or both) to be recognized as an authority. This person should be recognized as an authority not simply by the public but also by other peers in the profession. I am not an authority on car engines. So whenever my car is not running properly, I take it to a mechanic. But I do not take it to just any mechanic. I take it to someone I've known for a while. Someone whom I can trust.

2. That's right: trust. Anyone in a position of authority has, to some degree, power. And power can corrupt one's sense of duty and responsibility as an authority. So those in positions of authority should be consciously aware of and limit their ulterior interests, which could conflict with their positions as authorities. In other words, an authority should, more than anyone else, be aware of personal biases.

3. An authority must recognize and account for personal biases that could possibly distort the information he or she imparts to others. The awareness of one's biases is directly related to one's level of trustworthiness as an authority.

Think for a moment about the organization that produces the *Consumer Reports* magazine and website. In both forms of media, it discusses various products that we, as consumers, can purchase. *Consumer Reports* states up front what the tests are, which type of products it is testing, and which products did better and worse according to its tests. It is not in its interest to accept any financial contributions from any companies, for obvious reasons. By remaining disassociated from all consumer products, it is able to maintain a level of objectivity that is relatively free from bias. That is, it tests products as though it has no ulterior motives in its testing. To *Consumer Reports*, it does not matter if a Rolex® watch keeps better time than a Seiko® or a Bulova® or a Timex®. It does not receive endorsements from any companies. We can easily see why this is a virtue in the manner in which this company performs its services. This is a level of responsibility that we should find virtuous as an authority because it strives to be *fair* by acknowledging and accounting for ways to limit *bias*. Knowing in advance that *Consumer Reports* strives to be impartial and fair, we can believe it to be relatively trustworthy. Knowing that it has on staff engineers, scientists, and technicians, all of whom graduated from accredited institutions of higher learning (i.e., colleges and universities); knowing that it is relatively free from bias; and knowing that it is trustworthy, we can claim that *Consumer Reports* satisfies three very important conditions in being considered a good authority with respect to the operation and function of specific consumer products. But remember, an argument cannot stand on its own simply because it happens to be endorsed by a particular authority. We must consider the structure and content of an argument first. Only after it has passed a number of tests involving validity, consistency, and avoiding fallacies do we then consider whom is endorsing it.

Another aspect we need to consider in appealing to authorities to support our views is that we tend to seek out those authorities who endorse what we happen to already believe. Authorities take sides on important issues. It is not difficult to seek out and find those who happen to support the values and opinions we already believe. In a recent study conducted by political science professors Éric Montpetit and Érick Lachapelle at the Université de Montréal, they found that opinions about a fictional authority changed considerably depending on one's political position:

Students were presented with the description of Oliver Roberts, a professor of nuclear engineering at Berkeley and a Princeton graduate. To some, he was described as concerned about the impact of buried nuclear waste on human health and the environment. To others he was described as a defender of this safe practice. For 85 percent of students wary about nuclear waste, he was considered credible when he was also described as wary. His credibility dropped to 61 percent when he defended the practice.[13]

Although this is only a single study, it gives us at least some reason to keep in mind the fact that we do not simply accept any authority based on his or her ability to satisfy the previously listed criteria. We tend to be highly selective in this regard. This is all the more reason to be wary of our own biases as well as those of others who cite specific authorities as further support for their premises. And this is why an argument must stand soundly on its own support first before we can consider any further professional endorsements from authorities.

AD POPULUM OR APPEAL TO POPULARITY

This could also be called the "majority rules fallacy" or the "bandwagon fallacy." Can a billion people be wrong? The answer is yes! This fallacy occurs whenever anyone appeals to popular opinion alone as the reason for maintaining a position. The reason this is a fallacy is that the public can be (and has been) wrong in the past. Popular opinion on its own does not justify a good argument. It just means a lot of people subscribe to it. But a lot of people have subscribed to slavery, child labor, forced prostitution, human battles to the death, and so on, and the popularity of these practices does not necessarily make them right. On the other hand, of course, there are times when appeals to popularity are indeed justified. These are especially apparent in particular fields of expertise. Within technical scientific fields, for example, there is a level of professionalism in which groups of individuals monitor their behavior and create criteria of expectation and performance. Accordingly, members of such groups are quite justified in appealing to popularity. But we must recognize that such people are considered authorities because, as we just saw above in the appeal to authority section, they have satisfied the criteria of knowledge or experience, trustworthiness, and awareness of their own biases. As a collective of authorities in a given field, an appeal to ideas held by a group of such people is not a fallacious appeal to popularity; the ideas to which they subscribe have gained popularity because they have satisfied rigorous logical and scientific criteria. Those with authority recognize them as such, subscribe to them, and then they become popular within a particular group of authorities. So, for example, Einstein's theory of general relativity is an account of gravity widely accepted by many physicists because the theory has satisfied specific rigorous scientific criteria, in other words, it has stood up to theoretical and empirical tests time and time again. As such, it gains in popularity among physicists because it has yet to be falsified or considered doubtful, and dozens of experiments continue to confirm it. But remember that Einstein did all the hard work first, and then people began to subscribe to it. The theory stands on its own. The popularity of it came after people started to realize how relevant and descriptively accurate it was. The same can be said of the theory of evolution. The reason it is so popular among scientists (and much of the public) is because it stands on its own merits. Many of its components (e.g., natural selection, sexual selection, randomness, genetic drift, punctuated equilibrium) explain in great detail how life on this planet has functioned and continues to function. But as we shall see in part 3, it is one thing to talk about the functions of the cold, impersonal laws of the universe; it is quite another to talk about how we humans came to be in such a universe.

APPEAL TO EMOTIONS

This could also be called the "appeal to pity fallacy." We sometimes act according to our feelings of sorrow for someone or something rather than on what good reasoning and fairness tell us. Consider the following example in which Jason and Helen are applying for a teaching position at a university.

How could the dean have hired Jason over Helen? Jason is single, in perfect health, and with no family obligations whatsoever, while Helen has a broken leg and is a single mother with two children to care for!

We now need to ask the right questions, the most important of which is what are the qualifications of both applicants? If Jason is more qualified than Helen, then according to most hiring procedures, he should get the job. It is unfortunate that Helen experiences hardships in her life, but her suffering—that is, her unfortunate circumstances—should be irrelevant in the consideration of any job. There are times, of course, when one is justified in appealing to pity. If you promise your boss that an assignment will be done on a given day, and then you experience considerable hardship such as a death in the family, sickness, injury, financial devastation, disaster, and so forth, it would appear obvious that these become good appeals for not having completed the assignment on the proposed day. However, if the assignment was not completed because your favorite couple on *Dancing with the Stars* was eliminated from competition, then your appeal to emotion is fallacious and no longer relevant.

APPEAL TO FORCE

We could also call this the "scare tactic fallacy." We have most likely witnessed this type of fallacy of irrelevance either personally or on television. It involves a couple of men (or sometimes a group) who maintain a position on a particular issue. The usual setting is a bar or tavern, but it could also take place at a sports venue. One position is put forward while another is stated in opposition. Escalation of emotions and vocal support ensues. Sometimes one can hear the utterance, "You wanna take this outside?" These are times when appeals to force are clearly irrelevant. Determining the winner of an argument by beating up one's opponent may have a certain bravado in a rage of drunken stupor, but it has no place in actual argumentation. It was captured well in a bar fight in *The Simpsons* where Barney Gumble and former Boston Red Sox third baseman Wade Boggs get into a heated argument over who was England's greatest prime minister. The dialogue goes something like this:

BARNEY: And I say England's greatest prime minister was Lord Palmerston!

WADE BOGGS: Pitt the Elder!

BARNEY: Lord Palmerston!

WADE BOGGS: Pitt the Elder! [poking Barney]

BARNEY: Okay, you asked for it, bud! [punches Boggs to the ground]

MOE: Yeah, that's showing him, Barney! [scoffing] Pitt the Elder . . .

BARNEY: Lord Palmerston! [punches Moe][14]

There are, of course, more subtle ways of winning in this manner. In a scene from the movie *Boyz n the Hood*, members of one gang have a dispute with members of another gang. Suddenly, one of the gang members lifts his shirt to reveal a .45-caliber semiautomatic pistol and says, "D'we got a problem here?!" He then pulls the gun from his pants and cocks it. This sends the other gang members fleeing. The conversation is over in a hurry. Regardless of the practical implications of the gang member's activities, this appeal to force does not make his position any more true or right or justified. It just means that for now, there is no use arguing with a man with a loaded gun. It is far better to run away and live to argue another day. He keeps his gun; you keep your life.

There are, on occasion, times when appeals to force seem more justified than not. For example, during a time of war, if Country A is being brutally attacked by Country B, and Country B will not cease and desist despite countless efforts by the United Nations, NATO, and the like, then Country C may be justified in using military tactics to force Country B to comply (this is what happened with the United States in Kosovo against Slobodan Milošević). But notice how this differs from the gang-related incident just mentioned. In the case of US intervention, this seemed to be the last effort available to stop an atrocity, such as suspected genocide. In this case, the United States may be considered more justified in its appeal to force.

BEGGING THE QUESTION

This fallacy is a form of circular reasoning. Begging the question is a fallacy that occurs whenever anyone assumes as a premise what they hope to support as a conclusion. For example, consider the following:

> The word of the Bible is true. For it says right in the Bible that it is the word of God, and God would never allow the Bible to contain false information.

Even if the conclusion were true (which billions in the world believe), the premise does not support the conclusion—it presupposes it. This argument moves in a circle so that the conclusion supports the premises, which in turn support the conclusion. You may have heard the term *begging the question* used improperly by journalists over the last decade or so. I cannot determine who first coined the misuse of this phrase, but it somehow became quite fashionable to use it as a neat catchphrase. Consider the following improper use of the term:

> John, I'm standing outside of the airport right now. There is high wind, blowing snow mixed with ice pellets, and visibility is poor. The pilots of the plane that crashed were warned by the tower not to fly because of weather conditions; people on the airplane reportedly told the pilots to turn back on the runway; and the navigator himself told the pilot and copilot that he thought it was too risky to fly, which begs the question: Why did the pilots attempt to fly under such conditions?

What has happened is that somehow, somewhere, some journalists heard or read this phrase, used it incorrectly a number of times, and it caught on as a hip or sexy way of using a phrase. Feeling presumptuous enough to think that I have some obligation to enlighten the journalistic community, in 1995 I called CBC Radio's talk show *As It Happens* and told them (in a diplomatic way) that they were using this phrase incorrectly. I told them what the fallacy actually means, and instead of journalists saying X begs the question, what they need to say is that X *raises* the question or *poses* or *suggests* or *invites* the question—not *begs* the question. I still hear the phrase used incorrectly from time to time—unfortunately, even on *The Colbert Report*. In my research on this particular fallacy, I came across an interesting site called: Beg the Question: Get It Right.[15] The host(s) of this site and its followers wish to bring attention to the proper use of this informal logical fallacy and to issue cards of notice to those who use it improperly. Be forewarned, Mr. Colbert and all journalists.

CONFIRMATION BIAS

This fallacy could also be called the "hammer fallacy." In other words, when the only tool you have is a hammer, everything looks like a nail (see fig. 6.6).

It is very difficult to escape this type of bias. Once we start to see certain aspects of the world in a particular way, it is difficult for us to ignore opposing evidence. This happens in cases where we unjustly make judgments about people because of preconceived ideas. For example, if we are

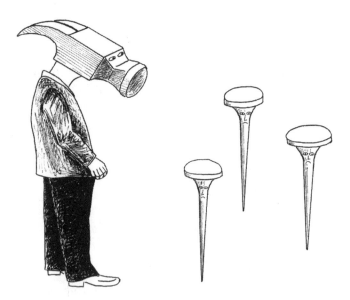

Fig. 6.6. Confirmation Bias. Image created by Sarah Sienna.

at a party and I tell you some rather nasty stories about one of the attendees named Jim, when you eventually meet him you might interpret much of what he says in light of the information I had already supplied. You might actively search out confirmation of your preconceptions of Jim in his discussion, mannerisms, or various references. And we can see why this is unfair. Jim may be a fine person, but your interaction with him was tainted or negatively biased because of what I told you. So Jim must now "swim against the tide of bias," as it were. His actions and mannerisms, no matter how benign, may be interpreted negatively simply because of a previously held bias that you are seeking to confirm. This is sometimes referred to as "poisoning the well." It is a preemptive attack on a person's character in order to discredit him or her prior to first introduction or, in a court of law, hearing the individual's testimony.

But there are other forms of confirmation bias. For example, whenever scientists become too attached to their cherished hypotheses, they may find it difficult to accept counterevidence. Sometimes referred to as the "fallacy of selective attention," scientists may ignore countervailing evidence against their hypotheses and instead actively seek out only information that confirms them. If we look long enough, any one of us could find patterns of behavior in all sorts of places as a result of our selective attention. For example, in the movie *The Number 23*, Jim Carrey's character finds significance in this number in seemingly disparate places. The plot involves Carrey's obsession with what's called the 23 Enigma, the numerological idea that many incidents and events are directly connected to the number 23.[16] Basically, if you focus on specific numbers long enough, you will, by coincidence, see them more. This is because you are deliberately looking for them. It's a sort of self-fulfilling prophecy. Because you are looking for something specific, you will remember the hits and discount the misses.

Focusing on hits and ignoring misses is exactly how psychics fool you into believing they possess supernatural powers, which allows them to tell you things about your past, present, and future (see fig. 6.7).

But they really cannot accomplish any such claims. What they do, instead, is speak in generalities, for example, "You are a caring person but

Fig. 6.7. Crystal Ball.
Image created
by Sarah Sienna.

can also be quite selfish at times." Show me five people who do not fit this description! "You don't like being bossed around, but you know how to get the job done." Such general statements could be true of just about anyone at any given time in history. People who see psychics and take their "readings" seriously do so because they want to hear something positive about themselves. Does anyone ever go to a psychic to hear things like, "You are *such* an asshole!" "I can't believe you even came here; you have no future!" Or how about, "I knew you were coming. There was no need to make an appointment. You're a loser. That will be forty dollars." I've never heard any psychic say such things about anyone. But clearly, if she were psychic, she would know all sorts of things about a person including the mundane, like, "You didn't wash your hands after going to the washroom last night at dinner."[17] Or the very personal: "You really seem to enjoy eating popcorn and masturbating while watching *The Daily Show*." But instead, the five main areas psychics focus on are health, wealth, employment, love, and relationships.[18] Since all these areas are extremely important to us, anything positive a psychic has to say will be accepted and *confirmed* by the attendee. Even if the psychic is wrong on 80 to 90 percent of her predictions, many will ignore this and focus on the hits. This is why I am so vocal about psychics and why I invite them into my classes every year (only one has accepted in over fifteen years). I believe psychics prey on the emotional vulnerability of their customers. One question we need to ask is to what extent are psychics aware of this type of predation? Many of the psychics I have met actually believe they have special powers. Even when you can demonstrate to them that I or anyone else could perform just as well or better, they still maintain that they have special abilities. James Randi, magician extraordinaire and überskeptic, has created the One Million Dollar Paranormal Challenge "to anyone who can show, under proper observing conditions, evidence of any paranormal, supernatural, or occult power or event."[19] So far, no takers. Here's something to keep in mind the next time you visit a psychic (if you or anyone you know is into that sort of thing):

1. Don't say anything after you say hello to the psychic.
2. Don't show any emotions.
3. Dress in a way you would not normally dress.
4. Record the event and listen to it afterward for accuracy.
5. When she is almost finished, ask her for the winning numbers in the next lottery.

I will assure you that after you subtract the gross generalities, the hits/misses ratio will be noticeably disproportionate. The hits will be well below 50 percent, and the misses will be far above 50 percent. The primary reason is because the psychic will simply have to guess about you regarding specific aspects of your life and put forward as many generalities (like the ones previously mentioned) as possible in a feeble attempt to accomplish some vague hits. If what I am saying as an argument still does not convince you that psychics do not possess the powers many claim to possess, at least consider this: Have you ever wondered why psychics should be in business at all? If they really do have the powers they claim to possess, wouldn't it be quite easy for them to know the winner of the next horse race? Or football game? Or lottery? They can apparently tell us so much about complete strangers and major events in world history, and yet they cannot determine whether the roulette ball is going to land on black or red (an almost 50 percent likelihood already given to them). Amazing! But what's truly amazing is that anyone would believe in psychics. And yet millions do! And the most common argument I get from critics of my skeptical view of paranormal phenomena is that, *for all I know*, some psychics might truly possess these amazing powers. This is a weak argument for anything, let alone psychic phenomena because it commits the *ad ignorantiam* or appeal to ignorance fallacy. Their claim is that since I have not disproven all psychics, there could very well be a real psychic out there that I may have missed. And that just happens to be the one they are now seeing.

I could use this same form of fallacious reasoning to confirm my belief in Flying Spaghetti Monsters, the Tooth Fairy, the Easter Bunny, or even Santa Claus (spoiler alert). No matter how many times I or anyone discounts sightings of Santa's sleigh and reindeer, the Easter Bunny, the Tooth Fairy, or the Flying Spaghetti Monster, a true believer could still say that I have not disproven all the reported sightings. Until I have, I don't know for sure that such beings don't exist. The reason this becomes exasperating at times is because some things have been proven false or unlikely enough times that we just shouldn't believe in them anymore. Keep in mind that the burden of proof must always lie with the claimant—the person who believes in the existence of such things. In reference to supernatural beings, all arguments live and die according to the evidence or lack thereof. Scientists will continue to falsify their existence, but until we can confirm any positive evidence on the side of the claimant, we have every reason to refrain from believing in the existence of such supernatural beings. This works equally well for UFOs, but I will keep a more skeptically open mind on the aliens than on dear old Santa. The fact of the matter here is that we need to keep the burden of proof squarely where it should lie, and that is with the ones who make the claims. Money talks and bullshit walks, as they say. If you have the special paranormal talents that you claim to possess or can prove the existence of supernatural beings, then, as the kids say: bring it, biotch! You demonstrate paranormal phenomena under a controlled scientific setting, and you get one million dollars [USD]. How tough could it be? If you are a psychic, you will be charging anywhere from $40 to $500 an hour to tell people some pretty amazing information. If you're that good, it should be easy to pull it off under a bit of scrutiny, wouldn't you think? Yet psychics don't take the Randi challenge, and they avoid my critical thinking classes like the plague. For the record, I think the world would be pretty cool if people did actually possess such powers.[20] But wishing something does not make it so. We just have to accept the fact that the world may not possess people who claim to have such powers. But that's okay. The world is still a mind-bogglingly interesting place. The many sciences, arts, and humanities show us this.

This section would not be complete without mentioning that a common display of confirmation bias appears commonly in conspiracy theories like the John F. Kennedy assassination, the Apollo moon landings, and even the 9/11 tragedy. No matter how much evidence to the contrary, it would seem that it is not enough to convince some people that Kennedy really was assassinated by a single individual; that astronauts really did travel to and land on the moon; and that the 9/11 disaster was not the result of anything other than a bunch of deeply misguided and sadistic fundamentalist Muslim extremists who believed themselves to be justified in the name of their religion to create terror, pain, and suffering for untold thousands of people in the United States. There is a close connection between having a confirmation bias and using *ad hoc* tactics to save your biased beliefs. The more cherished your personal hypothesis is, the more effort will be taken to continuously add more premises to your argument in an effort to provide support. But the premises are far and away exceeding Occam's advice, and in conspiracy theory cases, the simpler explanations really do seem to provide more acceptable explanations.

COMMON CAUSE

Sometimes referred to as the "third-cause fallacy," there are times when we see two things (A and B) occurring simultaneously and assume that the one causes the other to happen. This occurs occasionally in the observances of correlations. However, it is sometimes the case that neither A causes B nor B causes A, but that the cause of either or both was actually C. Consider the following example:

> Your baby wakes you in the middle of the night crying. She has a fever. So you conclude that the fever is causing her to cry. You conclude that if you reduce the fever, she will stop crying. However, the cause of the fever (and her discomfort) is due to an earache brought about by an infection.

If you are a parent or ever become one, you are going to use an enormous amount of causal reasoning in trying to figure out what is best for your child. In this example a parent is making the assumption that the fever is the cause of the child's discomfort. This is a perfectly normal assumption. The mind works in comparative ways. We may remember that when we had a fever in the past, we did not feel well. But the common cause of the baby's fever and crying is actually a microbe or bacterium that has caused her ear to ache. Because we can detect a fever with a thermometer but cannot see an earache, we need to investigate further into what is the actual (common) cause for the baby's discomfort. What we need to appreciate is the incredible complexities of causal relations, especially when dealing with human organisms. As humans, we generally like simpler explanations. Science itself appreciates and promotes simple explanations. In fact, as we saw with Occam's razor, it is often the case that the simpler and more elegant the explanation, the better. The same holds for the rest of us in the everyday world. We like easy solutions. The problem, however, is that sometimes there just aren't easy solutions. So we need to be aware of and on guard about the possibility of common causes and complex causal relationships.

CONFUSING CAUSE AND EFFECT

This could also be called the "cart before the horse fallacy." This is a relatively simple fallacy that occurs when one mistakenly identifies an effect as a cause or a cause as an effect. It is a way of misinterpreting the causal relationship between two things.

Example 1: A recent poll shows that more married couples are purchasing minivans than ever before. The popularity of such vehicles clearly indicates an incentive for young people to marry.

Here, the poll wrongly assumes that the minivans are the cause for people to marry. Rather, it is married couples who need minivans, usually due to an increase in family size. The poll has confused the cause-and-effect relationship.

Example 2: Every time I see dark clouds and I take my umbrella to work, it rains. I want nicer weather, so I'm going to stop taking my umbrella to work.

Here we can see it is not the umbrella that causes the rain but the clouds. The reason one takes the umbrella in the first place is due to the dark clouds, which suggest that rain is imminent.

DISANALOGY

This could also be called the "apples and oranges fallacy." It is often the case that people use comparisons when trying to make a point. This is a wonderful method for communication and probably one of the oldest forms of comparative reasoning. When an analogy is a good one, it is easy to make a connection. However, sometimes analogies are used that cloud our understanding and leave us wondering what they have to do with the conclusion at all. Consider the following analogy:

> In crossing a heath, suppose I pitched my foot against a stone, and were I asked how the stone came to be there; I might possibly answer, that, for anything I knew to the contrary, it had lain there forever: nor would it perhaps be very easy to show the absurdity of this answer. But suppose I had found a watch upon the ground, and it should be inquired how the watch happened to be in that place; I should hardly think of the answer

I had before given, that for anything I knew, the watch might have always been there. . . . There must have existed, at some time, and at some place or other, an artificer or artificers, who formed [the watch] for the purpose which we find it actually to answer; who comprehended its construction, and designed its use. . . . Every indication of contrivance, every manifestation of design, which existed in the watch, exists in the works of nature; with the difference, on the side of nature, of being greater or more, and that in a degree which exceeds all computation.[21]

In this passage, William Paley compares the finding of a watch as proof there must have been a watchmaker (see fig. 6.8).

And from this analogy, he concludes that seeing the complex things in the world and in the universe, there must have been a maker of everything—in other words, God. Is Paley's analogy weak or robust? Is he comparing apples to oranges? Is a watch and a watchmaker the same as the universe and a supposed universe maker?

Now consider the following analogy: In an episode of *Seinfeld*, Jerry Seinfeld tells his friend George Costanza that he is involved in a relation-

Fig. 6.8. Watch on Heath. Photograph by Matthew DiCarlo.

ship with a woman in which the sex is great, but everything else is meaningless. She is not an overly intelligent woman; they have nothing in common; and yet the sexual component is very rewarding because, as Jerry says, there are no inhibitions—that is, they are free to act out their wildest sexual fantasies. George responds by saying that he knows exactly what Jerry means: "It's like going to the bathroom in front of a lot of people and not caring." To which Jerry responds: "It's not like that at all."[22] The argument can be broken down to look like this:

(P1) Sex with inhibitions may be good, but not great (implied).
(P2) Jerry has sex with no inhibitions.
(C) Therefore, Jerry has great sex.

In this example, George is convinced he has understood what Jerry means and uses an analogy to prove this. George's understanding of the argument looks like this:

(P1) Sex with inhibitions may be good, but not great (implied).
(P2) Having sex with no inhibitions would be just like going to the washroom in front of a lot of people and not even caring.
(C) Therefore, uninhibited sex is great.

As it turns out, George has presented a disanalogy. That is, it is a really bad comparison, like apples to oranges. Uninhibited sex and public acts of toilet hygiene are quite dissimilar, and so George's disanalogy is irrelevant. George has presented what is sometimes referred to as a *non sequitur*, which is Latin for "it does not follow." It does not follow that uninhibited sex is great because it is just like going to the washroom in front of a lot of people and not caring. Some of the reasons uninhibited sex is great are because of the elements of freedom, exploration, and pleasure (or so I'm told).

EQUIVOCATION

This fallacy arises when one uses a term, phrase, or sentence in an argument with two different meanings. For example:

(P1) Power tends to corrupt.
(P2) Knowledge is power.
(C) Therefore, knowledge tends to corrupt.

Power in the first premise means the possession or control over people (a political context), whereas in the second premise the word *power* means the ability to control things (a scientific context). When discourse (either written or verbal) takes place between two or more persons, *equivocation* can take the form of a verbal dispute instead of a genuine dispute. In a verbal dispute, each person uses a key term or phrase with a different meaning. For example, suppose you and I are discussing the issue of the war on drugs. Our discussion is not going to be too fruitful if by "war on drugs" you mean the attempt to legally curtail the selling and use of street drugs (the intended and correct version) and my understanding of the phrase is that today's youth act as though they are at war on drugs. In a real dispute, each person must affirm what the other denies (to some degree), for example, you believe A and I believe Not-A. For there to be a real dispute, we must be referring to the same issue. Consider an oral sex example. If Auntie May thinks *oral sex* is actually *aural sex*, or discussing sex, and we know differently, there is no genuine dispute but only a verbal (um, oral) dispute.

The example of a fallacious use of equivocation I find most troubling is when those who disagree with the scientific findings of evolutionary theory do so because, as they claim, "It's only a theory" (see fig. 6.9).

In this case, they are using the term *theory* not as scientists use it, for example, the theory of gravity, quantum theory, and so on; *theory* comes from the Greek *theoria*, meaning a natural explanation of some aspect of the world which has been strongly supported by evidence. Instead, they are using the term to mean *hunch* or *guess* or *conjecture*. This is unfair. Part of the

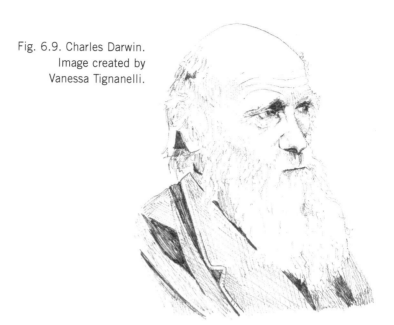

Fig. 6.9. Charles Darwin.
Image created by
Vanessa Tignanelli.

problem may come from a simple misunderstanding. On Dictionary.com, I found these two definitions for *theory* right beside each other:

1. a coherent group of general propositions used as principles of explanation for a class of phenomena: Einstein's theory of relativity.
2. a proposed explanation whose status is still conjectural, in contrast to well-established propositions that are regarded as reporting matters of actual fact.[23]

Notice how the way in which scientists use the term *theory* in the phrase "theory of evolution" is found in the first definition, whereas those who disagree with such a theory choose to use definition 2. Always be on your guard to make sure people interpret terms, concepts, and phrases in the manner that best represents your intention and the intentions of others. Otherwise, they will simply play word games with your ideas in an effort to undermine your power of persuasion.

EXTRAORDINARY CLAIMS FALLACY

If you are at a social function and a gentleman (let's call him Charles) says, "I just arrived and boy, does it look like rain!" You may assume, based on his personal testimony, that he would have at least some reason for making such a claim. Obviously, the claim will have been established by empirical methods, for example, the person simply noticed the weather conditions of approaching dark clouds, lightning, and so on. For the moment, there is really no use in demanding that this person back up his claim. This is where diplomacy comes in. He is simply making a commentary in the form of chitchat. It's an icebreaker, a way of introducing oneself. Requiring further support is uncalled for. However, if a person (let's call him Bob) arrives and says, "It looks stormy outside, and a tornado is going to develop soon," then we have good reason to ask why he maintains this belief because Bob is making an extremely strong claim—one that could affect the lives of everyone at the social function (see fig. 6.10).

We would expect him to provide more adequate—or extraordinary— evidence. To do this, Bob needs to satisfy a number of conditions:

1. What is his level of authority or expertise regarding, in this case, the development of severe weather patterns such as tornadoes? (He could just be an alarmist or someone who experienced a tornado once and jumps to hasty conclusions every time a storm develops.)
2. How reliable have his past judgments been? What's his track record?
3. How much experience does he have in spotting this type of storm activity? How long has he been studying such phenomena?

There are definite signs to look for in the development of tornadoes— unusual cloud color, high wind, a descending wall cloud, the presence of hail, and, eventually, a debris vortex. As well, most (but not all) tornadoes occur at the rear of a storm system, or after the rain and the lightning and hail. If Bob is able to satisfy the three conditions mentioned, then he will have provided adequate support for his extraordinary claim. However,

Fig. 6.10. Tornado. Image created by Vanessa Tignanelli.

one last note. Tornadoes are very volatile things. They can form and dissipate quite quickly. A more accurate assertion by Bob would have been, "It looks stormy outside, and a tornado *would* develop soon." But even with this qualification, we would still demand further strong support for the possibility of such an occurrence.

So when someone makes a claim, we need to assess first of all how strong the claim is before determining when the premises have provided adequate support. This also applies to very general claims. There seems to be a direct relationship between the generality of a claim and the number of premises required to support it. As we saw in the previous chapter, adequacy of evidence must be determined relative to the claim the evidence is intended to support. So if you state general claims like the following,

All people who wear glasses are smart.
All men with large feet have big hearts.

you are going to need a good deal of evidence to support these claims. It is important to keep your claims as specific as possible or, if your claims are quite grand, make sure you have plenty of premises—and the proper type—to back them up.

FALSE DICHOTOMY

This could also be called the "black or white fallacy" or the "only two ways about it fallacy." This fallacy occurs when someone attempts to state an argument in a way that leads us to believe there are only two alternatives. A false dichotomy is just that: it presents information in ways that mislead us into thinking the choices available have been completely represented. For example:

> Either you are with us, or you are against us.
>
> The choice for American university students is clear: they can choose not to smoke marijuana and live a healthy, happy life, or they can choose to become addicted to the deadly weed, which will inevitably lead them to harder drugs and a life of crime.
>
> DAVID: Boy, I hate this weather [walking in a snowstorm].
> ROY: Look at it this way: Either we get the snow or we get freezing rain. Which would you prefer?

In these examples, the speaker wrongly implies that the list of choices is complete. In the first case, one can be neither for nor against a particular group but can remain neutral. In the second case, one can easily imagine American university students who do neither extreme and engage in occasional marijuana smoking or who smoke heavily and never use harder drugs or commit crime. We can also imagine those afflicted by specific diseases who find smoking marijuana to be a relief from pain. In the third example,

Roy has neglected to consider that it doesn't have to be precipitating at all; it could be sunny and warm. We must always be on our guard against these types of false dichotomies because it is easy to assume that various facets of the world can be neatly polarized in this way. It can also falsely give the impression that the speaker has done some homework—that after careful consideration, it appears there are *only* two alternatives: A or B. Keep this in mind when doctors tell you or someone you care about that there are only two possible choices for an illness: taking the treatment they suggest or dealing with the harmful effects of the ailment. There is always more than one treatment available, and you need to ask for a second opinion and determine which is the best treatment in your individual circumstance.

HASTY CONCLUSION

This can also be called the "jumping to conclusions fallacy" or the "jumping the gun fallacy." In the extraordinary claims example, if Bob were to walk into a social function and mention that he believed a tornado were about to form, we would have every right to question the adequacy of his reasons for maintaining this position. It is entirely possible that Bob is jumping to conclusions. That is, for some reason he has determined the weather conditions are such that a tornado is imminent. However, if he does not have the education, expertise, or experience necessary to make such a claim, he may be jumping the gun, so to speak. I'll never forget watching *The Late Show with David Letterman* once when he showed a clip of some earthquake footage in California during a newscast. When the tremors began, the male and female anchors looked at each other in concern, and suddenly the man yelled out, "It's the big one!" and quickly dove under the desk. As it turned out, it was a rather minor earthquake by California or any seismic standards. It is safe to say that this gentleman may have made a rather hasty conclusion. But fear, ignorance, prejudice, and other biases can often lead us to make quick or rash judgments. Hasty conclusions are often drawn because we have been convinced of an argument before a sufficient amount of evidence has been gathered. See the following examples.

(P1) Because they save lives
(C1) Airbags in cars are good.

(P2) Air bags have actually caused severe injuries and deaths
(C2) So maybe they are bad after all.

(P3) Air bags have been modified to discharge under specific conditions in order to reduce the risk of injury
(C3) So maybe they are good after all.

As we saw in chapter 5, it is not always easy to know when enough evidence has been gathered in order to make a reasoned assessment of a claim. Just think about nutritional science for a moment. One year butter is bad for you. The next year butter is good, but margarine is bad for you. Coffee is bad one month and then good if one does not exceed three cups a day. High protein diets are the way to go. No, high carbohydrate diets are the way to go. No, high complex carbohydrate diets are the way to go. In life, the complexities of issues are staggering. We just have to accept the fact that evidence in some areas will be more adequate than in others. But we still need to keep asking the necessary questions to avoid arriving at conclusions too hastily.

LANGUAGE PROBLEMS

The following do not involve fallacies per se but reveal how misuse of language and concepts can give us good reason to reject a premise. The lack of conceptual clarity can more often than not lead to suspending our judgment or provisional acceptance of premises until such concepts have been clarified. To use words precisely, there are aspects of language that need to be identified and understood. The English language changes constantly. It is one of the more pliable languages on the planet. It grows according to technology (e.g., computers have generated concepts such as interfacing, downloading, hard drives, software, memory); subcultures (e.g., valley girls, hippies, punkers, grunge, hip-hop); the media (e.g., television, newspapers, Internet sources, movies, art). The English language also loses terms due to progress and the changes from one generation to the next. When was the last time you heard the expressions *nifty*, *scooters*, or *23 skidoo*? Language is a product not simply of time but also of geographic location. Although Canadians, Americans, Britons, and Australians all speak English, we have developed unique terms to describe similar objects, issues, and events (e.g., *elevator* versus *lift*, *car hood* versus *bonnet*, *TV* versus *telly*, *barbecue* versus *barbie*). Some terms gradually work their way into the language even though they may be grammatically or intentionally incorrect (e.g., the slang of "bad" for "good"). The term *irregardless* is often used but is not an actual English word. It resulted from the hybridization of *irrespective* and *regardless*. If you look carefully at the word, you will see that it is actually a double negative. Instead of saying that A exists without regard to something else, which is what *regardless* and *irrespective* both mean, the prefix *ir-* negates this meaning and states that A exists with regard to something else. Of course, George W. Bush created an interesting new hybrid. When asked about his presidential victory over Al Gore, he responded: "They misunderestimated me." You can misunderstand, and you can underestimate, but you cannot use the two together. Sarah Palin has given us the term *refudiate*. In commenting on Twitter, Palin called on Muslims to refudiate the planned development of a mosque near Ground Zero in New York City. You can refute something (prove something to be false), you can repudiate something (reject, cast off, dismiss), but Mrs. Palin made a hybrid of these two words. Often is the case that when we hear a term such as this, we can ignore the grammatically incorrect use (and apply the *principle of charity*) to appreciate the intended or contextual meaning of the word. We all misuse words. Hopefully, we can learn from our mistakes. Right, George and Sarah?

EUPHEMISMS

Euphemisms are expressions that clearly reveal the growth of the English language. They have several functions:

1. Substituting mild or indirect terms for those more harsh. For example, "passed away" is often used instead of "died." Animals are "put to sleep" or "put down" rather than "killed." And companies "downsize" rather than "massively fire" employees. The sensitivity of past phrasing spawned an entire set of descriptions and terms developed according to political correctness (e.g., "mentally retarded" became "mentally challenged" or "differently gifted," "handicapped" became "physically challenged," people were no longer called "old" but "elderly" or "senior").

2. Euphemisms can also be very harsh. In a memorable Monty Python skit, John Cleese brings in a parrot to a pet shop owner (Michael Palin) claiming that he has been swindled because the bird was already dead. The pet shop owner insists that the bird is just sleeping or is depressed, and so forth—anything but dead. John Cleese then goes into the most wonderful tirade of death euphemisms I've ever heard: "It's passed on! This parrot is no more! It has ceased to be! It's expired and gone to meet its maker! This is a late parrot! It's a stiff! Bereft of life! It rests in peace! If you hadn't nailed it to the perch, it would be pushin' up the daisies! It's run down the curtain and joined the choir invisible! This is an ex-parrot!"[24]

3. Euphemisms can also distort information, for example, using the term "police action" for "war," or referring to a "clean bomb," which kills people but leaves buildings standing.

Sometimes in the attempt to be less harsh or dramatic, euphemisms can distort what it is they are describing. And we should be on our guard to identify what others and ourselves are actually saying whenever we see, hear, or use them.

VAGUENESS AND AMBIGUITY

A *vague* term is one that is lacking precise definition or meaning, and an *ambiguous* term is one that has two or more distinct meanings. In other words, vague terms are "fuzzy" whereas ambiguous terms are clear but uncertain. Look at the following examples:

Ted is a liberal thinker.
Heather is a good student.

In both cases, we are left wondering what, precisely, the terms *liberal* and *good* mean. The problems arise because we all have our own understanding of these terms. To person A, *liberal* might mean that Ted believes in the political agenda of Canada's Liberal Party. To person B, *liberal* might mean that Ted thinks whatever he wants without caring what anyone else thinks. The same can be said of the second example. That is, how good a student is Heather? Does this mean she gets good grades? Or is it because she receives average grades but is attentive to the teacher in class? Or is it implying any number of other factors that could make a student good? When thinking about vagueness, think in terms of a scale where we have a wide area in which to establish a particular meaning. Since we cannot begin to determine what precisely the term means, we are left with conceptual obscurity. Until the vagueness is resolved, we really cannot accept such a premise. So we suspend judgment until such a time as the vague concept is clarified.

In reference to ambiguity, consider the advertisement shown in figure 6.11.

There are at least two ways we can interpret this very clever ad. There is the intended way—that the pig farmers are suggesting that we eat more pork because it is the meat we really enjoy. However, we can also interpret it to mean something a little more risqué. For those who are not familiar with euphemisms for sexual intercourse, the word *pork* sometimes means "to have sex with." So the ad, to use a colloquialism, can be taken to mean "Have intercourse with the one you love." I remember the first time I saw it advertised on a billboard as I was driving in Ontario one afternoon; I nearly had to pull over because I was laughing so hard. To this day, I think it is one of the best ads I have seen in a long while. Consider another advertisement: "Chi-Chi's. When you feel a little Mexican." Here it

P♥rk.
The one you love.

Sask **Pork**

Fig. 6.11. Pork. The One You Love. Reprinted courtesy of Sask. Pork.

appears obvious that someone in marketing was not thinking straight that day. For the ad can be taken to mean that either we should eat at Chi-Chi's when we feel like eating Mexican food, or we should feel a small Mexican person. When you think of ambiguity, imagine distinct definitions. For example, in the sentence "Bob loves sheep," the term *loves* could mean one of at least three things.

1. Bob likes eating sheep.
2. Bob likes raising sheep.
3. Bob has intercourse with sheep.

Although there are also forms of semantic ambiguity that arise due to multiple meanings of words, such as satire, pun, and irony, which exploit this aspect of the English language, in informative discourse, when the intention is to be linguistically clear, ambiguity can result due to the *equivocation* of terms. The clearer we are with our use of terms, the better and more effective our communication of ideas will be.

POST HOC FALLACY

Post hoc is a Latin phrase meaning "after this." The complete name of the fallacy is actually *post hoc ergo propter hoc*, which means, "after this, therefore, because of this." Often simply called a "post hoc fallacy," this occurs when someone assumes that because A precedes B, A *must* cause B. Consider the following examples:

> Example 1: Every Monday evening I put out the garbage on our curbside. And every Tuesday morning, a garbage truck picks it up. Therefore, my putting garbage out on the curb causes the garbage truck to come.

In this case, it is not the act of putting out the garbage that causes the truck to come. The truck will come regardless of whether or not I put out my garbage. If I miss my garbage night, I must either wait another week or take my garbage to the dump.

> Example 2: We should reactivate the World War II air-raid sirens in our town to signal when tornadoes have been spotted in the area. Knoxville did this ten years ago and hasn't seen a tornado since.

In this case, the person wrongly believes that because no tornadoes have occurred since the air-raid sirens were activated, it must be the sirens that have caused the decline in tornado activity. The actual reason may be due to coincidence or simply lack of turbulent weather.

> Example 3: In an episode of *The Simpsons*, Ned Flanders flees from a rogue bear. The city of Springfield assembles and establishes a group determined to keep bears out of the city. When Lisa talks to her father, who is on patrol, Homer tells her that since no bears have been seen, the patrol committee must be doing a good job. Lisa says that is specious reasoning: like saying the rock she is holding is responsible for keeping tigers out of Springfield. Since

no tigers have been seen, it must be due to the rock. Homer wants to purchase the rock.

It is not the patrol committee that is keeping the bears out of Springfield. It is simply because there are no bears around. The cause of the lack of bears is not the presence of the patrol committee but rather that there simply are no more bears in Springfield.

> Example 4: It's unlikely that I would be in a car accident while wearing a clown suit and driving on Highway 401. Therefore, whenever I drive on the 401, I should always wear a clown suit.[25]

If I were to drive on the 401 in a clown suit and not get into a car accident, it would not be the suit itself that has kept me safe on my travels. It would be my capabilities as a competent driver. In all cases, we can easily see how prior occurrences are not the real causes for eventual effects. The post hoc fallacy is often used hastily and anecdotally. One of the most public examples of this involves the much-publicized attempts of model/actress Jenny McCarthy to draw a causal connection between child vaccinations and autism. Just because her son developed autism *after* he was vaccinated does not necessarily mean the vaccination *caused* her son to develop autism. Since there is very little scientific evidence supporting Ms. McCarthy's claim, it would be more responsible to maintain that the causes of her son's autism are other factors. Should evidence arise indicating a causal connection between vaccinations of this type and autism, then it would be the responsibility of the National Institutes of Health, the World Health Organization, and statewide public health officials to stop its production and warn the public. Unfortunately, because parents are now vaccinating their children less often in California, the incidence of whooping cough and measles has risen noticeably.

RED HERRING

This could also be called the "something smells fishy fallacy" or the "beside the point fallacy," or even the "smoke screen fallacy." A red herring occurs whenever one uses a premise that is irrelevant to the conclusion, which distracts one away from the topic at hand—that is, when one shifts the topic in such a way that focus is no longer on the originally stated issue. See the following example

> BOB: How can you support the abortion of fetuses so that the brain tissue can be used in the treatment of Parkinson's disease?
> ANNE: Parkinson's is a disease that requires considerable funding. If we had more funding, we might not need to use such measures as treatments.

Bob's concern is with the treatment of fetuses as means to another end, in other words, to help patients of Parkinson's disease. Anne did not answer Bob but instead brought up the irrelevant point of funding. Obviously, if we had unlimited funding, we could stop a lot of questionable research. But the harsh reality is that organizations must operate on a fixed budget. Ask anyone involved in nonprofit organizations. The point in this argument is that, irrespective of funding, Bob maintains that abortion for use of the fetal brain tissue is wrong in and of itself, and Anne has failed to address Bob's concerns.

Keep in mind that for practically every situation comedy on television, you will eventually see reference to a red herring for comedic purposes. For example, whenever characters are caught doing something they otherwise should not be doing, a reference to an irrelevant point will be introduced. For example, when a husband is caught leaving to play golf with his buddies rather than stay home and finish the yard work, and his wife confronts him, he might blurt out any number of distracting red herring remarks, such as, "Have I told you how attractive you look today?" or "I think we should go out for dinner tonight," or "Have I told you how much I love you lately?" None of these responses deals with the fact that he was trying to get out of work or spending time with his wife. So they are irrelevant to the topic at hand.

Far and away, the people who use red herrings more than anyone else are lawyers and politicians. If you are careful, you can spot them in movies, on television, and in real life. One of the most famous (and obvious) red herrings in a twentieth-century trial in the United States involved the murder trial of O. J. Simpson. Mr. Simpson's defense team stated that O. J. was framed for multiple homicides because of collective racial hatred at several levels of police and forensic investigation. Mr. Simpson's lawyer, Johnnie Cochran, very successfully diverted the jury's attention away from the hard facts of the case and had them preoccupied with the incredibly unlikely possibility that O. J. Simpson was framed because of racial hatred. I can remember the case unfolding and thinking to myself about the defense team: "They're not going to play the race card." Then they did. And it worked extremely well. I am not saying racism does not exist in and around the greater Los Angeles area. I am saying that Nicole Brown Simpson and Ronald Goldman were viciously attacked and killed, and the evidence against O. J. Simpson was overwhelmingly in favor of his guilt. Two people died while a man got away with murder as the world watched the jury ignore the most important evidence of the case and instead chose to follow a red herring.

THE SLIPPERY SLOPE FALLACY

When you think of the slippery slope fallacy, imagine someone sliding down a hill with no possible way of returning upward. The slope is so slippery that once he or she starts sliding, there is no way to stop until the bottom is reached (see fig. 6.12).

This metaphor is used to argue for a chain of causal events. Once one cause starts, it will create an effect that will be the cause of another effect, and so on, until the final effect is something really terrible. We have probably all experienced either using or hearing someone use this form of reasoning at some time in our lives. Some of you may have been lectured about the dangers of smoking pot, that it is simply a "gateway drug" that

Fig. 6.12. Slippery Slope.
Image created by Sarah Sienna.

will invariably lead you to try uppers, downers, LSD, mushrooms, PCP, cocaine, heroin, and more; you will become a junkie who needs to steal and rob people to support your habit; and eventually you will end up either in prison or dead. All because of one joint. In all fairness, there have probably been people who have followed this exact path down the slippery slope. Perhaps people like Jim Morrison, John Belushi, Jimi Hendrix, Kurt Cobain, and so on. But does this mean that every person who tries marijuana will inevitably slide down that slope and die? Doubtful. In fact, I would be willing to bet that a good percentage of people who smoke pot maintain fairly active, healthy lives without ever having moved on to harder drugs. But this is something for a social scientist to figure out. What we are concerned with here is the structure of the slippery slope itself. The phrase *slippery slope* is a metaphor describing the compounding effect or long-term consequences of our actions. In other words, once we get started, we may not be able to stop. This metaphor becomes a fallacy when you can demonstrate that in starting with A, you will not slide down to B, and then to C, and finally to D—or, should you slide down to B or C or even D, that you can return or have returned to A.

Some people in the United States have argued that in allowing for the opportunity to discuss end-of-life care and considering the possibility of assisted euthanasia, there will be so-called death panels, which will execute Grandma at the first sign of a cold. The fear of the slippery slope with euthanasia is that once it becomes legalized for people with terminal issues, eventually the laws will become more and more relaxed and we will be inclined to euthanize people with non-life-threatening diseases or that many will simply give up and rush to the hospitals to be "put down." So far, in the United States, euthanasia is legal in both Washington State and Oregon. In both states, the reports indicate that people do not always choose euthanasia—even when it is legally accessible. In fact, in Oregon from 1998 to 2002, only 129 people opted for doctor-assisted suicide.[26] So it does not appear that a slippery slope effect for euthanasia is taking place in Oregon or in Washington at the moment. Currently, these figures suggest that fears driven by a slippery slope mentality have not been warranted.

STRAWMAN

This can also be referred to as the "mannequin fallacy" or the "dummy fallacy." We must take special care when interpreting someone's argument regardless of whether we agree or disagree with it. If we misrepresent an argument, not only are we being unfair to the speaker, but we also may be referring to aspects of an issue that the speaker never intended. In effect, we create our own model of the argument and proceed to comment on that. In other words, we have created a straw man (see fig. 6.13).

This metaphor is used because straw men were sometimes constructed during times of war preparation to give military trainees a practice target. By fighting the straw men, they are attacking not real enemies but constructed or fake men. The same holds for arguments. If we misinterpret a person's argument and then proceed to analyze it, this misinter-

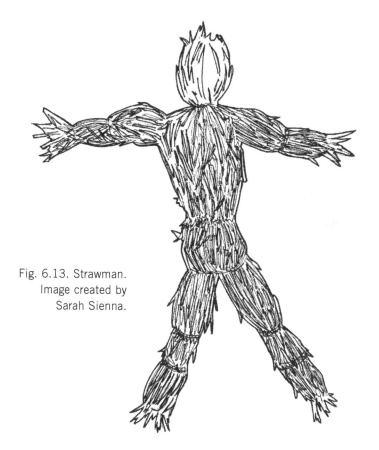

Fig. 6.13. Strawman.
Image created by
Sarah Sienna.

pretation leads to an irrelevant commentary—for we have not faithfully represented the argument. We owe it to any person to faithfully establish his or her intended position and support for it. This obligation is part of playing fair in critical thinking. How easy argumentation would be if we simply interpreted arguments to suit our own needs and thereby could dispense of them at our whim. You'd think we were politicians.

TU QUOQUE FALLACY

This could also be called the "you too! fallacy" or the "I know you are, but what am I? fallacy." Pronounced "too-kwoh-kway," this fallacy is committed when one makes an irrelevant attack against a person's similar actions in defense of an accusation by that person. It is another way of saying, "You too!" For example:

> BRIAN: Hey, Peter, you have to quit drinking so much. It's killing you!
> PETER: Oh, yeah? Well you drink too much too! So just shut up!

Regardless of whether Brian actually does drink too much, this does not mean that his statement is false or not relevant. Nor is it in any way refuted by Peter's retort. In fact, it is a type of red herring in the attempt to distract or mislead the relevance of Brian's comments away from Peter. Brian could be a terrible alcoholic; but this is not going to change the fact that Peter also has a drinking problem. Some people feel justified in acting immorally or illegally simply because others are acting in the same manner. They sometimes justify their behavior by claiming that others are acting in the same manner. This is how mob mentalities and riots can become triggered in desperate or seemingly desperate situations.

These represent a fair number of fallacies that people commit every day. It is important to know them well and recognize them when they are being committed and to avoid them in our own reasoning. This is something that comes over time and with practice. These fallacies apply not only to the Big Five but also to every aspect of our lives. Now that we have come to the end of part 1, we are equipped with some extremely powerful tools for better understanding our own views and those of others.

THE ABCs (AND DEFs) OF CRITICAL THINKING

Now that you have a good number of critical thinking tools at your disposal, you need to practice using them. The best advice I can give you at this time is to read the letters to the editors in a large newspaper. Start with the shorter letters and work your way up to the larger, more complex arguments you would find in the op-ed section. You will also find plenty of argumentative discourse on any blog. If you wish to check to see how you are doing, you can find a link on my blog at www.CriticalDonkey.com, which will provide you with some of my solutions to various letters I have found in my local newspapers.

First of all, use the techniques outlined in chapters 1 and 4 to diagram the arguments found in the letters to the editor or online in blogs. Remember that arguments look like houses. First determine what the person's conclusion is. Then look for indicator words and circle them. After you finish circling the indicator words, bracket and number the premises and, if necessary, the main premises. You may need to create a legend to list all the premises and the conclusion. Once this is completed, you can sketch the relationship between the premises and the conclusion. In this way, you will literally see what the argument looks like. This will empower you with the ability to more carefully determine to what extent you agree or disagree with the argument and respond accordingly.

After you know the structure of an argument, you can attempt to understand why the person may believe what he or she does. It may not be easy to determine the particular biases, but there may be clues that provide you with some insight into why the individual holds such beliefs. Recall what was said in chapter 2, and determine where you stand on the issues being discussed. This will provide you with time to reflect on your own biases as well. Do you agree with the person? Why or why not? What is good and what is lacking in the account? Keep in mind the advice in chapter 3. What are the circumstances and the context surrounding the letters? What motivated these people to take the time to write to the newspaper or to post a blog? Are they lonely? Are they looking for attention? Or do they have views that give others reason to reflect and consider?

Consider the evidence that has been provided or is lacking in their premises. What type of evidence is it? Personal? Scientific? Authoritative? Anecdotal? Have they provided enough evidence in relation to the conclusions they have put forward? Or are their arguments significantly lacking in some regard? If so, how?

Finally, search for fallacies. You have been given quite a few fallacies from which to choose. None of us is immune to them. But by knowing what they are and how they are committed, we can take better care to avoid them in our own reasoning and discussions and spot them in the arguments of others.

You have more than enough tools to become a really good pain in the ass. But before we consider the Big Five, we will look at some critical thinking methods from some of the greatest pains in the ass of all time: Socrates and the ancient Skeptics.

PART 2

THE BEST DAMN
PAINS IN THE ASS IN HISTORY

CHAPTER 7

THE METHOD OF SOCRATES AND THE MODES OF THE ANCIENT SKEPTICS

Now that we have covered the ABCs and DEFs of critical thinking, we will examine the methods and modes of some of history's greatest pains in the ass. Arguably, Socrates was one of the greatest pains in the ass in Western thought because he developed a method that enabled him to ask the right sorts of questions, which greatly bothered people. Known as the Socratic method, this technique was used as a means of questioning and cross-examining people about their beliefs— especially their most cherished beliefs. As you may already know, this did not go over very well with many of the local Athenians. The ancient Skeptics, on the other hand, developed an entire critical thinking system based on a series of *modes* that examined the reliability of the testimony of those who made various claims and their use of reasoning in support of their claims. The modes were individual examples that either demonstrated the relativity of a person's perspectives and beliefs or called into question the forms of reasoning that were used to justify such perspectives and beliefs. Both the Socratic method and the modes of the ancient Skeptics are extremely powerful tools that, when combined properly with the ABCs of critical thinking, will make anyone an extremely formidable pain in the ass to those who believe their particular answers to the Big Five are absolutely true or certain.

As stated in the introduction, there are limited ways in which anyone can respond to the Big Five. The two most distinct ways are *naturally* and *supernaturally*. In this chapter, we consider how Socrates and the ancient Skeptics effectively developed methods for critically examining the supernatural ways in which people have responded to and continue to respond to the Big Five.

THE SOCRATIC METHOD

In approximately 399 BCE, Socrates drank hemlock and died. Drinking poison was a form of execution—a death sentence—among the Greeks at the time. Why was he put to death? Because he was found guilty of several (trumped-up) offenses, such as corrupting the Athenian youth and not believing in the Athenian gods of the society (a charge referred to as impiety).

Much of what we know about the trial and death of Socrates comes from the great works of Plato.[1] What is important to know, historically, is that a man was sentenced to death because he tried to get people to think more clearly about why it was they believed and acted as they did. Socrates attempted to convince his fellow citizens that they were responsible for their moral beliefs and actions. He would question everyone—from the street merchant to the politician—about specific actions and closely held beliefs. In what has become known as the Socratic method, Socrates would feign ignorance regarding various ideas, concepts, and issues in order to get people to explain more clearly why they thought and acted in particular ways. It soon became clear that people quickly realized they were not as wise as they believed themselves to be. In fact, Socrates would expose their ignorance, a side of their understanding that people

Fig. 7.1. Socrates.
Image created by Vanessa Tignanelli.

were not comfortable either acknowledging or accepting. So it was often the case that people grew frustrated with his questioning.

The Socratic method is a means of questioning with which Socrates was able to reveal to people how little they really knew about a particular issue or concept, such as piety, justice, wisdom, courage, and so forth. It involved a dialogue (a discussion of sorts) between at least two people. Socrates would ask a person about a particular concept. As the person responded, Socrates would ask additional questions that would eventually demonstrate the inconsistencies of the individual's views, which would reveal how little he or she really knew about that concept. For example, in talking with a character named Euthyphro—a self-titled expert on piety—Socrates questioned him on the subject of piety. Today, a standard dictionary generally defines *piety* as the reverence one has for god(s). According to Plato's "The Apology," one of the charges of which Socrates was accused was impiety; as he is on his way to trial, he meets Euthyphro. Euthyphro informs Socrates that he, too, has been accused of impiety, and by his own family members. Socrates seizes the opportunity to find out from Euthyphro what piety is so he can better defend himself at his trial. However, Socrates quickly discovers that Euthyphro does not really know what piety means. At first, Euthyphro defines piety as the type of act he is performing (in his case, charging his own father with murder). Socrates quickly points out that Euthyphro is providing an *example* of piety rather than a *definition*, which could account for all such acts of piety. Euthyphro then modifies his definition by stating that piety involves those acts which the Greek gods admire. To this, Socrates points out that the gods could disagree with one another. Apollo might think one action to be pious while Cronos disagrees. Then Euthyphro states that those acts upon which all gods agree to be pious are, indeed, pious. To this, Socrates provides one of the most powerful arguments against any appeal to divine authority. (We will return to his response when we look at ways of answering the Big Five in part 3.) Socrates demonstrates the circularity of Euthyphro's third definition by asking him if the gods love pious actions simply because the acts are pious, or if the actions are pious because the gods love them? To this Euthyphro states that the gods love the actions because they are pious. Socrates responds by pointing out that there must be an independent reason for the piety of the actions other than the love from the gods. In other words, what is it about pious acts that makes the gods love them so? Such an account does not tell Socrates what makes the actions pious but only of how the gods react to them. We see here a fine example of someone, Euthryphro, who believes he is acting piously because of his particular beliefs. But is he? He changes his definition many times and only thinks he knows why he acts the way he does. Socrates was extremely adept at questioning others in this way. In regard to concepts, his method involved the search for commonality or the essence which all specific acts of piety, love, beauty, possess. People then, as today, did not like to have their most heartfelt beliefs undermined and their actions questioned. They were quite secure in their so-called knowledge of the world and their actions in it. Socrates likened himself to a "gadfly" that buzzes around society (metaphorically represented as a lazy horse) in order to get it moving. To better understand the importance of the actions of Socrates, ask yourself this: Has there ever been a time in history when we were so sure of ourselves and our understanding of the world that we no longer needed to critically reflect on what our beliefs were and why it was we believed and acted the way we did? As a society, we sometimes get lazy in our beliefs, either through feelings of apathy or because the system itself imposes particular fashions of activity that become entrenched and rarely questioned, or because we lack the power to critically think about important issues and express ourselves in logical and convincing ways.

Socrates is one of the finest historical examples of a person who thought for himself. He did not let society dictate to him what was right and wrong, good and bad. He thought very carefully about extremely important issues and questioned others whenever he could. He was, without doubt, a gadfly, and a very good one. Today, some would call him a pain in the ass. But he was a really good pain in the ass (one of the best, in fact) because he would force members of his society to consider matters that they believed were of the highest importance. Critically reflective people are (or often should be) pains in the ass because people do not like to have their beliefs challenged due to a fear of revealing weakness or lack of knowledge, or a fear of losing some form of control over their world. This is perfectly natural. However, if we are to be of any use to society, we should be capable of generating within people the capacity for critically reflective thought. People generally do not like to be shown to be ignorant or somehow lacking in certain respects. Excluding class clowns and other types of attention seekers, who likes to look stupid? To be a really good pain in the ass, then, is to get people (including ourselves) to examine their beliefs and actions in a thoughtful, responsible way.

It is not uncommon to see the Socratic method used by various people in different professions. Lawyers use the technique in cross-examining witnesses; police officers use it to question suspects; physicians and doctors use it in their attempts to uncover hidden information that might help in the diagnosis of an illness; psychiatrists and psychologists use it to help people better understand their own motivations and actions; and teachers at all levels use it to help students come to understand abstract ideas and concepts. It is a technique that allows people to talk about their views in an effort to come across potential problems, fallacies, or other inconsistencies in the hope of clarifying a position or understanding. Fake news journalists on both *The Daily Show with Jon Stewart* and *The Colbert Report* rely heavily on the Socratic method for their satirical analysis of the views of various guests, interviewees, and others. They do so in much the same way as Socrates did more than 2,400 years ago. Here, in a nutshell, is an effective way of using this method:

1. Begin by provisionally agreeing with your discussant's conclusion and maintain that his or her views are important or interesting or compelling. I know this may seem unusual, especially if you are in disagreement with the discussant's conclusion, but it immediately puts the other person at ease and identifies you as someone willing to listen. If you come across as too in-your-face, he or she can easily become defensive and guarded. Try to imagine what the person's argument looks like as a house. If you already know what the conclusion is, try to understand what its supporting premises and assumptions are.

2. As your discussant begins to tell you more about the premises in support of the conclusion, casually point out to him or her any inconsistencies or contradictions you notice. Remember to continue to agree that the ideas are still interesting. Your tone should not be sarcastic or condescending but one of genuine or feigned interest. At this point, you should be able to make a mental map of some of the biases in the argument. Appreciate the context in which the individual is presenting the premises and, although you might not be able to physically diagram the position, you should be able to determine what type of evidence is being used to further support the premises.

3. The more your discussant tells you about his or her ideas, the more likely it is that you will be able to identify further inconsistencies in the form of fallacies. You may tell the person that you still want to believe what is being presented or that you understand why he or she has this belief, but there is some work to do first. If you are able to point out specific fallacies the argument has committed, you can suggest that these need to be resolved before you can be fully convinced of his or her views.

At this point, you will generally find two possible reactions: your discussant will appreciate any clarity you may have brought to the discussion, or he or she will not appreciate your comments and will find you to be a bit of a pain in the ass. Either way, this method is designed for the purposes of generating dialogue in an attempt to establish greater clarity on why people believe and act the way they do.

In Plato's work, "The Apology," we find Socrates on trial for using his method in an effort to get people to think more clearly about their ideas and actions. It is one of the greatest pieces of philosophic writing ever written—both in content and in style—and it is an eloquent courtroom account of why Socrates acted the way he did (here, the word *apology* means "explanation").[2] In "The Apology," we find that, in defense of his life for allegedly corrupting the youth of Athens and not believing in the deities of the state (impiety), Socrates gives to humanity its greatest gift.

He makes the important—if not *the* most important—distinction between knowledge regarding matters of the natural world and knowledge regarding supernatural matters. The former deal with everyday, commonsense activities like eating, sleeping, going to work, paying your taxes, going to the washroom, having sex, raising a family, and so on. Over time, our rational and empirical understanding of the commonsense world eventually gave rise to a more consistent and comprehensive understanding that eventually developed into the sciences. Supernatural attempts to understand the world, however, deal with matters that lie beyond any naturalized understanding. So, by definition, such information cannot be studied and discussed in the same manner as other types of information, like commonsense and scientific matters. Today's scientific methodologies, which incorporate this same distinction, rest on a legacy more than 2,400 years old. We see the origins of such a legacy develop when Socrates begins his appeal against his charges. When asked by the jurors from whence such charges against Socrates could have arisen, he responds by saying that he has developed something of a reputation in and around Athens. His reputation arose, he believes, because of a statement by the Pythia or priestess of Apollo at the Oracle (shrine) of Delphi atop Mount Parnassus. The Pythia was considered to be a wise priestess who, for a price, used trance-induced powers of insight to offer advice and words of wisdom to people. She was considered a medium through which the god Apollo spoke—a sort of ancient cryptic psychic, if you will.

> Generals sought the oracle's advice on strategy. Colonists asked for guidance before they set sail for Italy, Spain and Africa. Private citizens inquired about health problems and investments.... The oracle of Delphi functioned in a specific place, the *adyton*, or "no entry" area of the temple's core, and through a specific person, the Pythia, who was chosen to speak, as a possessed medium, for Apollo, the god of prophecy.[3]

Many scientists today believe the site of the room in which the oracle received her "insight" was located directly over geologic faults from which vapors (or *pneuma*) would rise. Recently, geologists have discovered

Fig. 7.2. Oracle of Delphi. Image created by Vanessa Tignanelli.

deposits of methane, ethane, and ethylene in the travertine rocks of the ancient springs at Delphi. This has led some to believe that, essentially, the priestess would become intoxicated by the fumes and then, from a trance-like state, produce various messages to those seeking her advice (see fig. 7.2).

Often, the oracle's response would be in an enigmatic or riddle form. In the case of Socrates, his friend Chairephon had asked the oracle at Delphi if there were any man wiser than Socrates. Her response was that "no one is wiser." When Socrates heard of this reply, he asked himself:

> "Whatever does the god [Apollo] mean? What is his riddle? I am very conscious that I am not wise at all; what then does he mean by saying that I am the wisest? For surely he does not lie; it is not legitimate for him to do so." For a long time I was at a loss as to his meaning; then I very reluctantly turned to some such investigation as this: I went to one of those reputed wise, thinking that there, if anywhere, I could refute the oracle and say to it: "This man is wiser than I, but you said I was." Then when I examined this man—there is no need for me to tell you his name, he was one of our public men [a politician]—my experience was

something like this: I thought that he appeared wise to many people and especially to himself, but he was not. I then tried to show him that he thought himself wise, but that he was not. As a result he came to dislike me, and so did many of the bystanders. So I withdrew and thought to myself: "I am wiser than this man; it is likely that neither of us knows anything worthwhile, but he thinks he knows something when he does not, whereas when I do not know, neither do I think I know; so I am likely to be wiser than he, and I thought the same thing, and so I came to be disliked both by him and by many others.[4]

After questioning the politicians, Socrates questions the poets and the craftspeople in the same manner and discovered this:

As a result of this investigation, gentlemen of the jury, I acquired much unpopularity, of a kind that is hard to deal with and is a heavy burden; many slanders came from these people and a reputation for wisdom, for in each case the bystanders thought that I myself possessed the wisdom that I proved that my interlocutor did not have. What is probable, gentlemen, is that in fact the god is wise and that his oracular response meant that human wisdom is worth little or nothing, and that when he says this man, Socrates, he is using my name as an example, as if he said: 'This man among you, mortals, is wisest who, like Socrates, understands that his wisdom is worthless." So even now I continue this investigation as the god bade me—and I go around seeking out anyone, citizen or stranger, whom I think wise. Then if I do not think he is, I come to the assistance of the god and show him that he is not wise. Because of this occupation, I do not have the leisure to engage in public affairs to any extent, nor indeed to look after my own, but I live in great poverty because of my service to the god [Apollo].[5]

In other words, Socrates is on what might be called "a mission from god." He wants to disprove the claim of the god Apollo, who apparently spoke through the Pythia, who, while quite high in a trancelike state, stated that none is wiser than Socrates. In so doing, his method of investigation [the Socratic method] continues to keep him in public disfavor. Add to this the social phenomenon of young Athenian men finding his methods impressionable (what we might today call "cool"), and you have the recipe for a public nuisance. So in terms of corrupting the youth of Athens, if Socrates was influencing young men to question the concepts and knowledge claims that others believed to know with absolute certainty, it is not surprising to see how this would upset those in positions of social and political importance. In terms of not believing in the Athenian gods of his society, it is clear that Socrates's mission is one presented to him by none other than the Pythia of the Oracle of Delphi, who is the mystical speaker on behalf of Apollo. It is a matter for debate, of course, regarding whether Socrates actually believed in such deities. He could have simply been using the mythologies of the Greeks metaphorically in order to prove his overall point—that humans do not possess wisdom (or knowledge) of a supernatural nature. For if we dig just a little below the surface, what emerges from the Socratic method and the distinction of supernatural from commonsense beliefs is that the existence of Apollo clearly lies in the realm of the supernatural.

To further demonstrate his capacity for *reflective ignorance*, when confronted with the threat of execution for his crimes, Socrates maintains:

> To fear death, gentlemen, is no other than to think oneself wise when one is not, to think one knows what one does not know. No one knows whether death may not be the greatest of all blessings for a man, yet men fear it as if they knew that it is the greatest of evils. And surely it is the most blameworthy ignorance to believe that one knows what one does not know. It is perhaps on this point and in this respect, gentlemen, that I differ from the majority of men, and if I were to claim that I am wiser than anyone in anything, it would be in this, that, as I have no adequate knowledge of things in the underworld, so I do not think I have.[6]

It is both pretentious and arrogant to think that one is in possession of supernatural knowledge. Later in "The Apology," Socrates speaks of death again as consisting of only two possibilities: that there is either a continuation of our being (somehow and in some way), or there is no continuation of our being:

Let us reflect in this way, too, that there is good hope that death is a blessing, for it is one of two things: either the dead are nothing and have no perception of anything, or it is, as we are told, a change and a relocating for the soul from here to another place. If it is complete lack of perception, like a dreamless sleep, then death would be a great advantage. For I think that if one had to pick out that night during which a man slept soundly and did not dream, put beside it the other nights and days of his life, and then see how many days and nights had been better and more pleasant than that night, not only a private person but the great king would find them easy to count compared with the other days and nights. If death is like this I say it is an advantage, for all eternity would then seem to be no more than a single night. If, on the other hand, death is a change from here to another place, and what we are told is true and all who have died are there, what greater blessing could there be, gentlemen of the jury? . . . I think it would be pleasant. Most important, I could spend my time testing and examining people there, as I do here, as to who among them is wise, and who thinks he is, but is not.[7]

Those who believe that death is a state of a particular type lack the abilities to make such a claim. It is toward such people that Socrates directs his attacks:

I was attached to this city by the god—though it seems a ridiculous thing to say—as upon a great and noble horse which was somewhat sluggish because of its size and needs to be stirred up by a kind of gadfly. It is to fulfill some such function that I believe the god has placed me in the city. I never cease to rouse each and every one of you, to persuade and reproach you all day long and everywhere I find myself in your company.[8]

After the jury gives its verdict of guilty, Meletus asks for the death penalty. Socrates maintains that his penalty should consist of free meals for the rest of his life at the town hall of Athens (the Prytaneum). In response to the possibility of exile or, essentially, a gag order as a punishment, Socrates responds by saying:

If I say that it is impossible for me to keep quiet because that means dis-
obeying the god, you will not believe me and will think I am being iron-
ical. On the other hand, if I say that it is the greatest good for a man to
discuss virtue every day and those other things about which you hear
me conversing and testing myself and others, for the unexamined life is
not worth living . . . you will believe me even less.[9]

In his final address to the jurors, Socrates gives the haunting prophecy of
this book and for all of critical thinking:

Now I want to prophesy to those who convicted me, for I am at the
point when men prophesy most, when they are about to die. I say gentlemen, to those who voted to kill me, that vengeance will come upon
you immediately after my death, a vengeance much harder to bear than
that which you took in killing me. You did this in the belief that you
would avoid giving an account of your life, but I maintain that quite the
opposite will happen to you. There will be more people to test you,
whom I now held back, but you did not notice it. They will be more difficult to deal with as they will be younger and you will resent them
more. You are wrong if you believe that by killing people you will prevent anyone from reproaching you for not living in the right way. To
escape such tests is neither possible nor good, but it is best and easiest
not to discredit others but to prepare oneself to be as good as possible.
With this prophecy to you who convicted me, I part from you.[10]

And in the final lines of "The Apology," Socrates personalizes his mission
by applying it to himself and those he loves most—his sons:

I am certainly not angry with those who convicted me, or with my
accusers. Of course that was not their purpose when they accused and
convicted me, but they thought they were hurting me, and for this they
deserve blame. This much I ask from them: when my sons grow up,
avenge yourselves by causing them the same kind of grief that I caused
you, if you think they care for money or anything else more than they care
for virtue, or if they think they are somebody when they are nobody.
Reproach them as I reproach you, that they do not care for the right

things and think they are worthy when they are not worthy of anything. If you do this, I shall have been justly treated by you, and my sons also.[11]

If Plato's account of Socrates is accurate, we are witness to a man with considerable integrity. Staring into the face of death, Socrates chose the path of integrity by using the Athenian court as a means by which to demonstrate the absurdity of the beliefs of the majority of Athenians—including many of the jurors themselves. At the risk of sounding sexist, Socrates had balls the size of coconuts.

Socrates was willing to die for his beliefs. But unlike religious martyrs, zealots, or terrorists, Socrates did not die for a specific set of supernatural beliefs but for a *method* of analyzing others' beliefs. It was not his particular beliefs that bothered the Athenians of his day. It was the manner and method in which he questioned them. His method revealed ignorance, pretense, and arrogance in those who were deluded into believing that they possessed genuine supernatural knowledge. As you can imagine, this revelation deeply bothered them. Socrates stands as a wonderful model for what it means to be a really good pain in the ass. Societies need more people like him. Although his method was well suited to reveal the ignorance and pride of those claiming to have supernatural knowledge, we need to expand upon his method somewhat. Fortunately, history has taken care of this in the writings of the ancient Skeptics.

THE MODES OF THE ANCIENT SKEPTICS

In a story from the *Weekly World News*,[12] a headline reads: HELP! BIGFOOT BABY IS A HAIRY BRAT! Apparently, a Bigfoot offspring cub was found in Yellowstone National Park and was giving its caretakers a rough time. In another issue, headlines read: JESUS CHRIST RETURNS TO EARTH THIS FALL . . . AND EXACT DATE THE WORLD WILL END! and SECRET GOVERNMENT PLAN TO TATTOO EVERY AMERICAN WITH THE NUMBER 666![13] Should we believe these and other similar stories? We often find these stories to be ridiculous because they cannot possibly correspond to what we experience in everyday, normal life. They are inconsistent with the structure of our methods and means of explaining events in the world. These stories seem too bizarre to be true. So we look upon them with a certain amount of reservation. We *doubt* their truth, and we believe we have good reason to doubt them. In other words, we are *skeptical* toward them. At this point, I should point out that contrary to what many believe, the term *skeptic* does not mean "doubter." The Greek term *skeptikos* means "inquirer" or "investigator." Originally, skepticism was referred to as Pyrrhonism—so named after its founder, Pyrrho (pronounced "peer-oh"), a man who lived on the western side of the Greek Peloponnesus in a city named Elis.

Born around 360 BCE, Pyrrho, like Socrates, never kept a systematic method of his philosophy in writing. Most of what we have of Pyrrho today comes from the writings of his star pupil, Timon. Instead of elaborating a complex written system, Pyrrho offered his followers an *agoge* (pronounced "agg-oh-gay"), which basically means an exemplary way of living. Though not much is known as to the specific lifestyle that Pyrrho professed, we do know it involved living peacefully according to the laws and customs of the state. Now, this does not sound like a terribly radical or interesting lifestyle to pursue, considering we have just seen how Socrates was executed for teaching Athenians to question all aspects of society. But there is much more to Pyrrho's philosophy. To fully appreciate Pyrrho's contribution to critical thinking, we need to keep in mind that the central goal of much ancient Greek philosophy was happiness.

Fig. 7.3. Pyrrho of Elis.
Image created by Vanessa Tignanelli.

But this was no ordinary or base form of happiness. It involved a contentment of mind in the conduct of life. Contentment, it was believed, could be attained by satisfying one's curiosity regarding the really big supernatural questions of the day: What is the nature of Reality? How should one act toward others? Does God exist? Do we somehow survive death? From Pyrrho's student Timon, we learn that if a people are to be happy or content, they must ask themselves three questions and answer them to the best of their ability:

What Is the Stuff of Things?

Pyrrho's response is that all our senses—sight, sound, touch, smell, and taste—and all the proposed supernatural theories of his day, contradict one another when they refer to the nature or essence or "stuff" of things. For example, when we taste honey, is the sweetness in the honey, or is it in us? Certain foods may smell sweet but have a bitter taste. An object may look smooth but in fact be quite rough to the touch. Our senses, then, contradict themselves when we attempt to determine the true nature of things. So, too, do the supernatural theories about the nature of reality contradict one another. The prime component is air, or is it water? Or motion? Or atoms?

In What Relation Do We Stand to Things around Us?

This is one of the first places in recorded history where we see evidence of someone considering humans as possessing biases when it comes to making judgments about the world. Pyrrho is stating that humans affect the way in which the world is perceived, interpreted, and acted upon. When it comes to conflicting theories concerning the absolute supernatural essence of things, Pyrrho suggests that we refrain from siding either one way or the other because they are equally plausible or implausible. So we must engage in *epoche* (pronounced "epp-okay"): the suspension of assent or belief. In regard to supernatural accounts of the nature of Reality, it is the withholding of belief in the face of equally plausible or implausible claims. Like Socrates, Pyrrho explicitly recognized his own ignorance and, by so doing, acknowledged a lack of absolute knowledge concerning Reality. And in light of this realization, Pyrrho remained quiet concerning the supernatural essence of things. In other words, since one cannot determine one way or the other which supernatural doctrines are true and which are false, one should choose neither and remain silent—for nothing true can be said concerning their supernatural essence or being. This does not mean, however, that a Pyrrhonian simply remains quiet regarding natural issues. On the contrary, the skeptic is very interested and active in practical affairs but recognizes, as did Socrates, the very important distinction between what can be said about natural issues and how difficult it is to know information about supernatural issues.

What Is the Result, as Far as Our Happiness Is Concerned, of This Supernatural Detachment?

To Pyrrho, this detachment of belief (or *epoche*) led to a state of tranquility of the mind. By abstaining from fanaticism concerning supernatural matters that apparently cannot be proved, we can become content with living peacefully among our experiences without the need to know the nature of Reality or to impose our beliefs of supernatural Reality onto others. This peaceful state of contentment was not simply an anaesthetic that would numb one to the occurrences of day-to-day life. Pyrrho did not simply walk around Elis in a state of Buddhist indifference to life, staring at his belly button all day long. Nor was he so indifferent to the activities of life that he would disregard them. A biographer during the third century CE named Diogenes Laertius claimed that Pyrrho would walk through the streets of Elis completely oblivious to various obstacles and dangers. There are stories of Pyrrho citing that he would not look where he was going—for why should it matter one way or the other whether walking in front of an ox cart, or off a cliff, might cause him harm? If it were not for his commonsense friends who always managed to pull Pyrrho out of the way of traffic and away from cliffs, he would most certainly have forgone a most untimely death. There is also the story of

Pyrrho who, when seeing his teacher Anaxarchus stuck in the mud, refused to help him out, claiming that it did not matter one way or the other if he helped him. But many scholars today dispute the claims of Diogenes. Instead, they see the *agoge* of Pyrrho as being quite different. Many scholars believe that Pyrrho was a man of common sense who would never have endangered his life or any other for the sake of indifference to his own senses. So he avoided things like ox carts and cliffs and helped his friends in times of need. Pyrrho's indifference was directed mainly at the dogmatic and fanatical views of philosophers who held supernatural beliefs to be absolutely certain. Rather than trying to strip off or numb his ordinary human feelings, he exercised moderation in the face of the massive, unyielding forces of nature (like death and illness) that all humans must meet.[14]

Like Socrates, Pyrrho acknowledged his own ignorance regarding supernatural events and distinguished these from everyday practical activities. In such a manner, both Socrates and Pyrrho were among the first to distinguish two types of human ignorance: *reflective* and *nonreflective*. Both Pyrrho and Socrates were aware or reflective of their own ignorance regarding supernatural explanations of the world. However, they encountered many who believed (and today many more believe) to be in possession of supernatural answers to the Big Five. The difference between the two types of ignorance is that those who are reflective of their ignorance regarding supernatural matters admit it and accept it, while those who believe to have answered the Big Five with absolute certainty are often nonreflective, unaware, and oblivious to the fact that they really do not possess such knowledge. They tend to suffer from a condition which, to use the vernacular, might be called Head-Up-Ass Syndrome (HUAS). In order to be a really good pain in the ass, it is sometimes argumentatively necessary to figuratively help others pull their heads out from this particular orifice. Thus freed, they will be able to see more clearly that they did not possess genuine Truth about the nature of Reality. They might become humbled with this new clarity in recognizing their own ignorance on supernatural matters.

Historically, several skeptical schools of thought developed after

Pyrrho, and many skeptics helped contribute to the development of what would eventually become scientific reasoning.[15] Many, such as the Academic Skeptics, continued the tradition of doubt and inquiry made popular by Socrates and Pyrrho and continued to stress the importance of distinguishing between the appearance of things and the absolute nature of things. This distinction between appearance and reality became extremely important. It continued to make the very important distinction between supernatural matters—matters that could not be resolved by any rational or empirical means—and commonsense matters—matters that one must deal with on a day-to-day, practical level. Many of these Academic Skeptics continued to attack the views of those who believed to be in possession of absolute Truth: the dogmatists. The term *dogmatic* comes from the Greek *dogmatikos*, meaning "doctrinaire thinker." A dogmatist is someone who holds *dogmata*—not merely beliefs, but theoretical doctrines, tenets, or principles, to be absolutely true. The Academic Skeptics also introduced a detailed doctrine for living everyday life. They developed rules and a vocabulary for dealing with and interacting with their experiences, which have collectively been called the Practical Criterion (which we will look at shortly).

The first of the great Academic skeptics was a man named Arcesilaus (315–240 BCE). After Plato's death, Arcesilaus became the head of Plato's Academy (one of the first universities) and immediately rejected Plato's metaphysical doctrines. Arcesilaus focused his criticism mainly on the Stoics. The Stoics believed that certain perceptions are self-evidently true and cannot be doubted.[16] They believed these perceptions were so strong that they would force the mind to assent to them and, by so doing, one could grasp the absolute Truth of things in the universe.

> To this Arcesilaus answered that when a "wise man" points to a given perception and calls it the truth, we follow him and also call it the truth; but when a fool points out a given perception and calls *it* the truth, we laugh at him, call it an illusion. But this is to beg the whole question about what is the truth: We have no criterion for deciding who is indeed the Sage [the wise man] and who is the fool; and lacking an ultimate,

universally satisfactory standard, we cannot tell when we have indeed [certain representations] before us or when we have representations that only look certain. And so we should engage in *epoche* with respect to such perceptions, [and] should suspend judgment upon their truth.[17]

The problem of establishing a criterion or set of criteria upon which we can rely as justification for our various beliefs has been around for a long time. The problem has, to this day, always centered around our conceptual and intellectual limitations for devising or discovering a universal criterion, or what I have referred to as a Reality Measuring Stick. For example, ask yourself a supernatural question, such as "Does God exist?" If you answer affirmatively, you need to support this conclusion with appropriate premises. If you simply maintain that the absolute truth of this proposition is based on blind faith, then I could easily have similar beliefs about fairies, gnomes, Santa Claus, and so forth, and you would have no way to refute me. As we saw with the appeal to ignorance fallacy, it is impossible to sufficiently prove a negative. What we must remember is that the person who makes the claim is the one who has the burden to prove his or her conclusion with the use of supporting premises. This comes in the form of evidence. If you wish to offer support, or evidence, for the existence of such a being, you may appeal to the Bible (King James or other versions), the Koran, the Torah, or the so-called holy texts of more than one thousand other religious sects. If I ask you how you can know that the words of such texts are true, you will be at a loss. You may reason in a circle, claiming that the words of these texts are true because God says they are true within their pages. Or that God has spoken to you personally. Or that greater minds than yours have researched the holy texts and found them to be convincing, and you believe them. But ultimately, you will run out of appeals—that is, criteria, on which to rest your beliefs because you do not have a Reality Measuring Stick—a device that could measure and determine the absolute Truth of everyone's views regarding the Big Five (see fig. 7.4).

It is for this reason that all world religions rely on faith, which, in turn, makes most of their propositions quite dubious and impossible to measure.

Fig. 7.4. Reality Measuring Stick. Image created by Sarah Sienna.

It is for this reason that we have so many differences of opinions regarding the way people answer the Big Five. Having a Reality Measuring Stick would settle the score on such disputes once and for all. It would allow all people on this planet to see for themselves who is right and precisely why they are right. But we do not have such a device. The ancient Skeptics realized this a long time ago. So they developed a wonderful story to use as a tool to demonstrate this, called the "gold in the dark room" example.

THE "GOLD IN THE DARK ROOM" EXAMPLE

Imagine, if you will, a room filled with many people seated in chairs. Now imagine that the room is completely dark so that none of the people can see anything at all, not even their hands before their own faces. They are now told that metal cups have been placed under their chairs and each one is made of different metals: iron, lead, steel, silver, bronze, brass—and only one cup made of gold. Each cup weighs exactly the same, is shaped the same, and is predominantly made up of different metals with some alloys used to make their densities indistinguishable. No discernable difference can be determined by simply holding them, smelling them, clanging them together, or even tasting them. The people in the room are then asked to pass around the various cups to one another for a few minutes. After a period of five minutes a voice calls out asking for the person who possesses the golden cup to respond. The analogy here is quite simple. Stating supernatural beliefs is like saying you are holding the golden cup in the dark room. Even if you had the golden cup in your hands, you would not know it, because none of us can see in the dark. We may be in possession of supernatural beliefs, which may ultimately be absolutely true. However, the big problem is that we have no way of knowing this because we lack the ability to check them against any type of measuring device. In other words, we cannot turn on the lights. With supernatural beliefs, we are constantly in the dark. This is because we do not have a Reality Measuring Stick. If we did, we would be able to determine whose beliefs measure up more and less accurately to Reality. In other words, a Reality Measuring Stick would allow us to turn on the lights to see who is holding the golden cup. Until we can establish such a measuring device, we will all remain in the dark in determining who, if anyone, is holding the golden cup. What supernaturalists tend to do is not only claim to be holding the golden cup (for whatever reasons) but also maintain that we cannot prove that they are *not* holding the golden cup. This is a fallacious appeal to ignorance: "For all you know, we are holding the golden cup, and you don't know for sure that we're not." In this way, supernaturalists use the same ignorance that results from our not possessing a Reality Measuring Stick to give their views legitimacy or credence.

In all honesty, we must simply accept the fact that there is currently no way to determine the absolute Truth or falsity about supernatural matters. The responsible move would be to do as the ancient Skeptics and suspend judgment (*epoche*) and not worry about such speculations. Yet this is far easier said than done. Many believe so strongly that they have accurately answered the Big Five that they will claim all others are somehow lacking in "seeing the light." In so doing, they echo the words of Cassius in Shakespeare's *Julius Caesar*: "The fault, dear Brutus, is not in our stars, But in ourselves, that we are underlings."[18] How ironically accurate this statement is. Many supernaturalists will insist that their answers to the Big Five are true for all people on this planet; others simply cannot "see" this Truth because the fault is not with a particular god or deity but with us. The obvious problem with this, of course, is that logically they cannot all be right, for this is not consistently possible. All supernatural answers to the Big Five cannot all together, consistently, be absolutely True. In other words, they cannot all be holding the golden cup and seeing themselves to be holding it. To do so is to breach the law of noncontradiction. Look at it this way: Some people answer the Big Five through supernatural beliefs in a monotheistic god (or one god, e.g., Christians, Jews, Muslims); others answer the Big Five through supernatural beliefs in polytheistic gods (or many gods, e.g., Hindus, Pagans). It is logically and physically impossible for both sets of supernatural beliefs to be absolutely True simultaneously. However, it is perfectly consistent to maintain the possibility that all super-natural beliefs can be wrong, and if so, then no one is holding the golden cup and no one can "see the light."

In reference to such supernatural matters, the advice of Socrates and the ancient Skeptics is to admit one's ignorance and suspend judgment. If you do not wish to suspend judgment, anything that is said about such matters after such an admission to ignorance must be done with the awareness that you might be entirely and completely wrong. The great value of this realization and admission of ignorance is that we are *humbled* by acknowledging that we are limited in our knowledge. Once we have this realization, we can better get on with matters that affect us more directly—such as commonsense practical affairs. Humility, attained in this manner, is a responsible starting point in the acquisition of informa-tion. It is the type of humility that levels the playing field for all humans. Such humility is entirely egalitarian. Reflecting upon one's ignorance in a responsible manner is not privy to those with doctorates or only to white males. It applies to every human on this planet. It cuts through any and all barriers—naturally or culturally created. This is not to say that such a real-ization means supernatural matters are not important. On the contrary, we know that billions of people hold them to be extremely important. In recognizing this, we should be able to find ways to intelligently discuss such matters without the need for violent confrontation. But this will take some doing. The distinction here—and I will repeat—the very important distinction here, is the conscious recognition and separation between supernatural matters—the truth of which we currently cannot deter-mine—and commonsense (and eventually, scientific) matters, the truth of which we can determine, at least in a tentative, communal, and practical way. Historically, one of the greatest legacies that Socrates and the ancient Skeptics has given us is an understanding of the overall framework in which we attempt to understand the world and ourselves. It appears to be a very mature and well-conceptualized model in the way it looks at what is involved in everyone's attempt to understand the world. I believe this is one of our species' greatest cultural and conceptual accomplishments—the separation of *Big T* (or supernatural) Truth from *little t* (or common-sense and scientific) truth (see fig. 7.5).

As we progress through this chapter, we shall discover more valuable tools that the ancient Skeptics contributed to our understanding of ourselves and that have been forgotten or abandoned for far too long.

By the second century CE, the Post-Academic Skeptics had developed highly systematized means for demonstrating the shortcomings of the arguments of the dogmatists. The skeptics developed tools called modes that they would use when discussing any topics with the dogmatic thinkers. Some of the modes dealt with how our perceptions and observations of the world conflicted and disagreed, while other modes attacked the ways in which proof was offered by the dogmatists. These modes allowed the ancient Skeptics to ask the right sorts of questions to the dogmatists, which demonstrated the inability of people to acknowledge when they had attained absolute knowledge of Reality (or were capable of seeing that they were holding the golden cup). With these modes, all people can equip themselves with enough ammunition to become a consummate pain in the ass. For example, a second-century skeptic named

Fig. 7.5. Big T Truth and small t truth. Image created by Sarah Sienna.

Sextus Empiricus lists ten modes from what is arguably the greatest skeptical work ever written: *The Outlines of Pyrrhonism*. These modes, developed by a philosopher named Aenesidemus, deal with the relativity of conflicting appearances.

TEN MODES DEALING WITH CONFLICTING PERCEPTIONS AND OBSERVATIONS

1. The first mode depicts the type of relativity that exists between species, for example, a fish sees the world in different ways than a fly, who sees the world differently than a bird, who sees the world differently than a human, and so on. In this regard, who has the Reality Measuring Stick that would determine which species sees the world more accurately or closer to Reality than any other species? The fact of the matter is that we cannot determine this. We can only acknowledge our ignorance in this respect and must suspend judgment.

   For any dogmatist who answers the Big Five and believes himself or herself to be in possession of absolute certainty, one can simply ask: "How do you know it is humans and not, say, ants, cutthroat trout, African elephants, lions, or orangutans that more accurately see and understand the nature of Reality?" To appropriately address this question, the dogmatist must provide a way in which to measure human qualities against those of ants, cutthroat trout, African elephants, lions, orangutans, and every other existing species (of which there are approximately two million known and an estimated five to fifty million unknown[19]). Zoologists and ethologists know a great deal about animal behavior, but we have little idea as to what the animals are experiencing when they observe and interact in the world. Philosopher Thomas Nagel has written about this a great deal.[20] Nagel's point is that we can objectively understand the hardware of a species, but we will probably never be able to know what another species is actually experiencing. To the ancient Skeptics, since we lack a Reality Measuring Stick, we are at a loss to say which species is most privileged in this regard. Since we are quite ignorant with respect to the experiences of other species, the skeptic's advice is to simply suspend judgment.

2. The second mode is based on the differences between individual human beings. According to your particular physical and mental biases, you will understand and act in the world differently than those who are biologically predisposed differently than you. So how can we tell whose biases and filters best determine how to understand and act in the world? Again, we have no Reality Measuring Stick to determine this.

3. The third mode is based on the differences between the senses that can produce different impressions of things. For example, optical illusions in their many forms trick our senses; some foods and perfumes smell sweet but taste bad. As well, does an apple's qualities of smell, texture, and taste owe this to itself or to the structure of our own senses? Would such a fruit be experienced the same way by all humans? By all species? We do not know. So what is the absolute truth of an apple? We cannot determine this any more than we can determine absolute answers to the Big Five.

4. The fourth mode is based on the idea that our perceptions always depend on our circumstantial (or physical and intellectual) conditions at the time we perceive things. The ancient Skeptics were very adept in realizing that factors such as age, being awake or asleep, feeling tired or alert, being at motion or at rest, being in love or in hatred, feeling hungry or satiated, being drunk or sober, feeling happy or sad, and so on, are all circumstances that will affect the way in which we see, understand, and act in the world. If you have read a book, visited a city, or watched a movie several times at different stages in your life, you may experience it quite differently due to your age and life experiences. From the time I was a boy until now in middle age, I have experienced Shakespeare's *Hamlet* differently every time I have read it or seen it per-

formed. One may rightly ask: At which point in my life did I most accurately experience the play? The ancient Skeptics were well aware of human biases and used this knowledge to demonstrate the shortcomings of those dogmatists who professed to know, with absolute certainty, the nature of Reality. We can use these modes as well, to demonstrate the shortcomings of dogmatists who claim to answer the Big Five with absolute certainty.

5. The fifth mode is based on positions, distances, and locations. Things appear differently in different positions and at different distances. Observing an airplane at a distance gives the illusion that it is moving slowly, but viewing it at a closer range reveals the great speed at which it is traveling. The running lights of an automobile may seem dim during the day in comparison to when we see them at night. Our relative positions to objects observed can give us different perspectives. Which is the privileged perspective? In what position, distance, or location do we determine that observational position that is closest to Reality? Without a Reality Measuring Stick, there is no way to make such discernment.

6. The sixth mode is based on mixtures. Human perception is never direct but always through a medium. For example, we see things through the medium of air. As such, there will always be different ways of seeing things. For example, the reason some of the most beautiful sunsets in the world are in Los Angeles is because you must look through a great deal of smog containing pollutant particles that refract light and scatter it into many wondrous colors. The sun itself looks nothing like how we see it through such polluted air. The medium of smog in the air greatly affects our perceptions (and responses) to such beautiful sunsets.

7. The seventh mode is based on the composition of the perceived object. Objects will appear different according to variations in their quantity, color, motion, and temperature. The example provided by Sextus is that silver is generally perceived as shiny and bright, but silver filings appear dull and black. Which state, we

might ask, is the True composition of silver? Or for that matter, any object we perceive?

8. The eighth mode is based on relativity in general (to the judging subject, to circumstances, etc.). Modes 3 through 8 in general deal with the relativity of human experiences. From where we are physically in perceiving objects in the world, to our age, position, environment, and composition, all these factors will have strong influences over our understanding. Again, for each mode, we can rightly ask the dogmatists to demonstrate to us how they can determine that their age, position, environment, and so forth, are precisely the ones necessary to provide the most accurate understanding of the world. In order to do so, they would need to solve the gold in the dark room problem and provide us with a Reality Measuring Stick. Until they do so, we have no reason to accept their premises and conclusions as being absolutely certain and demonstrative of information that accurately describes Reality.

9. The ninth mode deals with arguments based on constancy or rarity of occurrence. As Sextus Empiricus states, "The sun is more amazing than a comet, but because we see the sun daily and the comet rarely, the latter commands our attention." In other words, we may have a difficult time determining the value or importance of objects and aspects of our world simply because of our local proximity to them. If you live in Paris and see the Eiffel Tower every day, it may not seem as interesting or spectacular as it does to a tourist seeing it for the first time. Who in this case would be seeing a more True image of the Eiffel Tower?

10. The final mode deals with arguments concerned with ways of life, customs, laws, mythical beliefs, and dogmatic assumptions, all of which can be put into opposition to each other. I find this to be one of the most prescient of all modes because it deals explicitly with the idea of cultural relativism. Imagine for a moment that you were born and raised in another country far away from where you were actually born and raised. You may see and understand things quite differently. This would have consid-

erable effect on the way you acted. For example, if you were born and raised in Pakistan and were educated strictly by the Taliban, you might see the world quite differently than if you grew up in Oslo, Norway. This mode speaks directly to the cultural biases of geographical location and ethnicity and demonstrates how difficult it would be to state which particular biases are more closely representative of an accurate understanding of Reality. In this regard, the ancient Skeptics were very much ahead of their time in recognizing many of the cultural biases outlined and discussed in the second chapter.

FIVE MODES DEALING WITH THE PROOFS OF DOGMATISTS

In *The Outlines of Pyrrhonism*, Sextus Empiricus refers to another set of modes that came from a philosopher called Agrippa. These modes were specifically designed to attack any references to proofs that the dogmatists might put forward in support of their views concerning the nature of Reality. Like the ten modes of Aenesidemus, these modes are very powerful tools that clearly demonstrate the shortcomings of any such dogmatic view. They deal with five relevant questions that we should ask whenever anyone puts forward supernatural explanations or answers to the Big Five. For these modes clearly question the grounds upon which any dogmatist can make such claims. Without a Reality Measuring Stick, a supernatural account is entirely without conviction, for we cannot even begin to measure its accuracy.

1. The first of the five modes deals with discrepancy or the realization that many aspects of common life are unknown, yet so many people attempt to take guesses at what they really are. Discrepancies and dissenting opinions as to the "True" nature of Reality exist between the various supernatural guesses regarding the absolute answers to the Big Five. But since we have not developed any defin-

itive way of determining which guesses measure up better on the Reality Measuring Stick, we cannot possibly say which dogmatic view is "more correct" in answering the Big Five.

2. The second of Agrippa's modes is concerned with the way in which dogmatists attempt to prove their conclusions. We can rightly ask any dogmatists on what grounds do they support their views. Once an appeal is made, we can then ask how they can know that the grounds to which they refer as support of their beliefs are sufficient to demonstrate Absolute Truth. In other words, without a Reality Measuring Stick, we can rightly ask dogmatists to justify their evidence in support of their conclusions. However, whenever they appeal to specific grounds, they require an unmovable measuring stick in order to convince us. Without such a device, Agrippa maintained that the dogmatist will continuously look for further grounds on which to base his or her views. This would lead to an infinite regress of appeals to further grounds, which appeal to further grounds, and so on. A Reality Measuring Stick would stop the infinite regression. But nobody is in possession of any such device, and so the dogmatist will forever continue to appeal to further grounds in support of his or her answers to the Big Five.

3. Agrippa's third mode deals again with relativity. This mode reiterates the difficult problem of determining to what extent our views and biases affect the ways in which we observe and understand the world. Not knowing who, if any of us, possesses a privileged view of the world, we are at a loss in determining absolute Truth in this regard.

4. The fourth mode is concerned with the notion of hypothesis or assumption. In part 1, we saw how inevitable it was to assume criteria as a basis for our understanding of issues and aspects (i.e., no assertion without assumption). Agrippa has brought explicit attention to this idea and reveals that any attempt by a dogmatist to demonstrate a bedrock form of criterion like a Reality Measuring Stick will be based purely on hypothesis or assumption. For when they state that they are in possession of such a measuring tool, we can rightly ask the dogmatists for proof or evidence indicating how they

know this is so. The tool of the Reality Measuring Stick would have to be self-justifying. In other words, it would have to be without assumption, thereby ending the problem of the infinite regress.

5. The fifth and final mode of Agrippa is a powerful tool that also attacks the proofs of the dogmatists. It is based on circular reasoning and denies the dogmatists' attempts to beg the question by asserting in their premises what they are attempting to prove in their conclusions. An easy demonstration of this occurs whenever a dogmatist introduces the notion of a god as an appeal to moral behavior. For we can rightly ask: Who or what made God moral? The usual response is that no one or nothing made God moral; he just is. We see a version of this in Socrates's criticism of Euthyphro's third definition of piety which, when applied to morality, goes something like this:

a. Is the good of an act that is approved by God good simply because it is good in itself, or is it good because it is approved by God?

b. If the good of an act is simply good by itself, then whatever is good about it is independent of God's approval. So what makes moral actions "good" would be independent of God's opinion and would not make God the basis of ethics.

c. If the goodness of a moral act is good because God approves of it, then this is purely a matter of the subjective will of God. Any such God could then arbitrarily decide that some actions were good while others were bad, for example, "Thou shalt sodomize squirrels on the Sabbath" might become an acceptable commandment because God approves of it.

Both Socrates's and the ancient Skeptics' criticism brilliantly demonstrates the two ways in which any appeal to God begs the question and raises more questions than it answers. For it shows quite clearly that either God arbitrarily chooses what is good without any further appeal other than that is what he likes at a given time; or God possesses some ability to recognize which actions are good (and bad), in which case determining value lies outside of his making such actions good, in other words, such actions are already good and do not require any appeal to God. The argument is circular because if we ask whether to act in a particular way and someone says, "Yes, because that is what God commands," we can now ask: Why? The answer might be: "Because God knows what is good." If we were to ask how God knows what is good, one might reply: "Because He's God." If we were to further inquire and ask what this means, one might again reply: "It means that he knows what is good." Why? "Because He's God." Which means what? "That He knows what's good." Why? "Because He's God." And so on in a never-ending circle (see fig. 7.6).

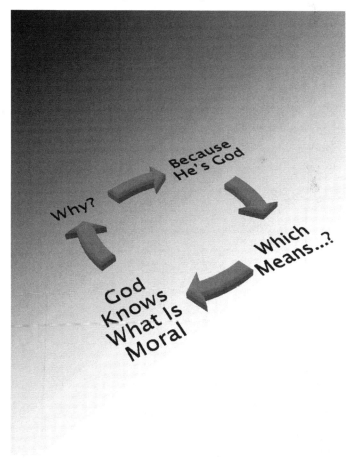

Fig. 7.6. God and Circular Reasoning. Image created by Robert Loucks.

THE MÜNCHHAUSEN TRILEMMA

When we look carefully at Agrippa's five modes, we can see that the first and third are really a brief summary or synopsis of Aenesidemus's original ten modes. Modes two, four, and five show a transition from these modes that dealt with conflicting perceptions and observations to three new modes that deal specifically with the proofs of dogmatists. These three modes have come to be called Agrippa's Trilemma or the Münchhausen Trilemma (see fig. 7.7).

The latter is named after a famous eighteenth-century baron who served in the Russian military and who, upon returning home from various battles, would spin tales about his supposed adventures.[21] Some of these adventures included traveling to the moon, riding on cannonballs, and pulling himself out of a swamp by his own hair.[22] The Münchhausen Trilemma is a powerful tool that can be used whenever one is engaged in dialogue with a supernaturalist who claims to be in possession of absolute Truth. It goes something like this: Whenever anyone claims to be in possession of certain knowledge, a pain in the ass can always inquire as to how he or she knows this (i.e., where is the Reality Measuring Stick). If proof is offered in any manner, we can now rightly apply the three modes listed as Agrippa's (or the Münchhausen) Trilemma:

1. Circularity of Reasoning: One's proof for a position ends up being supported by the position much like the "God knows what is moral" argument discussed earlier. Proof supports position, which supports proof, which supports position, and so on, ad infinitum.
2. The Infinite Regress: Offering proof requires further proof, which requires further proof, and so on, ad infinitum.
3. The Arbitrary Foundation: We eventually must arbitrarily pick some foundational criteria on which to rest our proof.

These modes in their various forms and numbers (10, 5, and 3) account not only for the numerous biases that affect and afflict human perception and understanding but also for the very tools of reasoning and logic we use in our attempt to understand whatever it is we perceive and try to understand.

Fig. 7.7. Agrippa/Münchhausen. Image created by Vanessa Tignanelli.

THE PRACTICAL CRITERION

According to Sextus Empiricus, after the skeptic has doubted the legitimacy to absolute Truth of the many various supernatural theories, one may rightly ask: How does the skeptic function in day-to-day life? You would think that, with the various modes, if the skeptic continues to doubt away the very things that attempt to provide an understanding of the nature of his experiences, he would be left in a state of catatonia—that is, the skeptic would cease to move or to function in any society (and as noted earlier with Diogenes Laertius, this is how some historians have wrongly caricatured the ancient Skeptics). But the ancient Skeptics did manage to function within society—in fact, they functioned very well and in a quite contented manner, which eventually set the stage for scientific reasoning. How did they achieve this? Very simply, the skeptic acquiesces to the appearances. In other words, the skeptic goes along with the appearances, neither affirming nor doubting the true nature of them. Sextus listed four main aspects that aid the skeptic in acquiescing to the appearances. These four aspects have collectively been called the Practical Criterion, and they summarize much of what we find in a commonsense and scientific understanding of our experiences.

1. *The Guidance of Nature*: The skeptic is guided by the natural human capacity for perception and thought—in other words, he uses his senses and his mental faculties to aid in continued survival. Objects seem to fall downward, fire seems to be quite hot, water seems quite wet, and so on, so we may want to avoid holding our hands over flames for long periods of time, walking off cliffs, or taking deep breaths while under water.

2. *The Constraint of Bodily Drives*: There are certain drives that the skeptic satisfies—hunger leads her to eat, thirst leads her to drink, sex to procreate, and so on.

3. *The Tradition of Laws and Customs*: The skeptic recognizes the necessity for laws and order in societies. Unless you live as a hermit, you have to determine how it is you wish to get along (or not) with others. And so there emerges the need for rules.

4. *Instruction in the Arts*: The skeptic practices an art or profession or gets a job (in Sextus's own case it was medicine) so that he or she can contribute to society as a whole. Some seem more gifted than others for specific types of activities. Fostering those natural abilities would be consistent with acquiescing to the appearances.

Notice how these criteria utilize the skeptic's acquiescence to the appearances to establish a pragmatic or commonsense understanding of human experience. For unlike the dogmatist, the skeptic does not hold any particular supernatural beliefs to be either true or false.

Like Socrates, the ancient Skeptics were extremely adept at agitating those dogmatists who were convinced of their supernatural beliefs. As we saw earlier, Socrates likened himself to a gadfly who buzzed around and bothered the self-satisfied Athenians. The Pyrrhonians described their views as a laxative that flushed itself out with all the rest of the waste. Today, some would call such people pains in the ass. A good skeptic today is, above all, responsible for the manner in which he or she attains, revises, and acts on information and only becomes a pain in the ass to someone who is unwilling to entertain the possibility of alternative beliefs. Like Socrates and the ancient Skeptics, these people are good for any society. For those who are overly dogmatic in their beliefs, this attitude may directly influence their actions, which could have harmful effects on other members of a society. Once we start to understand the framework within which we humans attain and exercise beliefs, we can better deal with conflicting viewpoints and ideas. Proper skepticism, then, requires a commonsense acceptance of an environment in which one develops concepts, ideas, behaviors, and the like. Philosophers sometimes refer to this as *hypothetical realism.* This position maintains a very basic framework of experience. That is, it presupposes or assumes a field of experience, which includes things like people, animals, plants, stars, planets, galaxies, and so on. In commonsense terms, we would call this the world and/or the universe. Unless future evidence warrants concern, a good skeptic treats these things *as though* they exist separately from one's thinking about them— that is, at the commonsense level of perception. In this way, skeptics *acquiesce to the appearances* and suspend judgment on supernatural matters. This attitude has directly contributed to the development of the scientific understanding of our experiences. For science allows us to extend far beyond our commonsense perception of the world to see things never before possible. What then should we be skeptical about? Generally speaking, we should be skeptical about the various ways we humans make claims about different aspects of our world. We need to be especially skeptical toward those who make absolute claims about the very nature of our world. For the onus of responsibility always lies with those making the claims. Remember the Sagan principle demanding that advice about extraordinary claims requires extraordinary evidence.

But if there is no absolute criterion (or set of criteria) that we can establish with certainty, how do we distinguish good ideas from bad ones? In other words, what is our measuring stick for matters at the *small t* level of truth? What can provide us with the ability to discern between good arguments and bad ones? At any given time in human evolution, we can be expected to utilize only the languages and modes of communication and expression available to us. This brute fact is called *historical facticity*; we are constrained by the influences of our generation. For example, Aristotle could not have discussed gene therapy, just as Newton could not have discussed downloading information from the Internet. Right now, we cannot discuss ways in which future generations will describe various aspects of their world. This is simply because scientific knowledge is gradual and cumulative—that is, we see as far as we do now because we have stood on the shoulders of the world's greatest thinkers from the past and we add to their cumulative effort. The measuring sticks we use today to distinguish good ideas or arguments from bad ones involve some of the various rules of reasoning and logic assisted in relevant ways by the various sciences, which we considered in part 1. We have established agreed-upon rules that are intended to be impartial and fair to all in an effort to establish universality. As skeptics, we have an obligation to continue to establish universal rules of reasoning in an effort to hold people accountable not only for their beliefs but, more important, for their actions, which may be harmful to others. We have a great tradition of ancient thought to thank for this. One of the central principles of all critical thinkers resonates from the collective works of Socrates and the ancient Skeptics and may be summed up in the following way: Think responsibly, act accordingly.

THE LEGACIES OF SOCRATES AND THE ANCIENT SKEPTICS: A CHECKLIST

Some of the most important legacies that Socrates and the ancient Skeptics gave us seem to have been long since forgotten. With the amount of worldwide belief in supernatural entities, untestable hypotheses, and all other manners and modes of pseudoscience, it would be good to refamiliarize ourselves with the greatest cultural contributions *Homo sapiens* have managed to develop so far. To conclude this chapter, let's summarize some very important tools that will allow us to become better pains in the ass to all dogmatists and supernaturalists.

Big T Truth and little t truth

Distinguish information and discuss it accordingly. Information regarding ourselves and our world and universe can be divided into at least two types: natural and supernatural. This has led to the responsible distinction and division of information that lies in the realm of what we can call Big T Truth and little t truth. Supernaturalists believe to be in possession of Big T or absolute Truth regarding the nature of Reality. Naturalists tend to understand the world at the small t level of common sense and scientific reasoning. If we can keep this division clear, I believe we will find ourselves on surer footing when it comes to discussing very important issues, so we do not talk past one another, and whenever anyone makes a claim—whether it is at the Big T or small t level of truth—we must keep the burden of proof squarely where it belongs: with those who make the claims.

The Method and the Modes

Remember that Socrates came to the very important realization that he did not know what was Absolutely True regarding the nature of Reality. The ancient Skeptics came to the same realization. Socrates developed a method that allows us to demonstrate this to dogmatists and supernaturalists while the ancient Skeptics developed a set of modes. The Socratic method proposes that we feign ignorance and begin a dialogue by initially agreeing with a dogmatist. By discussing his or her views as though we are in agreement, the dogmatist will be led to the inevitable discovery of inconsistencies and contradictions. By adopting the skeptical approach, we can apply any of the fifteen modes discussed in this chapter to demonstrate either the relativity of our views or the difficulties in maintaining the proofs of our views. Both the Socratic method and the skeptical modes are extremely powerful tools that clearly demonstrate the fallibility of dogmatic or supernatural claims.

Whip Out Your Reality Measuring Stick

Supernatural claims require far greater effort and ability by which to satisfy specific criteria than do commonsense claims. No supernatural knowledge about the universe or ourselves has been attained universally. This is due mainly to our inability to establish foundational criteria upon which universal agreement can be attained (remember the gold in the dark room example to demonstrate our lack of a Reality Measuring Stick). Supernatural beliefs lie in the realm of speculation and are removed from a commonsense and naturalized understanding of ourselves and our world. There is a genuine need to recognize and accept a default mode, given that we all cannot possibly agree on what the ultimate nature of Reality is—since there are so many different speculative views concerning what different believers actually believe and since we are unable to establish a universally acceptable criterion or set of criteria on which to base such views.

Show Us Your Assumptions!

As we saw earlier, a proposition is simply any statement that has a truth value. In other words, it is capable of being confirmed or denied. The act of presupposing simply involves an assumption on the part of any person when any claim is made. What this means is that we cannot make reference to any thing, nor can we state any proposition, without presupposing a foundation on which we rely in the transference of those statements. In the case of human communication, we assume and depend upon things like syntax, logic, and coherence. The underlying logical structure has to be relied upon at a very basic level for this type of communication to take place. Otherwise, as communicators, it would be very difficult—if not impossible—to make sense of the world and ourselves. So whenever we go about discussing anything—even at the commonsense level—we need to realize that there are always underlying assumptions or presuppositions. This is inescapable. It is extremely important, then, to determine the presuppositions or assumptions of those with whom you engage in discussion and to make clear to them your presuppositions as well.

Blind Ignorance

Many people not only wrongly believe they possess supernatural knowledge regarding the absolute nature of Reality but are blindly ignorant to this. As we saw earlier, these people are called dogmatists. Such people do not even know that they are ignorant of such information. They honestly believe not only that they are holding the golden cup but that they have been able to turn on the lights to confirm this. The worst form of dogmatism is evident in those who refuse to entertain the possibility that they could be wrong in their current (supernatural) beliefs and then act— sometimes in horrifically harmful ways—according to such dogmatic beliefs. These people suffer from severe cases of HUAS (head-up-ass syndrome). It therefore becomes the duty of every good skeptic to become a really good pain in the ass to such people.

Reflective Ignorance

Realizing the Big T and little t information distinction allows one to become reflectively aware of one's ignorance regarding information at the supernatural level. Becoming aware of and accepting one's ignorance is not intrinsically a bad thing, as so many have believed and feared and continue to believe and fear today. In fact, it is the first and greatest step toward becoming responsible critical thinkers. We can now confidently acknowledge and accept that there is a humbling and egalitarian nature to our reflective ignorance, in other words, it makes us all equal in not knowing what constitutes Reality. This, in turn, provides a liberating capacity to create and develop novel ways for understanding ourselves and our place in this world. Once we clear the field of supernatural explanations, we can begin a bottom-up approach by considering what we can know about ourselves at the commonsense and scientific level of understanding.

These are among the most important legacies left to us by Socrates and the ancient Skeptics. Collectively, they provide very powerful tools for becoming responsible thinkers and, when necessary, really good pains in the ass to any dogmatists oblivious to their own ignorance.

In the following chapters, we look at the ways in which we can answer the Big Five. As we have already discovered, there are generally two ways in which to answer these very important questions: naturally and supernaturally. Let's see how each holds up under the scrutiny of the ABCs of critical thinking, the Socratic method, and the modes of the Skeptics.

PART 3
ANSWERING THE BIG FIVE: PREAMBLE

You now possess more than enough tools to consider or reconsider how you would answer or respond to the Big Five. To reiterate, the Big Five are listed here:

1. What can I know?
2. Why am I here?
3. What am I?
4. How should I behave?
5. What is to come of me?

We also know that there are only four ways in which one can respond to the Big Five:

1. We can answer them purely naturally.
2. We can answer them purely supernaturally.
3. We can combine our answers with both natural and supernatural explanations.
4. We can choose not to respond at all.

For the purpose of clarity and brevity, I will focus only on the ways in which these questions can be answered naturally or supernaturally. As we witnessed with Socrates and the ancient Skeptics, those who wish to answer these questions supernaturally face a great deal of difficulty in trying to attain and demonstrate the perceived certainty of their answers.

We shall consider how these questions can be answered in these two ways for the remainder of this book.

But first, if we are going to compare the different ways in which people respond to the Big Five through natural and supernatural explanations, we should start by defining what it is we mean by *natural* and *supernatural*. The term *natural* will be used to refer to all matter or being that can be observed and studied according to knowable laws affecting and governing its behavior. This includes all things that can be observed and studied that exist in the physical world—from the infinitesimally small to the astronomically huge and everything in between. In other words, it comprises all that is found in nature. The term *supernatural* gets its meaning from the Latin *supra* or "above" and *natura* or "nature" and generally refers to anything above or beyond what one holds to be natural. Supernatural subjects range from mystical to theistic entities (e.g., gods, fairies, elves, gnomes, sprites, nymphs, angels, etc.), which we might call *theistic-supernaturalism*, and from the occult to paranormal activity (e.g., psychic activity, clairvoyance, the hereafter, ghosts, etc.), which we might call *paranormal-supernaturalism*.

There are generally two schools of thought when it comes to considering supernatural phenomena. Some believe that the subject matter of the supernatural simply lies outside the scope and ken of natural or scientific examination.[1] They believe that science, by definition, simply cannot study such matters. Others, however, maintain that any supernatural claims that state that supernatural entities or powers intervene with the natural world are open for scientific scrutiny and debate.[2] This school of thought maintains that whenever a supernaturalist makes an empirical claim, science has every right to investigate in the attempt to confirm or falsify it. Russell Blackford states that it is false to state that science

is, in principle, unable to investigate claims about such paradigmatically "supernatural" things as ancestor spirits, water nymphs, fire demons, magic dragons, or astrological influences. If these things exist and behave in fairly regular ways—like lions, elephants, kangaroos, crocodiles, and the flow of water—then science can investigate them. Of course, if they did exist we might come to think of them as part of "nature," but that's just the point. There is no clear and meaningful line between "natural" and "supernatural," such that science cannot investigate beyond that line. It is simply that certain kinds of things, notably disembodied intelligences, don't actually seem to exist; in any event, hypotheses involving these things have had a lousy track record over centuries. It is usually good practice for scientists to avoid those kinds of hypotheses if they can.[3]

We have seen how Socrates and the ancient Skeptics dealt with various responses to the Big Five. Those who respond to such questions supernaturally and believe themselves to be absolutely certain of their responses must provide proof in the form of evidence and then demonstrate how they are able to measure the accuracy of their absolute certainty. The naturalist, on the other hand, sees no way of knowing this and would never make a claim to possess such a Reality Measuring Stick. To say not only that such a measuring device exists, but also that it can be known and that one can demonstrate how it accurately measures the certainty of one's supernatural beliefs would require extremely extraordinary evidence in keeping with the Sagan principle. Natural answers to the Big Five are measured at the small t level of truth, which involves appeals to the type of criteria covered in chapter 5 on evidence. Evidence at the small t level of truth must satisfy criteria for consistency involving compliance with logical precepts like the laws of identity, noncontradiction, and excluded middle but also with the empirical evidence accepted within the various forms of scientific understanding. These criteria are generally accepted communally at the small t or natural level of understanding because they are pragmatic (i.e., they have worked in the past, and we can make predictions about future events that will be either confirmed or falsified by the data). This lends a certain amount of strength to natural answers to the Big Five. Natural answers at the small t level of truth never make claims to be absolute or certain because there is no known Reality Measuring Stick. Instead, naturalists attempt to understand themselves, the universe, and their place in it with the tools and methods that have been developed over a period of time and that inform us about how the natural world functions.

The most basic form of natural response is common sense. We make observations of patterns of behavior and then can predict, with some accuracy, how future situations will turn out. For example, if you have ever been taking a shower and someone flushes the toilet, the water in the shower usually becomes very hot (which is sometimes followed by your scream of discomfort or profanity and your family member's or house-mate's apology). Even if we do not know the physical plumbing reasons for why this happens, we simply refrain from doing it (unless we're trying to get even with someone). A little further inquiry will reveal, however, that when the toilet is drawing in fresh, cold water to refill the tank, it reduces the amount of cold water flowing to the shower—hence, the water in the shower becomes very hot. Most hotels and some houses have built-in systems that prevent these types of occurrences, but our house does not.

To further our commonsense understanding of the world, we have developed ways and means to better identify important patterns of behavior. Over a period of time, we have acquired tools and methods for understanding the world more consistently, coherently, and comprehensively than what our commonsense understanding has provided us. Much of our understanding of what can be known is dependent upon our language, logic, mathematics, ability to experience the world through our five senses of sight, smell, taste, hearing, and touch (the empirical approach); and upon our capacities to reason (the rational approach) and recognize patterns of behavior that are important to us in everyday life. A natural response to what we can know leads us to consider what our limitations are in terms of the tools available to us. For example, before the nineteenth century, there wasn't a well-developed germ theory as to why diseases developed and spread. There were various theories as to why people got sick, but there was no particular understanding of the pathogens and parasites that were causing people to become ill and, in some cases, die. At the time, people knew something was causing illnesses to occur, and some physicians could actually take measures to avoid such diseases, but they were not sure exactly what the causes of such illnesses were until tools and technology developed to the point at which physicians could observe them. So the invention and development of microscopes helped a great deal in understanding what types of organisms were at work when people got sick. Physicians could now literally see the germs and observe how they worked in the transmission of disease. We no longer needed to rely on older folk medicine ideas of "bad vapors" or perhaps religious explanations of "demonic possession" to explain such patterns of behavior. It is important to note that in no way am I making fun of the people who believed these explanations. They were trying their best to make sense of their world and were using the tools of understanding that were available to them at the time, just as we do today and just as our descendants will do far into the future. This is simply *historical facticity*. We can now understand our current acquired knowledge of the natural world as well as acknowledge our limitations because we are standing on the shoulders of giants who stood before us, which has allowed us to see as far as we can because of their hard work. We add to their great achievements in terms of understanding the world in a natural context. But this by no means allows us to claim that our knowledge in this natural way is absolute or even certain. Many of our ideas have been revised, altered, and changed; that's basically the way reason and science functions. Science builds upon past information regarding patterns of behavior that becomes, in time, a more consistent and comprehensive model of understanding various aspects of the universe. Nobody at the natural level can say he or she knows with certainty what is absolutely true about the universe. Commonsense and scientific knowledge come in degrees of probability. In other words, consider which scenario is a more likely explanation of the Black Death: that people living in western Europe between 1348 and 1350 who developed swollen lymph glands (buboes) and died within four to six days while vomiting and urinating blood had contracted the bacterium *Yersinia pestis*, which was believed to be carried by fleas, which were carried by black rats on merchant ships; or that nearly half of Europe's population died because of astrological forces, the wrath of God, or the poisoning of wells by Jews.[4] In this case, the scientific explanation seems to be the more likely because it satisfies criteria such as consistency, comprehensiveness, and coherence. It also does not violate Occam's razor and can be either falsified or confirmed. The astrological, religious, and racist explanations are lacking greatly in evidence and consistency and so are not considered as likely or probable explanations for the occurrence of the Black Death plague of Europe during the Middle Ages.

For a naturalist, given the information we have so far obtained, the most responsible thing to do would be to assume that specific criteria are better than other criteria at measuring the consistency of patterns of information that we observe on a day-to-day basis. Even though the naturalist could be entirely deceived in his or her understanding of the world, because we can imagine possible worlds in which magical demons or *Matrix* scenarios are making us believe all sorts of weird things about the world, which turn out to be entirely false, this would not appear to be a responsible set of beliefs to maintain given the past consistency of beliefs about the cause-and-effect relationships of our experiences. Every time I have tripped or stumbled on a level surface, I have fallen downward rather than upward. Gravity tends to work on a very consistent level. So we measure our past experiences and use them in an inductive way in considering that future episodes are going to behave similarly to past ones. This is not to say that they *must* behave this way. For all we know, the laws of the physical world may change drastically in the next five minutes. But since we have never experienced such laws changing, it seems the more responsible thing to do would be to act as though they are not going to change (and acquiesce to the appearances as did the ancient Skeptics). This seems to be about the best we can do at the small t level of truth. If anyone can attain information about the natural world in a better or more precise or accurate manner, more power to them; please provide it. But the burden of proof will befall anyone who makes such claims, whether naturally or supernaturally.

In reference to supernatural claims, once a supernaturalist makes a claim, it must be confirmed or falsified according to natural means, in other words, the types of criteria used to measure information at the small t level of truth, or the supernaturalist will have to produce a Reality Measuring Stick capable of measuring Truth at the supernatural level. I have never witnessed such a device, so I will assume that we will be forced to consider any and all supernatural answers to the Big Five according to natural criteria. Many examples of supernatural claims within the natural world can be studied through scientific means. Two such examples in the medical community involve the study of the potential effect of intercessory prayer (IP) on recovering cardiac patients and pregnancy rates in women being treated with in vitro fertilization–embryo transfer (IVF–ET). Prayer is defined as a request for supernatural intervention into natural occurrences. Clearly, we can see in many experiments that there is no significant difference in the pregnancy rates of women undergoing IVF–ET or in the recovery rates of hospitalized people for whom prayers for asssistance have been made.[5]

Other examples include the many instances of so-called miracles witnessed around religious statues. In November 2010, in Windsor, Ontario, a statue of the Virgin Mary measuring 4.9 feet (1.5 meters) high, encased in a shrine, sat on the front lawn of the home of a woman named Fadia Ibrahim.[6] Ms. Ibrahim made claims that the statue smiles during the day and at night weeps tears of oil. Much to the consternation of her neighbors, hundreds of people of faith have shown up at Ms. Ibrahim's house and believe this to be a supernatural sign from God. But when we think about this so-called miracle, it would not be difficult to examine such a claim according to naturalistic principles. An examination of how the statue is crying would be considered; the chemical composition of her tears would likely reveal a more earthly than otherworldly substance; and round-the-clock surveillance of the statue would determine if any tampering had been done in the form of less-than-divine intervention. So there are naturalistic ways by which to test supernatural claims. Such claims continue to be falsified, which gives us good reason to infer properly to the appeal to ignorance; in other words, because we have searched out and falsified all supernatural claims so far, it therefore stands to reason that they may all be falsified. But we will continue to examine any and all supernatural claims capable of being examined according to scientific analysis while keeping an open mind in considering them to be both falsifiable and confirmable (or at least nonfalsifiable). Any supernatural claims—regarding the Cottingley Fairies, psychic claims, UFOs, water dowsers, and those invoking a metaphysical deity or agency—can be falsified when people allow their evidence to be examined both rationally and scientifically.

Consider another example: According to the founder of Scientology, L. Ron Hubbard, an evil extraterrestrial being named Xenu was the dictator of a Galactic Confederacy, and seventy-five million years ago he reportedly transported billions of aliens to Earth aboard spacecraft that looked remarkably like human-built DC-8s. Xenu apparently placed these aliens around volcanoes and then blew them up using hydrogen bombs. So at this point, if these statements are considered to be true and used as evidence in support of a worldview like Scientology, we can proceed to confirm or falsify them naturalistically. We can drill for core samples around the world, especially near where these volcanoes were said to exist, and use various radiometric dating techniques to examine the findings of the precise period at seventy-five million years ago (and measure within, say, ten million years on either side of that time, just to be sure).[7] Using the six steps of scientific reasoning from chapter 5, we would predict that we should find data that would confirm the above statements (i.e., larger than average amounts of radioactive fallout, materials normally not be found naturally in the Earth at that particular time period). However, when core samples are analyzed in this way, we do not find such results. Clearly, if such a being as Xenu did come to Earth and detonate hydrogen bombs, we should find evidence for radioactive fallout at these levels. But we have not. So the lack of evidence that we predict to find indicates we are more justified in believing such events did not take place. Scientologists may now attempt to use *ad hoc* premises in an attempt to salvage their conclusion, but if such premises are not testable according to empirical study, then we arrive back at our original problem of needing something like a Reality Measuring Stick or a satisfactory response to the Münchhausen Trilemma.

Sometimes supernaturalists will say that the inherent nature of their answers to the Big Five is simply immune to empirical falsification. Creationists and Intelligent Design people like Michael Behe maintain that we cannot gain scientific information about a God or a Designer because God's reasons are simply beyond the scope and ken of mere mortals. To conceive of what God's plans are in any way would be purely speculative metaphysics. This is known as the *immunizing strategy* of the supernaturalists, which *insulates* supernatural explanations of the Big Five not only from criticism but apparently from any meaningful discussion at all. This immunizing strategy is simply a fallacious appeal to ignorance that acts as a type of force field surrounding such supernatural explanations, which disallows any criticism to penetrate. Such a force field simply stops the very chance for dialogue. So we may rightly ask: Why bring in such beings, entities, causes, or agents at all? Is not such a move a clear violation of Occam's razor? If we cannot even talk about such entities, why bring them into an explanation? Then to say such a being does in fact exist but in such a way that we cannot really know anything specific about it, and it is foolish to even try? Upon what, then, do supernaturalists base their conclusions? In other words, how can supernaturalists know anything about the qualities or characteristics of any such entities? And how would we measure this? Again, the burden of proof must always lie with whomever is making a claim. If anyone answers the Big Five by using supernatural claims, the onus is on him or her to show us the money by convincing us using sound reasoning and solid evidence.

The important takeaway point here is that whenever anyone makes empirical claims—whether natural or supernatural—by definition, they fall within the natural realm of scientific inquiry and can therefore be scrutinized and examined according to specific procedures and criteria. As we have seen, information attained and understood at the small t or natural level does not require a Reality Measuring Stick. I do not know any naturalists who make claims that their views of the natural world are absolutely true. Instead, naturalists, like the ancient Skeptics, live according to a provisional and pragmatic understanding of the world, in other words, they acquiesce to the appearances and have no need to determine the absolute Truth of their understanding of the universe and our place in it. If their views consistently work in the natural world, that is good enough for naturalists. As David Hume pointed out to us long ago, if it's absolute Truth you want, you may be waiting for a very long time. Let's now consider the natural and supernatural responses to the Big Five.

CHAPTER 8
WHAT CAN I KNOW?

As for me, all I know is that I know nothing.
— "THE REPUBLIC," SOCRATES

While I know myself as a creation of God, I am also obligated to realize and remember that everyone else and everything else are also God's creation.
— MAYA ANGELOU

We don't know a millionth of one percent about anything.
—THOMAS EDISON

W e now have a pretty good idea of what it means to answer the Big Five either naturally or supernaturally. So where does this leave us in terms of the ways in which we can provide answers to the question, "What can I know?" We saw how the legacies of both Socrates and the ancient Skeptics have provided us with a clear acknowledgment of our limitations in making knowledge claims. They were among the first in recorded history to recognize and separate blind ignorance from reflective ignorance. As well, they went to great lengths to develop systems that clearly distinguished information that can be understood at the common-sense level of the natural world—the realm of little t truth—in contrast to claims about the supernatural world—or the realm of Big T or absolute Truth. Both Socrates and the ancient Skeptics were aware of how difficult it was for anyone to answer questions like the Big Five with absolute certainty. Through analogies like the gold in the dark room example, we have seen how, without the ability to turn on the lights to see who is holding the golden cup, everyone is in the dark when it comes to making such supernatural claims. In other words, we do not possess any type of Reality Measuring Stick that can demonstrate how close our ideas and beliefs are to what Reality may actually be. This realization of supernatural ignorance led both Socrates and the ancient Skeptics to become humble in accepting such limitations and this, in turn, produces an egalitarian effect; in other words, we are all equally ignorant. None of us appears to knowingly possess absolutely true responses to any of the Big Five questions. The ancient Skeptics took this one step further and, in recognizing their ignorance in this regard, acquiesced to the appearances and developed a four-stage commonsense approach to life that is called hypothetical (or provisional) realism. In other words, the skeptics will acquiesce to their appearances provisionally unless and until they have good reason to believe otherwise. Forces in nature, observations of causal factors, laws, customs, and so on, all seem to be essential parts of the world that can be observed and adhered to. This practical outlook on knowledge and experience is very much influential to the manner in which the sciences eventually developed. For science, in general, produces information about the natural world that extends beyond our commonsense understanding of it. The legacies of both Socrates and the ancient Skeptics contributed greatly to what has become known as *methodological naturalism* as the predominant manner in which scientists attempt to understand the natural world. This simply means that the scientific method (discussed in chapter 5 on evidence) is used to understand cause-and-effect relationships in the natural world.

THE NATURAL RESPONSE

First of all, when providing natural responses to the question regarding the limits of our knowledge, we have already seen how limited we are in regard to attaining absolute certainty. We can recognize that we are limited by a given time period in which we now exist. So what we can know about ourselves, the universe, and our place in it is limited by the tools and the languages that we now have available to us. We can now talk about heart transplants or downloading porn off the Internet, whereas for the majority of humankind's history this was not possible. Neither Plato, Galileo, Newton, nor Einstein could have discussed such things because they simply did not exist in the same time and place as we now do. We have little knowledge of what ideas and technologies may develop well into the future. But what we do know is that our understanding of ourselves and of the universe is always dependent upon where and when we find ourselves in history. This is known as historical facticity. In other words, we are bound to a large degree by the time and place in which we find ourselves. This is why time-travel movies are such fun. We get to imagine scenarios in which our current ways of dealing with the world compare to those of the past or future. To better understand the natural means by which to answer the first of the Big Five questions, we need to understand some of the vast complexities of nature and all that is contained within it. To do this, I have developed a way for understanding the many different ways the various sciences understand us and our place in the universe, called the Relations of Natural Systems (RNS). This physical understanding of the natural world can then be combined with our understanding of the many different cultural ways in which our lives develop, which is called, appropriately enough, the Relations of Cultural Systems (RCS). Together, both the natural and cultural systems demonstrate just how vastly complex our lives, the world, and the universe are. Taken together, the two systems are interconnected in a complex interplay of activity resembling the multiple layers of the skin of an onion. I have appropriately named this model of understanding the Onion Skin Theory of Knowledge (OSTOK). Using an onion as a metaphor for our combined systems of knowledge, we can understand how information about ourselves, our world, and the universe relate. The more we can understand the complex causal interplay among various systems, the deeper into and the farther around the onion we go.

The Relations of Natural Systems (RNS)

The Relations of Natural Systems began as a project I started more than a decade ago. I wanted to be able to present to students a concept of the *big natural picture* in a single glance. To do this, I had to demonstrate the relationships all humans have with everything in the natural universe. This was no easy task. I began to think in terms of systems and the relationships that exist between them. When we take a good look at life around us, on this planet, and elsewhere throughout the stars, it becomes apparent that everything we see is either a part of, or a conglomerate of, systems. Take yourself, for instance. What are you, physically, but a fleshy package of systems? You have a skeletal system that supports your body; a muscular system that allows for locomotion; a nervous system for communication within your body; an immune system to ward off parasites and pathogens; an endocrine system to allow for hormonal transfer of information; a circulatory system to provide oxygen to your organs, and so on. If all these systems work well in conjunction with one another, you can maintain a fairly healthy lifestyle. However, if some of these systems or their parts falter, you may find yourself experiencing the need for medical attention. Now ask yourself: What is a human as a conglomerate of systems? We are a species (like many others) that functions within ecological and cultural systems. These collective systems make up cities, municipalities, countries, and so forth. Together, we find ourselves functioning within political systems that overlap into other geopolitical systems. All these function on a fairly small planet we call Earth. Planet Earth is but one of eight in a planetary system.[1] Our planetary system functions largely because of the star at its center (our sun). As an open system, the sun provides light and heat and is but one of many stars that are revolving in a system called a galaxy. Of all the many stars that make up our Milky Way galaxy, this is only a single collection of billions of stars. This single galaxy is one of millions that make up a cluster of galaxies. There are millions upon millions of galaxies in each galaxy cluster. And there are millions of galaxy clusters throughout the known universe, which is continuously expanding and increasing in immensity and which we define as all space-time (see fig. 8.1).

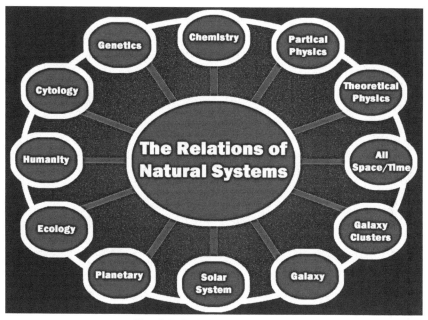

Fig. 8.1. Relations of Natural Systems (RNS) Flowchart. Image created by Robert Loucks.

Just as we can recognize our interconnectedness on a grand scale, if we move in the opposite direction from ourselves and examine systems in smaller and smaller detail, what we see is that all our systems within our bodies are made up of cells. Each type of cell works as a system to communicate how each cell is to behave. Cells themselves are made up of smaller and smaller units: macromolecules, chromosomes, DNA, RNA, and so on. Each of these macromolecules is made up of smaller units, such as atoms. These, in turn, are made up of smaller units such as quantum particles. Once we move into the smaller realm of subatomic particles, we enter the arena of theoretical physics, which maintains there might even be smaller units that make up quarks (and everything else in the universe), called superstrings.[2]

The point is that we must learn to recognize the immense complexity of cause-and-effect relationships between ourselves and the physical universe. Causality at one level seems to operate differently from causality at another level. For example, the forces that cause atoms to behave as they do is quite different from the forces that cause planets to behave as they do. However, we must recognize that we are connected in this very complex manner to the rest of the universe. In this way, we can see ourselves as being intimately connected to the world in many complex ways. If we can see ourselves in this way, then there is a possibility that we can establish some form of universal agreement regarding commonalities about ourselves as human beings.[3] The nature of the Relations of Natural Systems project is interdisciplinary. It combines the various ways in which the sciences have contributed to our understanding of the physical universe and our place in it in an attempt to give us a very broad understanding of the current limits of scientific knowledge. It is important to understand this synthetic view of humanity with the rest of the known universe. What this collaborative and collective view of the natural universe will provide is a more comprehensive view of the complexities of humankind in relation to all known causal factors with which we are associated.[4]

When a naturalist considers the question "What can I know?" the Relations of Natural Systems is a fairly comprehensive way to demonstrate the interconnectedness of scientific knowledge and understanding. A natural understanding is reliant on language, logic, syntax, mathematics, and a community in which to socially recognize criteria to which statements about the natural world can be considered acceptable or warranted. Naturalists are limited in their knowledge of the natural world by the symbols used to represent their observations and findings and by the historical facticity in which they find themselves at any given time. A natural understanding is one that is continuously ongoing and incomplete. It is a self-monitoring and self-correcting approach to gathering information, and it is one that makes no claims to establish absolute certainty about Reality.

The Relations of Cultural Systems (RCS)

Just as we can imagine a complex interplay of natural causes related in intricate ways, the same can be seen in the manner in which cultural systems have developed. To a naturalist, much of what we can know is the result of the ways in which cultural systems have developed over thou-

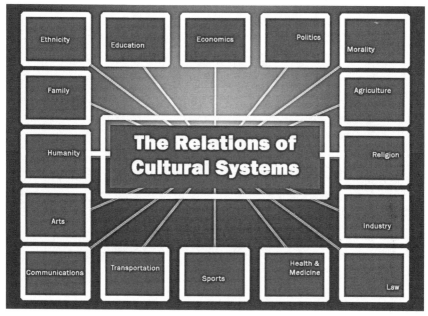

Fig. 8.2. Relations of Cultural Systems (RCS) Flowchart.
Image created by Robert Loucks.

sands of years. These systems include family, ethnicity, education, economics, politics, morality, agriculture, religion, industry, law, health and medicine, sports, transportation, communications, the arts, and so on. Humans interact according to the many complex relationships of these varying cultural systems (see fig. 8.2).

The Onion Skin Theory of Knowledge (OSTOK)

We noticed in the chapter on biases (chapter 2) that many cultural factors are going to affect the way we understand and act in the world. The world has close to seven billion people inhabiting it and a great many diverse forms of cultural systems that have developed over a fairly short period of time. We must now try to envision and understand how the Relations of Natural Systems (RNS) and the Relations of Cultural Systems (RCS) interact in a complex whole. Imagine these two systems intertwined into

Fig. 8.3. Onion.
Photograph by
Matthew DiCarlo.

a ball with layer upon layer of complex interplay between them. Now imagine that the layers are like the skins of an onion (see fig. 8.3).

I hope this analogy will give you some idea of how naturalists view the vast complexities of the natural world.

The Relations of Natural Systems (RNS) + The Relations of Cultural Systems (RCS) = OSTOK (Onion Skin Theory of Knowledge)

The Onion Skin Theory of Knowledge is a very complex model that demonstrates the enormously complex interplay of natural linear and nonlinear systems. Our knowledge is limited by the manner in which we can identify and attempt to understand what might be called *causal clusters*. These clusters are connections between events within these two overlapping systems. The better we can understand the causal forces influencing various effects in our lives, the better we can predict and control the natural world in an effort to survive and maintain a particular lifestyle. However, there's a bit of a problem: it's called *randomness*. Naturalists have become so adept in understanding natural and cultural systems that they have even been able to identify a major problem in understanding causal clusters in the physical world.[5] They have discovered an the immense amount of sheer complexity in the world due to the many ways in which the natural and cultural systems interplay inside the onion. How complex? Ask the meteorite guy, Orvil Delong. My cousins from Cambridge, Ontario, have informed me that an acquaintance of theirs, Mr. Orvil Delong, has come very close to having his life cut short several times through extremely random events. On one occasion in October 1977, Mr. Delong was in a very serious car accident. In the same year, he was struck by lightning while golfing in August. On a third occasion while golfing, he was nearly struck in the head by a meteorite. A cast of the extraterrestrial stone can be seen at the Doon Valley Golf Course in Kitchener, Ontario. Now think of the many events that placed Orvil ("Orv," as his friends call him) in the near direct path of that meteorite, lightning bolt, or automobile accident. What if, at any time in his life, he had missed a bus rather than caught it? Or decided to have steak instead of chicken for dinner on a given night? Or decided to watch a playoff sporting event rather than play golf? Any of these changes might have led to a series of events that would have taken place in slightly different ways because Orv's decisions could, according to specific models of chaos theory, contribute significantly to vastly different outcomes. In one possible world of Orv, he acts slightly differently on a given day and ends up being struck by the meteorite. In other possible worlds, we can imagine Orv not even on the course that day or that he had recently won a lottery and was instead on his new yacht.

Another example of randomness and causal complexities involves a brief e-mail relationship I had with highly respected American neuroscientist and neurobiologist Patricia Goldman-Rakic, who was known for her pioneering study of the frontal lobe and her work on the cellular basis of working memory. On July 22, 2003, at 8:05 a.m., I e-mailed Dr. Goldman-Rakic to ask her a question regarding research I was doing at the time. Here is my e-mail:

Hello Dr. Goldman-Rakic,

My name is Chris DiCarlo and I teach philosophy at the University of
Guelph. My interests are interdisciplinary and extend into areas of cognitive science and evolutionary psychology. I am currently working on
a paper and I am considering cognitive aspects which may extend into
your area(s) of expertise. I want to know if problem-solving produces
any endorphin activity? In other words, does one get a bit of a high
through the act of solving problems? If this is the case, any references
related to this would be greatly appreciated. Thank you for your time
and consideration.

Best regards,
Chris DiCarlo

Shortly thereafter, I received the following response from Dr.
Goldman-Rakic:

Christopher—I am sorry that I have no information on the subject and
I doubt that anyone has. But introspection suggests that there is a high
from solving problems whether or not endorphins are involved. Where
there's smoke, there's fire—certainly one can expect a biological foundation for euphoric experience.

P. Goldman-Rakic

On July 31, just nine days after corresponding with Dr. Goldman-Rakic,
she was struck by a car and killed in Hamden, Connecticut. In trying to
understand the complexities of the known natural world, we may inquire:
To what extent did my e-mail correspondence contribute to the vast
number of events prior to Dr. Goldman-Rakic's accident? Her obituary in
the science journal *Nature* stated:

She died of injuries sustained after being struck by a car as she was
crossing a heavily trafficked street in Hamden, near her New Haven,

Connecticut, home. While she did not go gentle into that good night, we, in the scientific community, her friends, and colleagues, alternately rage, and grieve, and remain in stunned disbelief that this vibrant and brilliant woman was taken from us by a freak accident that revealed the cruel menace of impartial chance.[6]

Had I never e-mailed her, would this have been enough of a missing causal factor to have led her course of actions to be slightly altered to the point where she would not have been crossing the street at exactly the same time or in the same place in Hamden? In some ways, I would like to think not; but in others, how could my e-mail not have had at least some causal effect on her chain of actions leading up to that fateful day?

My hope is that Mr. Delong's and Dr. Goldman-Rakic's experiences can demonstrate to you the vast complexities in which humans live out their lives. In trying to determine what can be known from a natural perspective, we must submit to humility and admit to ignorance in many ways. But although randomness plays a large part in the natural world, we can understand clusters of local causal elements quite well. Although scientists continue to examine the breadth of the degrees of separation between events, it is apparent that our understanding of natural causes has grown significantly. From work done by economist Steven D. Levitt in *Freakonomics*, we find many cause-and-effect relationships we might not have thought existed (e.g., the cheating rates of sumo wrestlers and high school teachers, and the negligible effects of good parenting on education). A considerable amount of scientific study has demonstrated the vast complexities of social networks and unusual causal clustering. In their book *Connected*, Nicholas Christakis and James Fowler examine how behaviors, habits, and other traits ripple along chains of friends and are contagious to three generations of separation. So if you are a smoker and are trying to quit, this may impact the success or failure of your friend's friend who is also trying to quit smoking.

It is hoped that understanding such complexity within the context of the Onion Skin Theory of Knowledge will make it a bit easier to understand just how complex our lives really are at the natural and small t level of truth and understanding. So whenever anyone discusses ideas and concepts at the natural level, we can talk in terms of how far we can go around and into the onion. For example, with regard to the very limited depth and breadth of my particular understanding of, say, quantum physics, I can travel only a few scant layers into and around the onion, whereas someone like Stephen Hawking can travel much deeper in it and navigate broadly around it. On other topics, I may have greater depth and breadth. The broader and deeper our understanding is of varying causal elements involved in the natural world (causal clusters), the greater our abilities to predict novel outcomes. And with prediction comes control and greater perceived security.

Based on this understanding, the naturalist might now maintain that given our knowledge of ourselves within the natural world, it follows that with so many systems, we, like all other species, attempt to manipulate these systems to the best of our perceived advantage. In other words, like all other species, humans are *system manipulators*. And there are many systems to manipulate. Biologically, humans, like all species, must be concerned most with two things: survival and reproduction. How we manipulate various cultural systems in an attempt to survive and reproduce as a species is carried out in extremely diverse and unique ways. This is because humans can alter their environments more than any other species on Earth. Politics, employment, education, healthcare, the media—all represent important cultural systems through which our species tries to survive and reproduce. Where you live in the world will affect how much political freedom you have to gain the type of education or employment you want, which may in turn provide you with enough resources to live the type of lifestyle you want. If you do not have access to sufficient healthcare, however, you may not live long enough to manipulate the other cultural systems in an effort to attain the types of resources you desire. So the many cultural systems through which we all must function determine to what extent we will be successful in surviving and reproducing.

What Can I Know?

In answering the question regarding what we can know, a naturalist will begin with an admission of reflective ignorance, acknowledge that no one has yet to produce a Reality Measuring Stick, and pursue information at the small t level of truth based on specific criteria of consistency. A naturalist will not necessarily state that no supernatural knowledge is possible but that none claimed has satisfied the criteria for knowledge at the small t level of truth, nor has any supernaturalist been able to produce a Reality Measuring Stick that could effectively and convincingly demonstrate knowledge at the Big T level of Truth. So, much like Socrates and the ancient Skeptics, the naturalist will acquiesce to the appearances and utilize tools of understanding such as logic, reason, and science in an effort to better understand the many aspects of the world. Based on the complexities of the Onion Skin Theory of Knowledge, naturalists recognize the incredible complexities that network through the natural and cultural systems. Acknowledging the role that randomness plays in understanding aspects of these systemic networks leads to the development of understanding causal clusters in an effort to make more accurate predictions and gain greater control over their environment.

THE SUPERNATURAL RESPONSE

In terms of supernatural responses to the question of what is or can be known, things appear quite differently. As we have seen from theistic-supernatural responses, some people will claim not only that they have knowledge of themselves, the universe, and their place in it but also that they have absolute knowledge of such things; and that this has been guaranteed to them because of their sources, such as books, texts, and scriptures; or this was told to them by family members, clerics, imams, rabbis, and so on; or it was personally experienced through an epiphany or an act of revelation. In terms of supernatural responses involving the existence of deities, many people would be willing to say that they possess certain or absolute knowledge. That is to say, they believe they are in possession of information that is absolutely true about Reality and cannot possibly be false. At this point, we need to take a moment to think about this and consider the magnitude of such claims. For individuals to say that they are in possession of absolute knowledge regarding the way the universe *actually* functions is to hold the most important information anyone could possibly attain. Quite a serious position. If we think carefully about such claims, we realize that just as Socrates and the ancient Skeptics demonstrated, we need to be wary of them. For in making such claims, the onus or burden of truth must always lie with those claiming to be in possession of absolute knowledge. So far, any supernatural claims that have been stated empirically—theistic or paranormal, or miracles, psychic phenomena, divine interventions of various sorts, and so on—have been shown to be lacking in consistency, and their premises have not been well supported or warranted. To date, no one has collected the one million dollars from the James Randi Foundation for demonstrating, under rigorous scientific conditions, the existence of any paranormal activity (e.g., ghosts, water dowsing, clairvoyance, telekinesis, ESP, homeopathy, astrology). This does not mean that phenomena such as these do not exist. It just means that no one to date has been able to demonstrate that they do, in fact, exist. So we would be justified in using the argument for ignorance in this case; we have responsibly given every opportunity for supernatural claims to be demonstrated and they have all failed, so it is a warranted provisional conclusion to believe that all such supernatural claims will be falsified. Opportunities for supernatural claims will still be provided according to rigorous scientific investigation. Should any such claim satisfy the conditions of such testing, we would have to revise our current ways of understanding the natural world to include such new phenomena.

When we consider exclusively those supernatural responses to the Big Five that invoke deities as causal forces in the universe, we see a pattern emerge. To the first question, the response from such supernaturalists usually (though not always) has a common pattern.

What Can I Know?

1. I can know what is absolutely true about the nature of Reality—including the absolutely true answers to the next four questions of the Big Five.
2. I am in possession of this knowledge because I have experienced it in any or all of the following ways:

Learned:
- a. The information can be found in written form (e.g., the Bible, the Koran, the Torah, the Granth Sahib, the Vedas).
- b. People who claim to know a great deal about this written information (e.g., rabbis, imams, priests, sadhus, gurus) teach it to others.
- c. This information is often discussed, taught, or shared among family members (e.g., from parents to children, from sibling to sibling), and often from birth.
- d. There are often indoctrination procedures involved that signify important rituals related to the written and spoken information (e.g., circumcision, baptism, bar mitzvah, etc.).
- e. This information is often the basis for community activities and gathering at specific places of designation (e.g., churches, mosques, synagogues, schools), which allows for communal reinforcement of the importance of this information.
- f. Theologians, scholars, and academics study, comment, and discuss various aspects of these views.

Revealed:
- a. An epiphany: when one experiences a sudden flash of insight into the reality or essential nature of some aspect of the universe.
- b. Revelation: when one experiences the presence of a divine being that somehow communicates words of insight and understanding.

This represents the basic pattern of the variety of ways in which a theistic-supernaturalist might respond in answering the first of the Big Five questions in regard to the limitation of knowledge. The differences between this type of supernatural response and a natural response are quite clear. Right away we can see how the points of Socrates and the ancient Skeptics reveal how the absolute claims of the theist do not amount to absolute knowledge or information regarding Reality. Instead, we find references to gods, written works, teachings, rituals, and so on, as though these things actually represented what is found in Reality. We cannot accept such claims or information as being absolutely True because the theist would need to demonstrate how his or her particular views measured up on the Reality Measuring Stick. Since we are without such a device, the theist must rely on something much weaker: *faith*. But faith, as the devout often say, can move mountains. (Not really. It's explosives and heavy machinery that do the job.) Faith is what is actually taking the place of scientific reason and methodology when reference is made to such deities as causal agents.

Let's review. Theists believe that the knowledge they have of their god or gods is absolutely true and indicative of the way in which the universe actually functions. This is their conclusion (or the roof to their house). The premises (or walls) that support this conclusion come from written works (the Bible, the Koran, etc.), the spoken words of "holy" people (imams, priests, rabbis, etc.), family experience, personal experience, schools, indoctrinated rituals, and possibly epiphanies and revelatory or mystical experiences. The underlying assumptions (or foundations) will vary, but some of the most common ones include the idea that an all-loving god would never deceive its followers (a form of begging the question/circular reasoning); the tradition or age of the views (it's so old, it must be right); the accuracy of the texts (divine intervention was recorded so it must have happened); the authority of the experts (people have devoted their entire lives to the study of such views—they wouldn't waste their time on something frivolous or wrong); and the power of their personal experiences (you just have to feel the power of the Lord to truly believe). Combine all this with the power of cultural and family indoctrination (context) and you have the recipe for some extremely hardened biases. Penetrating these biases with reasoned argumentation will not be easy because supernatural beliefs speak far more to human emotions than to human reason.

Some may argue the following: How do we know that what the theists claim is *not* absolutely true and indicative of the way in which the universe actually functions? Here we see a fallacious appeal to ignorance. As noted earlier, we cannot absolutely provide negative proof for such a claim. Just as you cannot absolutely refute my belief that there are exactly twelve invisible elephants eating pink popcorn on the dark side of the moon, so I cannot dispute absolutely any such supernatural claims of the theist. As Bertrand Russell so eloquently wrote:

> If I were to suggest that between the Earth and Mars there is a china teapot revolving about the sun in an elliptical orbit, nobody would be able to disprove my assertion provided I were careful to add that the teapot is too small to be revealed even by our most powerful telescopes. But if I were to go on to say that, since my assertion cannot be disproved, it is an intolerable presumption on the part of human reason to doubt it, I should rightly be thought to be talking nonsense. If, however, the existence of such a teapot were affirmed in ancient books, taught as the sacred truth every Sunday, and instilled into the minds of children at school, hesitation to believe in its existence would become a mark of eccentricity and entitle the doubter to the attentions of the psychiatrist in an enlightened age or of the Inquisitor in an earlier time.[7]

Russell's point is the same as those put forward more recently in the satirical beliefs in flying spaghetti monsters, invisible pink unicorns, or invisible dragons in my garage (see fig. 8.4).

The point of the reference to all these so-called entities is that the onus of proof must always lie with those making such claims. And according to the Sagan principle, since extraordinary claims require extraordinary evidence, we have every right to ask those who maintain such supernatural beliefs to provide extraordinary but warranted and convincing premises as evidence in support of their conclusions. The reason why all theists' premises fail to convince us of the absolute certainty of

Fig. 8.4. Russell's Teapot. Photograph by Matthew DiCarlo.

their conclusions is because we have no way of determining this outside of their devotion to and faith of such a belief system. But faith and devotion are not enough to warrant an acceptable argument. Please be advised that I am in no way doubting the passion with which supernaturalists maintain their beliefs and supposed absolute knowledge. Supernatural responses to the Big Five often elicit very powerful emotional feelings, which sometimes makes calm and levelheaded discussion very difficult. The fact is that without the ability to know that they are in possession of Big T Absolute Truth, in other words, without producing a Reality Measuring Stick, supernaturalists must rely on much weaker claims to knowledge. References to so-called holy texts, holy people, and so on, are really just holy smoke when it comes to reasoning and argumentation. This in no way denies anyone the civil right and freedom to religious belief and practice, nor does it deny anyone the freedom to believe in ghosts, UFOs, telekinesis, homeopathy, or any other forms of the supernatural or pseudoscientific. It simply points out what is entailed when answering the Big Five supernaturally. Let's now take a look at the different ways in which naturalists and supernaturalists answer the next question: Why am I here?

CHAPTER 9

WHY AM I HERE?

Don't go around saying the world owes you a living. The world owes you nothing. It was here first.

—MARK TWAIN

Why am I here? I want answers now or I want them eventually!

—HOMER SIMPSON

Now that we have a clearer understanding of the differences between natural and supernatural responses to the first of the Big Five questions regarding the limitations of knowledge, we can better understand why each subsequent question is answered accordingly. In this chapter, it should not be much of a surprise for many of us to acknowledge the stark divisiveness that exists between identifying ourselves either naturally or supernaturally. We might even make the case that it is precisely the manner we define ourselves according to the ways we answer these questions that has led to considerable misunderstanding and disagreement throughout the history of our species.

THE NATURAL RESPONSE

If we take a purely naturalistic view of ourselves as beings on this planet, we would maintain that we are here, alive on this planet today, because of many cosmic forces, biological and chemical reactions, and a huge amount of luck. Astronomers generally maintain that the age of the universe is approximately 13.7 billion years old and that our own planet within this solar system came into existence around 4.6 billion years ago. But one might ask: How do they know this? What are their premises and assumptions in support of these claims? As discussed earlier, many good sources of information discuss the varying types of radiometric dating techniques that are used to measure the age of things in the universe (including our very planet).[1] In principle, these techniques use the naturally decaying rate of specific types of matter (e.g., uranium to lead, potassium to argon, rubidium to strontium) to measure the age of our planet and many other things found throughout the planet (see fig. 9.1). But how do such decaying elements tell us how old something is? From the United States Geological Service we find this description:

> A chemical element consists of atoms with a specific number of protons in their nuclei but different atomic weights owing to variations in the number of neutrons. Atoms of the same element with differing atomic weights are called isotopes. Radioactive decay is a spontaneous process in which an isotope (the parent) loses particles from its nucleus to form an isotope of a new element (the daughter). The rate of decay is conveniently expressed in terms of an isotope's half-life, or the time it takes for one-half of a particular radioactive isotope in a sample to decay. Most radioactive isotopes have rapid rates of decay (that is, short half-lives) and lose their radioactivity within a few days or years. Some isotopes, however, decay slowly, and several of these are used as geologic clocks.[2]

So by measuring the amount of parent matter of one substance (e.g., uranium-238) to the amount of daughter matter (e.g., lead-206), geologists can measure the age of rocks quite accurately. This is because the consistency of the rate of decay from parent to daughter is constant

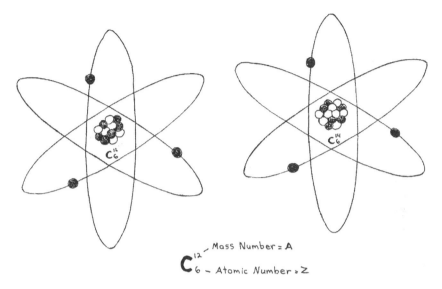

Fig. 9.1. Carbon Isotopes. Image created by Sarah Sienna.

regardless of other forms of effects; in other words, no matter how you alter the rock's structure or temperature, it still maintains a constant rate of decay. Naturalists feel quite confident in the ways in which scientists are able to discover such information about ourselves and the universe.

Naturalists claim that the universe is 13.7 billion years old and Earth is 4.6 billion years old, but this still doesn't answer the question of *why* we're all here. The simple answer is that we're here because we're here. There is no real rhyme or reason; we just got lucky. We could have just as easily not been here. No buildings, roads, technology, no Ice Capades. But surely the universe and all that is contained within it could not simply have come into being just like that? Not without a bit of a push from some supernatural agent. Right? To a naturalist, the universe and everything in it simply came to be. Whether it was a Big Bang or an enormous number of starts and failures, or whether there are other types of universes existing in different dimensions, or we are all just holograms,[3] the fact of the matter is that naturalists see no need to inject a creator into the mix to help explain why we're all here. Many believe that our universe came into being without cause and out of nothing.[4] For some, this is impossible to imagine. "Something cannot come from nothing," they will say. I can deeply sympathize with them, for they are abiding by the law of non-contradiction as it applies to causality on a human-sized scale. In other words, when we look out our window, it is contradictory to see every effect preceded by a cause and then say that the universe itself did not need a cause (like a god). To many, this just does not make sense. If it were not for the quirky world of quantum physics, they might be right. As Plato, Aristotle, and Thomas Aquinas argued many years ago, there had to be a prime mover—something to get the ball rolling, as it were. However, quantum fluctuations happen without apparent cause all the time. If we can observe the effects of such unusual behavior happening before our eyes today, then why is it so difficult to imagine that something could have come from nothing billions of years ago? I cannot even begin to pretend to understand some of the unusual aspects of quantum physics. I can only go a few scant layers into and around the onion when discussing some of the bizarre activities that take place at this infinitesimally small scale. I must, at some point, defer to those whose mathematical knowledge exceeds mine by huge magnitudes. Be forewarned. This is not easy stuff. Nor should it be. We are talking about the very nature of what our mathematical concepts can tell us about the nature of matter—a field that was once the domain of philosophy and religion.

Many physicists will refer to what is called the Lambda-Cold Dark Matter (Lambda-CDM) model to explain how something can come from nothing. According to this model, prior to the existence of our universe, the nothing that existed allowed for unusual space-time quantum fields. Accordingly, the smallest possible amount of volume allowed by quantum mechanics (with a linear Planck length[5]) is a volume of 10^{-99} cubic centimeters. This is an incredibly small amount of space. The largest amount of mass that could fit inside this unbelievably small cube without collapsing into a black hole is a speck of matter that would weigh 1/100,000th of a gram (see fig. 9.2).

According to Heisenberg's uncertainty principle, this amount of matter can come into being for a very short period of time: 10^{-43} seconds.

Physicists believe that if this amount of space and matter come into existence simultaneously within a particular type of scalar field, then a universe can be successfully created. In other words, if the conditions are just right, this is a sufficient amount of both time and matter to create all the stuff that is currently in our universe. At this point, physicists introduce a concept called *inflation*: a period when the scalar field divides space into a

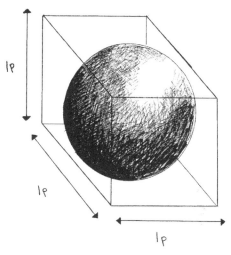

Fig. 9.2. Planck Volume and Matter. Image created by Sarah Sienna.

brief period of extreme exponential expansion. During an inflation, space erupted from its tiny beginnings into an incredibly huge volume. This expansion generated an enormous amount of what physicists call gravitational binding energy. This in turn produced an enormous amount of matter, estimated to be at least 10^{85} grams (that's a 10 followed by 85 zeros). Many believe that this huge amount of matter was counterbalanced by a corresponding group of positive energy in the scalar field. So what started as an infinitesimally small bit of virtual energy has now become all matter and energy in the expanding universe. Yet the total energy of the universe is within a quantum fluctuation equaling zero. Weird, huh? As the universe continued to expand at an exponential rate, tiny quantum fluctuations grew into macroscopic fluctuations in the density of the scalar field, making it possible for the planets, stars, and galaxies to form, which gave rise to the current structure of the universe. As the inflationary period ended, hot space continued to expand and gradually cooled. The energy of the scalar field now decayed into what physicists call dark matter, dark energy, and normal matter: things like photons, quarks, and electrons, gradually formed into protons, neutrons, and atoms, which make up the type of normal matter we see in our universe.

If you find this mind-boggling, consider what physicist Lawrence Krauss has to say about all this.

According to Krauss, "Nothing isn't nothing anymore in physics."[6] To Krauss, according to the laws of quantum mechanics and special relativity, on extremely small scales nothing is "really a boiling, bubbling brew of virtual particles that are popping in and out of existence on a time scale so short you can't even see them."[7] He maintains that although physicists cannot measure these virtual particles directly, they can measure their effects directly, which give rise to some of the best predictions in physics. Krauss mentions that the empty space inside of a proton that exists between quarks means most of the mass of the proton comes from empty space. These fields of empty space that pop in and out of existence provide about 90 percent of the mass of a proton. Since protons and neutrons are the particles that make up most of what we are, empty space is responsible for about 90 percent of our mass. So empty space is crucial for understanding our place in the universe and why we are here.

> Our new picture of cosmology is that we live in a universe dominated by nothing. The largest energy in the universe—70% of the energy in the universe—resides in empty space. This tells us that we are more insignificant than we ever imagined. If you take the universe, everything we see—stars, galaxies, etc.—if you get rid of it, the universe is essentially the same. We constitute a 1% bit of pollution in a universe that is 30% dark matter and 70% dark energy. We are completely irrelevant. Why such a universe in which we are so irrelevant would be made for us is beyond me.[8]

So we can understand not only how we came from nothing but also that we are predominantly nothing as well. So to naturalists, the reason we are here is because of a quantum fluctuation in a negative vacuum. We, along with everything else, could have just as easily not been here.

The natural answer to the question "Why am I here?" involves a number of physical processes that range from quantum fluctuations in a negative vacuum that initially gave rise to the origins of the universe 13.7 billion years ago; to the cataclysmic cosmic forces that formed Earth and its solar system 4.6 billion years ago; to the gradual development of continents and Pangaea; to the first developing single-celled organisms; to the gradual evolution of more complex organisms; to invertebrate sea dwellers, to vertebrates that eventually crawled out of the sea and onto land; to the origin of reptiles, insects, birds, and mammals. From here, the line of descent through modification of various traits allowed our ancestors to pass through mammalian stages that eventually gave rise to apes, from which we split with a common ancestor of the chimpanzee some seven to eight million years ago. To naturalists, this is why we are all here. We shall consider the evolutionary stages of human development in greater detail in the next chapter when we consider a naturalistic perspective of what we are.

THE SUPERNATURAL RESPONSE

I suppose the quickest way to give a supernatural response to the question of why we're all here is: God did it. But we must realize that people have devised thousands of ways in which to explain their existence from a divinely inspired and creative process. In fact, billions of people—from Jews to Christians, to Muslims and Hindus—all believe that the reason they are alive today is due to a particular divine power that willed their existence into being. But where should we start when there are so many different versions of supernatural human creation? From Aztecs to Zoroastrians, there are literally thousands of ways in which humans have attempted to answer the question of why we are here in a supernatural context.

In some Eskimo cultures there is a myth involving the first man who falls from a pea pod and is visited shortly thereafter by Raven, a man-bird who made, feeds, and nourishes the first man (or Man). The Raven then shows Man how he makes all the other animals out of clay. Raven then makes Man a Woman. From this first Man and Woman, all the world became populated.

In Assyro-Babylonian cultures from the seventh century BCE, we find life emerging from the sea in the form of two serpents: Lakhmu and

Lakhamu, who gave birth to the first man, Anshar (the heavens), and the first woman, Kishar (the earth). They begat two great gods: Anu, the powerful, and Ea, of great intelligence. Then other divinities were born: the Igigi, who took to the sky, and the Anumnake, who roamed the earth and the underworld.

In Egyptian cultures, it was believed that in the beginning, there was only a chaotic scene of bubbling water called Nu or Nun. It was from out of Nu that all things were created. The sun god Ra rose out of a giant blue lotus flower that had appeared on the surface of Nu. Ra then gave light to the universe. Ra then created the air god, Shu, and his wife, Tefnut, the goddess of moisture, who then gave birth to the sky-goddess, Nut, and the earth god, Geb, thus creating the physical universe. At this point Ra takes a bit of a breather while his kids finish the task of creation. Geb and Nut apparently get married against Ra's wishes; Ra then orders Shu to separate them. However, Nut is already expecting, so Ra decides to disallow Nut's giving birth in any month of the year. Meanwhile, Thoth, the god of learning, was gambling with the moon for extra light. Thoth wins five more days of light, which are added to the 360-day calendar and allows Nut the time in which to give birth to Osiris, Horus the Elder, Seth, Isis, and Nephthys. Meanwhile, another god named Khnum[9] was busy creating all the living creatures of the planet on his potter's wheel. Khnum, who is believed to have a ram's head, was a god of fecundity and creation and is said to have modeled all the animals, plants, and people of the earth.

Then of course there are the Greek myths with Zeus, Poseidon, Hermes, et al.; the Roman myths with Jupiter, Neptune, Vulcan, et al.; the Norse myths with Odin, Thor, Balder, et al.; the Japanese myths with Ho-Masubi (god of fire), Inari (god of rice), Izanagi (creator god), and so forth.

The Old Testament provides a six-day account of creation starting with light, the heavens and the earth, the seas, and so on. Eventually, humans come along from two progenitors: Adam and Eve. The Old Testament gives us two versions of the Adam and Eve myth—one in which the two were created together in Genesis 1:27: "So God created man in his own image, in the image of God created he him; male and female created he them," and another in which Adam is created first and then Eve is created out of one of his ribs in Genesis 2:7, 21–22: "And the Lord God formed man of the dust of the ground, and breathed into his nostrils the breath of life; and man became a living soul . . . and the Lord God caused a deep sleep to fall upon Adam, and he slept: and he took one of his ribs, and closed up the flesh instead thereof; and the rib, which the Lord God had taken from man, made he a woman, and brought her unto the man."[10] The Koranic version is somewhat different, in that Adam figures quite prominently from the beginning and Eve comes in quite a bit later. At 3.59 of the Koran, it states, "Surely the likeness of Isa is with Allah as the likeness of Adam; He created him from dust, then said to him, Be, and he was." We do not hear about Adam's wife until much later when God informs both to enjoy the heavenly wonders but stay away from the (ironically titled) tree of knowledge.

Aboriginal accounts of creation provide stories of a great sky woman in various forms.

> The first people were the Sky People, they lived beyond the sky because there was no earth beneath. One day the chief's daughter became very ill and no one was able to provide a cure for her sickness. A wise elder was consulted and he told them to dig up a tree and lay the girl beside the hole that remained. The Sky People respected the elder and began to dig up the tree. Suddenly the tree fell down through the hole and dragged the chief's daughter with it. As the girl fell she saw that below was only an ocean of water. Two swans were alarmed by the girl falling and decided she was too beautiful to drown so they swam to catch her. They landed her on the back of the Great Turtle, and all of the animals of the earth gathered. . . . The Sky woman lived on the island on top of the Great Turtle's back. She gave birth to twins, one good called Tharonhiawagon, one evil called Tawiskaron. From the breast of Sky Woman grows three sisters, corn, beans, and squash.[11]

And there are hundreds of other such aboriginal stories of creation. The question that now stands before us of course is which creation account should we accept and why (see fig. 9.3)?

Since it is logically impossible for each account to be true but logically

Fig. 9.3. Gods and Prophets. Image created by Vanessa Tignanelli.

possible that they could all be wrong, we are left with the extremely diffi-cult task of determining what amount of truth, if any, can be attributed to any of the various creation myths that have developed over the last several thousand years.

Some people will say, "Oh, but you can't compare some of these cre-ation myths to the truths found in the Bible, the Torah, or the Koran." It is true that few people today believe in Thor anymore or Zeus or Quet-zalcoatl. Those stories are just fairy tales and metaphors. But are they really any less believable than a virgin birth, a talking burning bush, taking six days for an all-powerful being to create everything, prophets flying off to heaven on winged horses, walking on water, coming back from the dead, and so on? The fact of the matter remains the same: the evidence provided by supernatural accounts appeals to verification at an ultimate level, which requires a Reality Measuring Stick. Since no one is in posses-sion of such a device, supernaturalists have no way of measuring the perceived absolute Truth of their creationist accounts. If supernaturalists wish to present some of their views in a manner that can be tested according to empirical or scientific criteria, then they should be able to stand up to scrutiny if, in fact, as their followers claim, they are absolutely True. Yet no empirical evidence for the existence of such deities has ever been scientifically demonstrated; no modern-day miracles or divine interventions have ever passed such tests of verification.

So supernatural responses to the question of why we are here fail miserably in the realm of empirical proof. What about rational or logical proof? There are several different proofs for a supernatural creative power that is believed to be responsible for our presence on this planet. There is the *ontological argument* for the proof of God's existence that was first formulated by a medieval theologian named Anselm (of Canterbury) in the eleventh century CE. This argument basically states that when one imagines the greatest conceivable being (i.e., one capable of bringing into existence a universe such as ours), one must conclude that if such a great being existed only in the imagination, that would make it less great. Therefore, the greatest conceivable power *must* exist because an existing greatest being is greater than an imaginary greatest being. There are many different formulations of this argument.[12] But the important thing to consider is whether we can, by reason alone, prove the existence of such a supernatural being in such a fashion. One of the problems with such a proof is that it assumes the existence of something is made necessary by the definition of a thing's qualities—in this case, the quality of greatness. To use an analogy, I could use a version of the ontological argument to will into being practically anything. For example, I can imagine right now the greatest conceivable banana ever imaginable. If this banana existed only as a thought in my mind, it would not be as great. So I must conclude that, somewhere, such a banana must exist; otherwise, it wouldn't be as great. The important point to note here is that thinking about something does not necessarily make it so. Otherwise, we could will all sorts of things into existence.

The second major proof for the existence of God is called the *cosmological argument*. Sometimes referred to as the first cause or prime mover argument, this proof received its origins with, among others, Plato and

Aristotle and gained further refinement with St. Thomas Aquinas. The idea is that if we look at anything or any person, for example, your parents, they must have had parents who had parents, and so on. You cannot have an infinite number of parents causing children, nor can you have a loop of causality of parents causing children who eventually cause the same parents. So there must have been a first parent or creative force that brought the first parents into being. Hence, God. Or look at the universe itself. Some will argue that the universe could never have been created from nothing (or *ex nihilo*, as the medieval theologians used to say). Speaking of medieval theologians, St. Thomas Aquinas developed the cosmological argument into five sections (called the *quinque viae* or the five ways). All the arguments follow a similar pattern, so we will concern ourselves with just a few of them. Aquinas believed God to be omnipotent (all-powerful), omniscient (all-knowing), omnipresent (all-present), and omnibenevolent (all-good). In his first argument, he states:

(P1) Physical objects are in motion.
(P2) Whatever moves is caused to move.
(P3) The chain of movers cannot be infinite.
(P4) Therefore, there must be a first mover.
(C)   This first mover is god, the unmoved mover.

In his second argument, Aquinas states the following:

(P1) Some events cause other events.
(P2) If an event occurs, it must have been caused by something other than itself.
(P3) There can be no infinite chain of events and causes.
(P4) Therefore, there must have been a first cause.
(C)   The first cause is god, the uncaused cause.

But notice how Aquinas's second argument contains contradictory premises:

(P2) If an event occurs, it must be caused by something other than itself; and

(P4) (It follows that) there is a first uncaused cause.

If we think about this for a minute, we will see that if the fourth premise is true, the second cannot be; and if the second premise is true, the fourth cannot be. So there is an internal *inconsistency* to Aquinas's cosmological argument. Today, people like William Lane Craig have put forward the so-called Kalam cosmological argument, which states practically the same thing:

(P1) Whatever begins to exist has a cause.

(P2) The universe began to exist.

(C) Therefore, the universe had a cause.

Here, Craig, like Aquinas, wrongly assumes that an Aristotelian notion of cause and effect must take place. It is easy to see why. According to the classical laws of thought discussed earlier in the book, our daily lives are largely governed according to the laws of noncontradiction, identity, and excluded middle. However, when it comes to the origins of the universe and the bizarre nature of quantum mechanics, we saw earlier in this chapter how many physicists have demonstrated how quantum fluctuations can exist prior to the existence of our current universe. But if we return to the notion of a God bringing the universe into existence, the supernaturalist will find great difficulty in explaining why God can be injected into the argument without having a prior cause. The usual response is that God has always existed. How does a supernaturalist know this? What evidence is there in support of such a statement? Why couldn't we say that the universe has somehow always existed? Since there is no empirical evidence for the existence of such a being, a supernaturalist must rely on rational grounds, which we have found to be lacking in conviction and proof.

The fifth argument for the existence of God that Aquinas provides is commonly known as the *teleological argument*. This term derives its meaning from the Greek *telos* meaning "end" or "purpose." The argument's structure looks something like this:

(P1)   Among objects that act toward an end, some possess minds and some don't.

(P2)   An object that doesn't possess a mind must have been designed by one that does.

(P3)   So there must exist a being with a mind that designed all mindless objects that act toward an end.

(C)   Therefore, God is the being that designed all mindless objects.

This argument was later reformulated by William Paley in the nineteenth century in his famous watch analogy. As noted earlier, the argument assumes that if one finds a watch (a mindless object), one can rightly conclude that there must be a watchmaker (a being with a mind). Hence, since humans and other species are far more complex than any watch, there must exist a being, God, who has the intelligence to design such beings. This argument has been reformulated and used by intelligent design creationists who argue for God's existence in much the same way. A great blow was dealt to this argument when Charles Darwin released *On the Origin of Species* in 1859.

Darwin demonstrated that although nature looks like it has been designed (e.g., the hummingbird's beak fits nicely into the flower to retrieve nectar, frogs eat flies, fish eat frogs, and so on), nature actually selects which species get to survive and reproduce based on their characteristics. It just so happens that birds with specific types of beaks can exploit their environments in ways that increase their likelihood to survive and reproduce. Those species less adapted to changing environments are naturally selected to die out. A natural explanation for apparent design was given in place of a supernatural explanation.

We have briefly looked at three of the most often used rational or logical arguments for the proof of a supernatural creator. Although historically interesting, each argument lacks the ability to provide the type of evidence required to convince us that such a supernatural agent actually exists as the reason for why we are all here. This generates considerable problems in answering the Big Five supernaturally. For if there are no solid empirical grounds upon which a supernaturalist can base his beliefs, and the rational grounds are equally lacking in evidence and conviction, upon what do supernaturalists base their views?

At this point we need to mentally step back, as it were, and look at the natural and supernatural responses to why we are here as two possible explanations. If we were to ask ourselves, "What was the cause of everything?" where "everything" can be defined as all that has been, is, and will ever be (i.e., the universe with us in it), we arrive at a disjunct of plausibility, which could be stated like this:

$$Ui \lor \sim (Ui)$$

(Universe Intended or Universe Not-Intended)[13]

For something to come into being, it can be either an accident or an intention. I did not intend to run over the squirrel; it was my car that caused its demise. So too, with the universe—either it came to be purely by chance perhaps in a quantum fluctuation, or something *intended* it to come into existence. These are the only two possibilities. There isn't a third or fourth possible way for the universe and us to exist. Either the universe and all of us were intended to be or we were not. *Intentionality* is the key idea here. It indicates causal purpose or, in its absence, a lack of causal purpose and an accident. Faced with such a disjunct, we have a number of choices. We can say outright that the universe was unintended. Or we can say outright that the universe was intended. Or we can suspend judgment on the disjunct and decide neither way. The latter of course, is the safest way to go and would be the choice of the ancient Skeptics and Socrates. Even though naturalists have no compelling reasons to believe that a supernatural force is responsible for the existence of the universe, they must still allow this to be possible in ways that, according to their historical facticity, may not be immediately recognizable to them. But having said this, if the universe was somehow intended to be as it is, the supernaturalist can find no direct evidence to indicate this either. If there is no God as an intentional creative force of the universe, then the universe is simply accidental and we, as humans, are here as a product of that accidental occurrence. As such, we are on our own. The universe would be devoid of any absolute meaning, purpose, or moral sense. It is not difficult to see how this idea frightens some people.[14] The psychological effects of considering the possibility that no such supernatural agent exists is similar to a child's fear of losing his/her parents. It is disruptive to the comforting feeling that a parent figure is somehow looking over us to make sure that everything is all right. This supernatural parent is often looked upon as an intervening being who will see to it that the just are rewarded and the unjust are punished. But the thought of losing a holy, divine, supernatural parent figure, is far worse than losing one's own parents because it means one is all alone in this immense universe. And as such, we would be existential orphans—free to decide for ourselves what we should and should not do without any divine parent or guardian telling us what to do. Many supernaturalists do not know what to do with such freedom. The thought of it can be quite frightening. They may run to the comfort of their religious communities, their synagogues, temples, mosques, and churches. There they are adopted by like-minded individuals who foster group support and maintain that, collectively, they cannot possibly all be wrong. But of course, they can be. As discussed, it is an impossibility for all defined world religions to be right, but it is entirely possible for them all to be wrong.

The problem with supernaturalism in general is that not only is faith in the existence of God proclaimed (i.e., choosing one of the disjunctive sides), but He is given numerous qualities, character traits, and attributes, and He tells us humans (through revelation, intervention, commands) not only how the universe came to be but also how we should act as well. There are specific traits and qualities attributed to God found in many creationist accounts that result in several tensions. There is a direct correlation between the number of qualities attributed to a supernatural agent and the likelihood of contradiction and error, for it moves one further and further away from the knowable disjunct of Ui or $\sim$(Ui). Instead of maintaining an epistemically responsible position by suspending judgment on such a disjunct, supernaturalists often multiply entities far past necessity (another violation of Occam's razor). Instead of suspending judgment on Ui or ~(Ui), the supernaturalist not only chooses Ui but then calls it "God" and subsequently proceeds to add a great string of conjuncts in the form of qualities, commands, and descriptions (e.g., the supernaturalist will claim to know that there is a creator, and it is all-powerful and all-knowing and all-present and all-good, and it created humankind, and it told humankind what constitutes the world, and it told humankind how to act/behave). So any definition of God as a supernatural agent starts to look like this equation,

$$Ui = God = x_1 \,\&\, x_2 \,\&\, x_3 \ldots x_n,$$

where x = qualities, attributes, commands, descriptions, and so on. In other words, the supernaturalist believes the universe to be brought into existence intentionally by a creator whose qualities, attributes, and commands can be known with absolute certainty. All supernaturalists tend to define such agents in fairly complex ways by attributing to them many different qualities and attributes. But the more attributes a supernaturalist adds to his or her definition of God, the more likely it is to find unsolvable tensions, inconsistencies, contradictions, and fallacies, and the more likely such a position is likely to die the death of a thousand *ad hoc* justifications.

We have now considered the natural and supernatural responses to the question "Why am I here?" No matter how you choose to respond to this or any other of the Big Five, you must constantly review your responses according to the ABCs of critical thinking. What are your arguments, your biases, the contexts in which you formulated your responses, your diagrammed arguments, your evidence, and your fallacies? If you disagree with those who answer the Big Five differently from you, why? What are they lacking, and what can you do to demonstrate that your arguments are more warranted according to acceptable criteria than theirs? Now that we have considered the first two questions of the Big Five, it is time to consider how naturalists and supernaturalists answer the next question: What am I?

CHAPTER 10
WHAT AM I?

I am who I am.
—EXODUS 3:14

I am a deeply religious nonbeliever—this is a somewhat new kind of religion.
—ALBERT EINSTEIN

Man is descended from a hairy, tailed quadruped, probably arboreal in its habits.
—CHARLES DARWIN

We define ourselves in many ways: by ethnicity, by gender and sexuality, by nationalist pride, by employment, by wealth or lack of it, by religion or lack of it, by our love of art, sports, music, and video games. There are countless ways in which we, as a species, give identity to ourselves as individuals, family, community, and citizens of the world. But no distinction seems to generate as much contention as the ways we define ourselves naturally and supernaturally. In fact, throughout the world, and especially in the United States today, there is considerable divisiveness over the manner in which citizens respond to this question.

THE NATURAL RESPONSE

If the universe is 13.7 billion years old and Earth is around 4.6 billion years old, then what are we? If the universe came into being so long ago, what was happening all that time? Why did it take so long for us to arrive on the scene? The basic understanding of biological development on this planet goes something like this:

After the universe came into being around 13.7 billion years ago, various forces of nature were forming: gravity, the strong and weak nuclear forces, and electromagnetic forces. Over millions of years, the universe cooled, so that today the average temperature of deep space is about three degrees above absolute zero. Various elements, such as hydrogen, helium, lithium, and others, accumulated, and by the force of gravity created stars, planets, moons, asteroids, comets, meteors, and so on. Around 4.6 billion years ago, Earth began to form. As its molten mass cooled, there was massive condensation that released gases such as hydrogen, carbon dioxide, ammonia, and water vapor, creating a primitive atmosphere. It is important to note there was no free oxygen (O_2) for the first third of the Earth's history, for over one billion years. As Earth continued to cool, water vapor condensed and flooded the planet with rain, causing oceans to form. These oceans contained basic chemicals, such as alcohols, carbon-rich acids, simple carbohydrates, and the like, which formed the first amino acids in chemical reactions brought about by the electrical influence of lightning. These protomolecules were the initial requirement, the very first organic building blocks that brought about the first forms of life on this planet about 3.5 billion years ago.[1] The first life-forms were called *prokaryotes*—bacterialike single cells without nuclei (see fig. 10.1).

The earliest instance of natural selection began to take place in what is called *biochemical evolution*. Prokaryotes began to use up the supply of organic molecules in the oceans, and those that had the ability to synthesize their own energy source survived and those that could not perished. Around three billion years ago, self-feeding (or autotrophic) prokaryotes, such as blue-green algae, evolved. These single-celled organisms developed the ability to perform photosynthesis—or undertake the metabolic

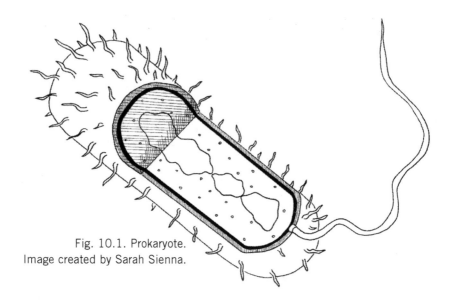

Fig. 10.1. Prokaryote.
Image created by Sarah Sienna.

process whereby energy from the sun combined with carbon dioxide (CO_2) and water (H_2O) causes the formation of simple sugars (food) as storage for energy and releases oxygen (O_2). Once blue-green algae developed the capacity for photosynthesis, there was an ever-increasing rise in the production of oxygen (O_2). Gradually, prokaryotes became more diversified, and we find in the fossil record the emergence of the first organisms with nuclei—the *eukaryotes*. These cells reproduced asexually—that is, they cloned themselves. But by about 1.5 billion years ago (perhaps longer), evolution got an incredible push—the origin of sexual reproduction (a sort of second Big Bang).[2] Now, instead of cellular cloning, we saw for the first time genetic variability, and the gene pool got a lot bigger. In other words, two different organisms now contributed to the genotype (the genetic makeup) of the offspring. This could be either beneficial or disadvantageous to an organism, depending upon its current level of environmental stasis. But undeniably, sexual reproduction led to greater and greater diversity, which led to an increased rate of differences appearing in plants and animals (*flora* and *fauna*).[3] About 750 million years ago, plants and animals comprised of more than one cell appeared. These multicellular organisms had specialized cells for specific functions.

Around 535 million years ago, something remarkable happened on Earth: the level of free oxygen increased dramatically. With this new abundant supply of oxygen (created from photosynthesis), multicellular organisms were better equipped to extract energy from carbohydrates. As well, the free oxygen created a layer of ozone in the upper atmosphere that better protected the organisms' DNA from the sun's harmful ultraviolet rays. In British Columbia, there is a section of mountain called the Burgess Shale. There, scientists are discovering new species of organisms (sometimes dozens a day) that were evolving during this period of increased oxygen (called the Cambrian Explosion). Multicellular organisms gradually evolved into more and more diverse organisms, such as land plants, soft-bodied vertebrates, shelled arthropods, and, eventually, the first vertebrates—fish. By around 395 million years ago, bony fish species diversified and expanded, and amphibians and insects appeared. By around 350 million years ago, we see in the fossil record evidence of the first land reptiles that evolved from amphibian ancestors. By 280 million years ago, we see fossil evidence of large mammal-like reptiles, like sail-backed lizards (*Dimetrodon*), which would have been an ancestor to early mammals. During the Mezozoic Era (225 million years ago to 65 million years ago) dinosaurs flourished, mammals appeared, and birds appeared.

During this period, known as the Permian Period, all the continents were grouped together in a single landmass known as Pangaea. Approximately 200 million years ago, due to continental drift, the Pangaea landmass separated into two distinct landmasses: Gondwanaland and Laurasia. By 135 million years ago, Laurasia had drifted and separated into North America, Europe, and Asia, while Gondwanaland separated into Africa, Antarctica, Australia, and South America. At this point, what is now known as India was a large island in the middle of the Pacific Ocean. It would not be until around 30 to 35 million years ago that India would meet with mainland Asia to create the enormous land buckling that is now the Himalayan mountains. What is now the US eastern seaboard was once connected to Chile, as was California to Australia; Brazil was connected to Nigeria.

About 65 million years ago, a giant meteor crashed into Earth, causing a mass extinction. This event devastated the populations of dinosaurs. Once dinosaurs became extinct, the surviving mammals had far fewer predators to contend with, and early primates appeared and radiated from 65 million years ago to 38 million years ago. From 38 million years ago to 23 million years ago, Old World and New World monkeys appeared and radiated. While species continued to diversify, global forces were influencing evolution. After the continents had drifted to their current positions, weather patterns had changed the northern and central African jungle into a more arid grassland (the savannah). Between 6 and 8 million years ago, human and ape species split from a common ancestor. Human species evolved from a smaller, apelike ancestor—the australopithecines (*afarensis, africanus, bosei/robustus*)—to the taller, larger-brained *Homo* species (*habilis, erectus, sapiens*). The "savannah hypothesis" proposes that as the jungles of Africa became grassland, our ancestors were forced down from the trees and became bipedal (walking on two feet). Whether or not this hypothesis is true, bipedalism undoubtedly led to important developments, such as free limbs (arms) by which to create and use tools; it allowed for greater visibility and smell of predators and prey; it led to greater locomotion; change of diet from plant-eating to both plant- and meat-eating (omnivorous); and it led to an increase in brain size (from 400 cubic centimeters 3.5 million years ago to our current size of 1,350 cubic centimeters).

There were many different species of hominins or humanlike apes. As recently as 30,000 years ago, there were at least four different species of hominin still in existence: *Homo neanderthalis, Homo erectus, Homo florensiensis*, and *Homo sapiens*. Gradually, most species of early humans became extinct. However, one survived: *Homo sapiens sapiens* (the "smart ape"). The human species used tools to some degree and perhaps had crude languages. It is now believed that our ancestors left Africa around 60,000 years ago.[4] The archaeological records indicate that at about 35,000 to 70,000 years ago, the manufacturing and diversity of tool use increased dramatically. The fossil records show that, in some hominin species, tool use and technology remained unchanged for long periods of

Fig. 10.2. Hand Axe. Photograph by Matthew DiCarlo.

time, for example, the use of the stone hand axe remained virtually unchanged for about one million years (see fig. 10.2).

But a fairly short time ago, human culture changed, and we began to see signs of complex tool use, clothing, and the origin of art. Why did this happen only about 40,000 years ago? Perhaps it was due to our ancestors' relatively sudden ability to communicate in complex ways. The greater one can articulate about one's environment, the greater one can modify it (just watch children of different ages play with Lego building blocks). Or perhaps it was due to increased migration, socialization, and communal development. Or perhaps combinations of these and other factors. What we do know is that up until about 10,000 years ago, our ancestors were still hunter/gatherers. They were largely nomadic and moved about scavenging, trapping, hunting, and foraging where food was plentiful. But something quite remarkable happened about 10,000 years ago. Perhaps due to another ice age and a scarcity of food, our ancestors' numbers began dwindling. It was around this time that our ancestors invented something that would change the world forever: the domestication of plants and animals—agriculture. Once our ancestors became agrarian, they did not have to continue moving around after herds. This new form of survival gave way to the development of economics, social commerce, trading, and more sophisticated forms of survival. Art and economics began to gradually flourish as central depots became communities, towns, and so forth. We have seen the rise and fall of the Mesopotamians, Egyptians, Greeks, Romans, Chinese, Japanese, Arabs, Spanish, French, British, and now Americans, to name but a few. Our ideas about the natural world have gone through amazing transitions, revisions, and fluctuations. Just when the Romans were at their height of commerce, science, and technology, western Europe plummeted into the Dark Ages for nearly one thousand years. Then, through the Renaissance, we began to see the power of human reason once more. With the advent of the printing press, ideas could be circulated throughout Europe, and science and technology began to thrive. Scientific methodology evolved to become more rigid, systematic, and objective. We have accomplished much in a relatively short time. We are a very young species in terms of culture, science, art, technology, commerce, and so on. Our brains are doing advanced things while our bodies are still trying to catch up. We are very creative, imaginative creatures. In a very short time, our technological achievements have made this large planet seem very small.

This naturalistic answer takes a look at what we are from a very long period of time. Our ancestry lies in the primordial oceans of a very young Earth. Over billions of years, life became more and more complex until our ancestors moved through stages of development: from single-celled organisms to more complex organisms; through aquatic life, to amphibian and reptilian, and eventually to mammalian. It is at the mammal stage that our evolutionary history becomes most interesting and, for some, most contentious. If we just look at the past six or seven million years, we find our line of descent splitting from that of the chimpanzee. They went their evolutionary way; we went ours. Our ancestors went through some interesting changes along the way, and there were many different species of humans throughout the last several million years. Some might be quite surprised to know that in just the last four million years, there have been more than a dozen different species of humans on this planet. And they all came from Africa. It follows then that *we are all African*. For naturalists, this is perfectly acceptable, since many of the evolutionary sciences produce very convincing evidence in support of this conclusion. But for others who are more inclined to answer this question supernaturally, they might think otherwise. In fact, in Gallup polls from 1982 to 2004, almost 50 percent of Americans polled maintained that "God created man pretty much in his present form at one time within the last ten thousand years." There is no doubt that supernatural beliefs can stand in the way of accepting scientific information about human origins. But what are the premises and evidence in support of such a natural understanding of ourselves? I present some of the most recent evidence that supports the claim that all human lineage descended from a small group of ancestors in Africa around sixty thousand years ago, and then we will examine some of the important political, philosophical, and moral implications that result from such an understanding of human origins.[5]

When Charles Darwin said in *The Descent of Man* that "it is somewhat more probable that our early progenitors lived on the African continent than elsewhere," this claim was "somewhat more probable" in the late 1800s. However, today, there is overwhelming scientific evidence to support this conclusion. Scientists in various fields have compiled evidence from fossils, climatological records, geological trends, migration patterns, tool use, and the like, to provide premises and evidence with which to demonstrate our African ancestry. But what appears to be the most compelling evidence today does not come from bones, skulls, radiometric dating, or even tools. It comes from us. Molecular anthropologists and geneticists have examined DNA samples of living humans and can identify specific genetic markers that indicate when and where mutations arose in our distant past. In other words, we all carry time machines in our DNA. By examining where and how these mutations converge, they have been able to demonstrate a common lineage of all humans alive today. And it points directly to central–eastern Africa.

Fossils and Hominin Lineage

One of the things we must acknowledge about fossil evidence is that fossilized remains of our ancestors are very rare and difficult to discover, and they require an enormous amount of planning, money, and luck to find. But as difficult as it is to discover primary evidence, scientists do keep finding more bones and skulls (see fig. 10.3). The picture of the puzzle of human origins prior to genetic anthropology still maintains an "Out of Africa" migration pattern. But hominin[6] fossils can tell us what genetics cannot: what our ancestors looked like. Even though fossilization is quite rare for many species—including hominins—archaeologists have amassed enough evidence to paint a fairly accurate picture not only of our ancestors but also of the ancestors of species of humans that did not survive as long as *Homo sapiens*. We must not forget that throughout much of our ancestral time, we were not alone. As mentioned, as recently as thirty thousand years ago there were at least four different types of hominins alive on this planet: *Homo erectus*, *Homo neanderthalis*, *Homo floresiensis*, and *Homo sapiens*. Think about this for a minute: aside from ourselves, there were at least three other distinct species of humans inhabiting this planet. Would this fact alone not give one pause to think of how we (that is, *Homo sapiens*) could have been specially created if there were three other types of

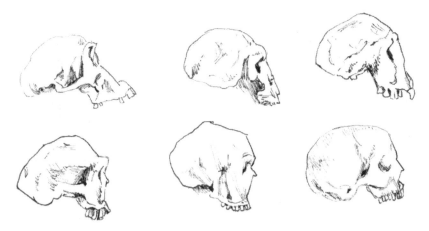

Fig. 10.3. Hominin Skulls. Image created by Vanessa Tignanelli.

humans living alongside our ancestors? Although much of the fossil record is incomplete prior to five million years ago, paleoanthropologists have pieced together some compelling evidence for the first types of hominins that stood upright in Africa. One of the most famous of these ancestral beings is named Lucy, after the Beatles song "Lucy in the Sky with Diamonds." Lucy was a species prior to *Homo* called *Australopithecus afarensis*, which lived approximately 3.5 million years ago. She was discovered by Don Johanson in 1974 in the Afar region of Ethiopia. Through radiometric dating (as well as other dating techniques), bone physiology, dentition, and so on, Johanson estimated her height to be around three and a half feet, and she weighed approximately sixty pounds. Lucy represents one of the oldest and most complete upright-walking human ancestors. Many other fossilized remains have been found that demonstrate an ancestral hominoid/hominin bush, dating back to six million years ago with *Sahelanthropus tchadensis*, where our ancestors and chimpanzee ancestors split from a common ancestor. Although many of the connections and relations between species are still unclear, the latest model from the Smithsonian Institution's Human Origins Program connects the lineage of Lucy to *Homo habilis*, then to *Homo ergaster*, then to *Homo heidelbergensis*, and finally a split to *Homo neanderthalis* and *Homo sapiens*.

A fairly recent technique that further corroborates the "Out of Africa" model was carried out by population biologist Andrea Manica from Cambridge University. Manica and her team analyzed 4,666 male skulls and 1,579 female skulls from 105 worldwide populations. By 200,000 years ago, *Homo heidelbergensis* had evolved into *Homo neanderthalensis* and *Homo sapiens*. *Homo sapiens* became the only surviving hominin species, which migrated out of Africa approximately 60,000 years ago. Genetic studies corroborate the "Out of Africa" model because genetic diversity is greatest in Africa and decreases steadily the further populations move from the continent. Using techniques based on thirty-seven measurements, Manica's team found that skull shapes of humans around the world closely match the genetic data, in other words, the diversity of skull shapes within a given population changes consistently the farther they are from Africa.

Climatology/Meteorology/Migration/Tools

The changing landscapes and weather conditions also contributed greatly to the evolutionary constraints on our ancestors. Some close relatives left Africa long before our ancestors did. Around 2.5 million years ago, we find evidence of the first ice age. Africa's climate had gone through radical changes: from a vegetative forest to savannah grasslands; it had become a much warmer and drier place while Asia and Europe became much colder and drier. Some *auststralopithecines* were specialists in diet (like *A. robustus*), which maintained a diet of roots and leaves and could chew with massive molars several times the size of our own. Other australo-pithecines became generalists and turned to a meat-based diet. This caused their digestive tracts to shorten and their brain sizes to increase. By 1.8 million years ago, *Homo erectus* was lean and slender—an adaptation as a means for reducing heat—and also had a brain size about half of ours today. *Homo erectus* was making stone tools quite prodigiously. There would be six more ice ages, some lasting 90,000 years, with the last one ending about 10,000 years ago. Other hominins, including the Neanderthals, had moved out of Africa long before our ancestors. They were in Europe by about 300,000 years ago. Most of our ancestors would not leave Africa until about 60,000 years ago. By this time, they would have been traveling in rather small numbers, foraging, hunting, and constantly moving as nomadic tribes.

The Genetic Evidence

The history and field of molecular anthropology is fairly recent. Among the first contributors was Allan Wilson, a New Zealander and scholar at the University of Carlifornia at Berkeley. In 1967, he copublished a paper in the journal *Science* with doctoral student Vince Sarich titled, "Immunological Time-Scale for Human Evolution." Wilson believed that the origins of the human species could be seen through a *molecular clock* by dating the genetic mutations of humans which had accumulated since we parted from a common ancestor.

When Wilson and Sarich analyzed and compared genetic material from humans with chimpanzees they found the material to be 99 percent identical. From this, using the "molecular clock" reasoning (bigger differences equate to greater time since their last common ancestor) they deduced that the earliest proto-hominids evolved only five million years [ago]. This was fifteen million years younger than stated by conventional anthropology.[7]

So whenever you read or hear someone say, "You know, our DNA and a chimp's DNA is about 99 percent identical," you can thank Wilson and his team for figuring this out. Due to academic politics and the difficulty involved in changing accepted norms, Wilson's work would remain on the fringes of the anthropological community for twenty years. Nonetheless, Wilson appeared to enjoy his status as a cutting-edge dweller. He attracted some of the best students in the world to work with him at his Berkeley lab. By the early 1980s, his findings were starting to become more widely accepted. One of Wilson's brightest students, Rebecca Cann, applied his techniques to a number of specimens taken from people whose ancestry originated from different parts of the world. By examining the differences in mutations that had accumulated since their mitochondrial DNA shared a common ancestry, she constructed a matriline (or matritree) connecting them.

The result was a revelation. Whichever way you drew the tree, its root was in Africa. *Homo sapiens* was thus unveiled as an African species. Cann and Wilson did some matridendrochronology. The result suggested that all lines converge on the ovaries of a single woman who lived some 150,000 years ago.[8] Sometimes referred to in the media as the matriarchal African "Eve," there would have been perhaps some 2,000 to 10,000 women containing the same mitochondrial DNA mutations. However, if anything had happened to them, we might not be here at all. When you consider the evidence carefully, our ancestors' trek out of Africa is one filled with staggering odds and amazing consequences. From a time when our ancestors were living in trees to climatological events that led to a radical change in flora throughout Africa, to descending down from the trees to the African savannah some five to six million years ago, to walking upright, developing smaller guts and bigger brains, inventing stone tools, and utilizing fire, it is quite an epic story that today we have evolved to the point where we can actually make sense of our origins. We no longer need to simply philosophize about who we are or where we came from. We no longer need to contrive supernatural stories; we have evolved to the point where we can accurately look back on history within the time machines of our own DNA.

The Genographic Project

Sponsored by the National Geographic Society and IBM, the Genographic Project is a worldwide effort to establish a large database (two hundred thousand samples) of human DNA in an effort to chart the migration history of our ancestors. But what is DNA? How can it tell us anything about our ancestry? Cells in our bodies are given instructions on how to produce proteins in order for specific cells to grow and function in particular ways. If the instructions are interrupted or interfered with, in other words, mutated, then cells may function in ways that may be harmful—or on rare occasions—beneficial to the organism. There are two ways in which molecular anthropologists can study such mutations:

1. As we have already seen, one method is through an analysis of mitochondrial DNA, which is passed from mother to offspring, thereby allowing scientists to trace the female line of descent.
2. Through an analysis of the Y chromosome. This is passed from father to son.

Many mutations become repaired or eliminated at birth and do not get passed down to subsequent generations. However, some mutations, known as *germ-line mutations*, are passed down to offspring without serious medical consequences (there are more than one thousand known mutations). Founder mutations get passed down intact over generations without change. All people possessing founder mutations have a damaged section of DNA identical to that of the original founder. This shared region of DNA is called a haplotype. If you share a haplotype, you share an ancestor all the way back to the original founder. The age of founder mutations can be determined by examining the length of the haplotype: the shorter the length, the older the mutation. Between 50,000 and 55,000 years ago, our ancestors migrated to India and Australia. Around 45,000 years ago, the African descendants reached the Middle East; and as the second-last ice age waned by 40,000 years ago, they moved into the open steppes of Central Asia. As Spencer Wells, director of the Genographic Project, puts it so aptly: "If Africa is the cradle of humanity, Central Asia served as its nursery."9 From Central Asia, we find *Homo sapiens* reaching Europe around 35,000 years ago. By 20,000 years ago, a separate group of Central Asians moved north into Siberia and the Arctic Circle. Eventually, there were at least two separate migrations to the Americas: The first appears to have come from western Europe where we now see evidence of migrations along the ice flow of the last ice age, which stretched from western Europe to North America. The second appears to have come from a land bridge from Siberia to what is now Alaska. Although molecular anthropologists such as Wilson, Cann, and Wells have given us our greatest discovery about ourselves, geneticists still wish to track markers more comprehensively throughout all human populations and create an even more detailed map of our ancestors' journey across the globe. Anyone can now participate in the Genographic Project. At a cost of around $100 (USD), it allows any person to track the movement of his or her ancestors out of Africa. My family and I purchased a kit, and we decided to send in a DNA sample of our youngest son, Matthew. His lineage was traced out of Africa, through what is now Saudi Arabia, into the Fertile Crescent (Iraq/Iran), and into western Europe.

Some Inferences

Since the empirical evidence that backs the premises is quite strong in warranting the naturalists' belief that all human ancestry comes from Africa, we should consider some of the inferences and broader implications for our species if we are to honestly and humbly accept that *we are all African.*

1. In accepting our African origins, we see a genetic coalescence of the entire human population. We now know that we descended from inhabitants of Africa who began migrating out of Africa around sixty thousand years ago. In this way, it is impossible for us not all to be, in some ways, related. Think of it as the past union of all degrees of separation.

2. We are forced to consider how this discovery of our origins was made. In so doing, we see an immediate appeal to the many wondrous evolutionary sciences that individually support our African lineage and collectively make this discovery highly warranted. It is intrinsically valuable whenever any scientific discoveries are made. They tell us something we previously did not know and, in so doing, enrich our lives with the reward of discovery and enlightenment. To those who have supernaturalist beliefs regarding who and what we are, there should be no fear to embrace science and incorporate it into their current supernatural beliefs. But at the same time, supernaturalists should not be biased against scientific discoveries of our ancestry simply because they do not happen to fit in with a particular supernatural account.

3. We must accept that evolutionary theory about human origins is a responsible means for establishing scientific facts about who we are and where we came from. We will continuously add to our already vastly large accumulation of information about our ancestry. We may make new discoveries that challenge current views. But this is the very spirit of science itself. It is a self-building and self-correcting process. It is by no means perfect, but this has never been one of its claims. At the end of the day, there are simply more and less responsible means for attaining and disseminating information about the cause-and-effect relationships of the natural world. Our current sciences aspire to be the most responsible in this regard.

4. We now have definitive proof that racism is a human invention. Yes, it is true that by nature, most species—especially mammals—are intrinsically xenophobic, that is, wary of species different than themselves. But this is simply a hardwired response to the possibility of

threat and danger. However, once there is evidence of an absence of threat and the potential for increased security and resource acquisition through cooperation, there is no further need for fear of foreignness. Robert Kurzban has referred to this hardwired xenophobic response as an "otherness detector" that exists in us because of its use in judging the trustworthiness of strangers. I have spent much of my academic career analyzing how all humans (and many mammals) possess a highly comparative brain. Kurzban believes that humans have traditionally used skin color as sign of uniqueness and a way to make comparisons. But he says other factors can have the same effect, for example, unusual accents, colored T-shirts at athletic competitions, flags of different countries, gang colors, and so on. But skin color has a specific evolutionary function:

> [Skin color] balances the need to protect the skin from damage by ultraviolet light (which requires melanin, the pigment that makes skin dark) and the need to make vitamin D (which results from the action of sunlight on a chemical in the skin). This explains the dark, opaque skins in the tropics and the light, transparent ones nearer the poles.[10]

It is possible to conceive that if all people on this planet were to accept that we are all African, there might be less racial hatred, violence, and bloodshed. As William Hamilton has written extensively, we tend to care more for our kin and less for strangers.[11] This appears to be a hardwired, inherent trait known as *kin selection*. Perhaps it is possible to transcend our biological constraints and, with the help of science, recognize that we have the ability to treat one another as an extended kinship. For if we turn the evolutionary clock backward just a few thousand years, all Jews and Arabs are brothers and sisters. The same is true for Turks and Greeks, Japanese and Chinese, Hutus and Tutsis. If we turn back the clock further, we all coalesce into a common ancestry: "Each of us bears biochemical witness to the fact that all humans are indeed members of a single family, bound together by the shared inheritance of our genome."[12]

So racism is really just a social construct with lingering natural biases—leftover baggage from our mammalian xenophobic tendencies. Once these tendencies are transcended through reason and science, it is possible to reduce one's fear of the other. Shared values become more important than the less relevant characteristics that distinguish one group's members from another's. More thought and energy can be devoted to searching for a commonality of ideas and values between different groups. If there is to be anything like a universal charter of rights, we must first determine those values that are most common to the populations of the world.

5. By acknowledging that we are all African, we are all humbled, liberated, and equal. One obstacle to this sense of humility may come from the belief that one's in-group is somehow more privileged or chosen in some ways than other out-groups. Instead of viewing one's group as the "chosen people" of a particular supernatural agent, a naturalist sees our African origins as liberating us from any self-imposed status onto a specific group. We are all exactly the same. The discovery that each one of us is descended from African ancestors means that we no longer need to segregate and distinguish ourselves through the use of artificial inventions of importance, whether politically, philosophically, or supernaturally motivated. We now know, without doubt, that we are all the same. This egalitarian realization liberates us from any delusions of self-imposed importance and makes us all equal. This may not be easy for some to accept; especially if their supernatural answers to the Big Five elevate their moral or civil status above others. But then again, many of us can only stand so much fairness.

Let's now consider what we are from a naturalist understanding in current times. Throughout the various stages of the evolution of our species, we have been in a constant struggle—a sort of arms race—to fight off predators and attain prey. But in today's world, we generally do not need to avoid lions or other large predators on the way to work. Instead, the predators that seek us out are much, much, smaller. As we saw earlier, we are a conglomerate of physical systems. Pathogens and parasites manipulate our systems as hosts in which to survive and reproduce. Essentially, our bodies are similar to huge microbial ecosystems in which wars far greater than any conceivable in fact or in fiction take place every day between invading organisms and our immune systems. One way we can understand this part of our identity is to consider what happens when new factors are introduced into our body's own ecology. For example, consider the ubiquitous use of antibacterial soap. With an ever-increasing desire to be more hygienic, there has emerged an apparent need and eventual market demand for higher-quality products for personal hygiene. This has led to the use of a chemical agent called triclosan in our personal bodily ecosystems, introduced through the use of antibacterial soap. Although we cannot literally see what is happening at this microbial level, manufacturers are claiming that triclosan kills 99.9 percent of the types of bacteria it is intended to kill. However, the 0.1 percent of bacteria that it does not kill will survive and spread, and we will begin to see the development of what have been called "super bugs" or "super germs." With a better understanding of what we are and how these types of natural systems work, perhaps we will be better able to develop social policies that act in our best interest and in the best interest of future generations in regard to our health and well-being. However, this requires that we have a firm understanding of what we are from a naturalistic perspective.

Another striking piece of information that emerges from the way in which a naturalist would respond to the question "What am I?" is that our species along with all others, has a limited amount of time on this planet. Few people alive today are aware that 99 percent of all species that have ever lived on this planet are extinct. There were no less than eight mass extinctions throughout Earth's history: the Precambrian, the Vendian, the Cambrian, the Ordovician, the Devonian, the Permian, the End-Cretaceous, and the Holocene. Most of the mass extinctions were due to advancing glacial and volcanic activity, but the End-Cretaceous (the one that wiped out the dinosaurs) was due to meteor impact. Keep in mind that when scientists say "mass extinction," they're not fooling around. The volcanic activity that sparked the Permian extinction, for example, which happened around two hundred fifty million years ago, wiped out an estimated 95 percent of all marine life and 70 percent of all terrestrial life. That is a lot of life gone in a fairly short period of time. Scientists in Luoping in southwest China have recently unearthed more than twenty thousand marine fossils from a fifty-foot layer of limestone—the first fully functional ecosystem that was trapped in sediment at the time of the Permian extinction. They estimate that it took over ten million years for life to recover after such a devastating mass extinction. And to think that there were seven other known major extinctions leads us to conclude that when we ask ourselves "What am I?" we must, at least on some level, respond by saying: extremely lucky. We can see how this luck of our species came to be within the causal complexities of the Onion Skin Theory of Knowledge that has influenced 99 percent of all species to diverge, prosper, die, and become extinct—taking with them all surviving members. This is simply the natural process of all organisms—plant or animal. In all likelihood, this will happen to us as well. When and how this will happen are the really relevant and interesting questions to us. Battling our own extinction is going to take some consideration, careful planning, cooperation, and thoughtfulness.

A final point a naturalist might discuss in responding to the question "What am I?" requires us to go back toward the beginning of the universe when stars were forming and exploding, galaxies were coming together, and solar systems were coming into being. If we evolved from nonliving matter from this planet,[13] and the planet is made up of swirling debris left over from exploding stars, it would follow, then, that every atom inside your body was once inside a star. If you think about yourself as a conglomerate of systems, and you consider what makes those systems, you will realize that the physical "stuff" or "bits" that make you what you are had to have come from somewhere at some time. According to a naturalist account, all the stuff that composes your body has existed for a very long time. After you are dead and gone, the stuff that makes you what you now are will change its form, but its substance will not go out of existence.

If you are buried, your body will rot and change form. If you are cremated, your body will become a form of carbon ash. The patterns of information that compose your identity will alter in distinct ways, but the underlying substance will not cease to exist. The bits that make you what you are were forged billions of years ago in the Big Bang and in subsequent astronomical activities like solar formations, super novae, and so on. In this sense, Joni Mitchell is quite correct in saying that we are all made up of stardust. This is a profoundly important understanding of who and what we are. For like the fact that we are all descendants from Africa, it also provides greater insight into our egalitarian origins on a cosmological scale. These are only a few of the more striking features we can see in ourselves when we take a naturalistic look at what we are.

THE SUPERNATURAL RESPONSE

As discussed in the last chapter, supernatural responses to the Big Five will vary dramatically depending on which particular supernatural response you choose. Unlike natural responses to the Big Five, supernatural responses vary in extremely diverse ways because there is no Reality Measuring Stick by which to determine their level of truthfulness. This means that we have no real tangible way of measuring their claims at the Big T level of Truth. So it would be best to consider some overlapping themes of personal identity that are found in some of the world's more popular supernatural belief systems, such as the Abrahamic systems (e.g., Judaism, Islam, and Christianity) along with Hinduism, Buddhism, Sikhism, and various folk beliefs.

What we generally find in many of the world religions is the supernatural belief that humans are made up of at least two parts: a body, which is physical, and a spirit (or mind or soul), which is immaterial. So there is the physical part of a person, and then there is a spiritual part. This is called *dualism* (see fig. 10.4).

With supernatural accounts defining us in this way, far more importance seems to be placed on the spiritual aspect of a person than on the physical aspect. The physical body is considered merely a vessel in which the soul or spirit somehow resides. After one dies, the soul continues to live on and can inhabit other worlds, for example, nirvana, heaven, hell, purgatory, Hades, and so on, or it can simply be regenerated and recycled back onto Earth in another physical body in a karmic cycle. Certainly not all but many supernaturalists believe that the way in which one behaves while in this physical body will have a direct effect on what happens to one's spirit or soul after one

Fig. 10.4. Dualism.
Image created by Vanessa Tignanelli.

dies. For example, many Christians believe that if you abide by the words of the Bible and live a life that emulates various Christian principles found in the Bible, your soul will be rewarded at the time of your death and you will spend an eternity in heaven alongside past dead relatives, historical figures, saints, angels, Jesus Christ, the Virgin Mary, the Holy Spirit, and, of course, God (depending of course, on your particular take on the notion of the Trinity). If you choose not to live according to Christian principles, your fate is somewhat nastier. You get to live eternally in hell, which has been described and defined as a very cold place, a very hot place, the place furthest from light and God, a torturous place filled with horrific entities, and so on. Muslims believe that if you live a life that abides by various Islamic principles found in the Koran and submit to the will of Allah, your soul will be rewarded at the time of your death, and you get to reside in heaven. Otherwise, you end up in a similar type of hell-like place as the Christians describe. Hinduism and Sikhism are somewhat similar to each other, with both promising a continuous cycle of reincarnation until you get it right and then are rewarded by either gaining enlightenment or merging with God. Judaism varies from the nonexistence of an afterlife to some type of nebulous shadowy world to a world to come or heavenlike plane of existence. And there are hundreds of other supernatural accounts of what our souls are like and what becomes of them. We will consider these in more detail in the final chapter.

The common theme emerging from such supernatural accounts is that there is a strong belief in some type of eternal substance that underlies our physical bodies. Right away we should be able to spot a bit of a problem with such claims. First, when we ask for evidence in support of such claims, how can a supernaturalist possibly demonstrate this? Empirically or scientifically, there have been a grand total of zero accounts of observing anything remotely close to a "soul." "Ah," says the supernaturalist, "but you can't see a soul." Such a tactic incorporates the insulation technique of protecting the claim from the very possibility of testing it empirically. It's Russell's teapot all over again. And of course, in like fashion, such a claim would obviously violate the Sagan principle by making quite an extraordinary claim and then not providing the extraordinary evidence required for anyone to evaluate it in a relatively unbiased manner. For those who claim that things like souls exist but can be neither confirmed nor denied by empirical methods—which, by the way, would immediately win the Randi challenge money of one million dollars—we can now ask, "Then how do you know it's there?" The appeals will usually refer to a particular text like the Bible, the Koran, the Torah, and so forth, which then starts us back to the problem of trying to confirm or falsify various pieces of scripture. We do not have a Reality Measuring Stick, so there is no conceivable way to prove such things as souls actually exist. The existence of things like souls, then, becomes purely a matter of faith and resides in the same realm as gnomes, elves, or fairies. The eighteenth-century Scottish philosopher David Hume had something to say about souls:

> The Soul therefore if immortal, existed before our birth; and if the former existence no ways concerned us, neither will the latter. Animals undoubtedly feel, think, love, hate, will, and even reason, tho' in a more

imperfect manner than men; are their souls also immaterial and immortal?... The souls of animals are allowed to be mortal; and these bear so near a resemblance to the souls of men, that the analogy from one to the other forms a very strong argument.[14]

By way of analogy, Hume considers the death of animals to our own, and since he can find no compelling evidence (nor could anyone else during his time) to believe that such species possess things like souls, he infers that this might give us good reason to think that no such things exist in humans as well. He also questions the manner in which one who believes in such things as souls could possibly prove their existence:

By what arguments or analogies can we prove any state of existence, which no one ever saw, and which no way resembles any that ever was seen? Who will repose such trust in any pretended philosophy as to admit upon its testimony the reality of so marvelous a scene? Some new species of logic is requisite for that purpose, and some new faculties of the mind, that may enable us to comprehend that logic. NOTHING could set in a fuller light the infinite obligations which mankind have to divine revelation, since we find that no other medium could ascertain this great and important truth.[15]

In an eighteenth-century manner, Hume is stating that those who make extraordinary claims require not only extraordinary evidence but also a "new species of logic" or "new faculties of the mind" specifically for this purpose. In other words, they would need a Reality Measuring Stick.

But there are still many more questions to consider in pondering the nature of a soul. If a soul is physical, then it would have to comply to physical laws. If it is not, how does it interact within a physical body in a physical world? Philosopher Daniel C. Dennett uses an analogy to demonstrate this problem.[16] If you remember Casper the Friendly Ghost,[17] in some scenes he could easily fly through walls, but in others he would be able to lift chairs, throw balls, and interact with the physical world at will. How does he turn on his ability to both slip between the physical and still interact within the physical world? This seems to be a violation of the law of noncontradiction, as though Casper gets to eat his cake and have it too. In this way, the concept of a human soul seems to raise more questions than it answers. Perhaps he's a "quantum ghost"?

Then of course there is the problem of how the soul originally comes into being. Were souls created at the beginning of the universe? Have they always existed? Will they always exist? What happens to the souls of miscarried fetuses? Do they become supernaturally recycled? Is God a green soul recycler? Does the soul change at any time? For example, when children die at a very young age, do their souls mature after death? Or are they always young? The same goes for the severely mentally challenged. Do their souls gain knowledge and insight after death? Or would there be mentally challenged souls? Where exactly do these souls reside, and what do they do for eternity? Do they simply sit on clouds and play harps? Do they haunt the physical world in shadowy dimensions? Do they have afterlife parties? According to some faiths (e.g., Islam), why does sex play so prominently in the afterlife? How can there be physical pleasure in an immaterial world? That's a tough one (though by worldly measure, a not altogether undesirous one).

We must think about how the soul, an immaterial substanceless form of ectoplasmic fog—somehow enters into and rides along with the physical body until it dies. When, precisely, does this happen? For most Christians and Muslims (who make up about half the world's population), this occurs at the point of conception. This is when they claim life begins. It would be internally inconsistent of them to say that humans can live or be alive without a soul. If the soul enters the body at conception, *how* does this actually happen? It must be a process. It cannot be otherwise. Sperm meets egg and *wham!* you not only have meiosis but the incorporation of an immaterial substance with that biological process happening simultaneously. This is an extraordinary claim indeed. Yet this process is also not empirically testable. If, by its nature, such a claim is not testable, then the insulation tactic is again used along with an obvious violation of the Sagan principle. So we are back to the lack of a Reality Measuring Stick problem yet again. But nobody said finding absolute Truth was going to be easy. Billions of people on this planet believe with absolute certainty that they are in possession of the correct answers to the Big Five. So many millions of people have abandoned the Skeptical and Socratic ideas that so clearly demonstrate our lack of knowledge and suggest a genuine acceptance of humility in realizing our shortcomings to knowledge at this Big T level. How different this world might be if all we ever worried about were matters at the small t level of truth. Imagine. Would there be less bloodshed in places like the Middle East? Would we be more inclined to envision all humanity related to one another in a not-so-distant past? With such an understanding of our shared ancestry, would we treat one another differently? These are interesting thoughts to ponder as we move on to consider the ways in which we might answer the question of how we should behave.

CHAPTER 11
HOW SHOULD I BEHAVE?

There is nothing more frightful than ignorance
in action.

—GOETHE

You've got to have something to eat and a little
love in your life before you can hold still for any
damn body's sermon on how to behave.

—BILLIE HOLIDAY

On December 26, 2004, an earthquake measuring 9.0 on the Richter scale occurred on the bottom of the Indian Ocean. It created a tsunami that devastated much of the coastline of Southeast Asia. The United Nations estimated that more than two hundred thirty thousand people lost their lives that day. It was a devastating natural disaster. But it occurred without any intent to take human or animal lives. Tidal waves don't have brains, wishes, intentions, desires, drives, wills, or volitions. However, we *Homo sapiens* do. But if humans, like all other animate or inanimate things in the universe (like tidal waves), function as a product of a complex series of causal events (as we saw in the Onion Skin Theory of Knowledge model, OSTOK), then wherein lies their virtue or their vice? As we saw in chapter 10, if we cannot locate anything like a soul within each of us that is somehow responsible for not only our essential identity but also our free will, then how much control does any one of us have over our actions? It's reminiscent of the old joke: "We have to believe in free will; we've got no other choice!" But if a naturalist does not believe in dualism (i.e., the idea that there is a separate ectoplasmic part of us that controls our behavior), then are people "good" simply because they have been lucky enough to be able to control their volitions, desires, and intentions in ways that are approved by a given society? And are others "bad" simply because they have not been so lucky? How much control did Tiger Woods have over his actions? How much control does an alcoholic have? Or a serial killer? Or you?

When we ask ourselves the question of how we should behave, we are faced with the consideration of a branch of philosophy called *ethics*. For millennia, much has been said about ethics and moral behavior. I make no promises to state what I think are definitive guidelines for one to use in making ethical decisions. Instead, I shall keep my focus squarely on the different ways that naturalists and supernaturalists answer this very interesting and extremely difficult question. But before we look at these two sides, we should take a bit of time to clarify matters first.

WHAT IS ETHICS?

As a working definition, we can say that the field of ethics involves the study of how and why we *value* human behavior or actions. Values are those estimations of worth that we place on specific actions (and inactions). Value is often measured in terms of how we judge particular actions to be good or bad, right or wrong, fair or unfair. In many cases, ethics acts as a system of rules designed to reflect the values of a particular social group. In other words, it is a list of do's and don'ts that acts as a guide to social behavior. Often associated with such rules are rewards and punishments. Acts that are highly valued tend to be rewarded, while less valued actions committed by individuals or groups are punished.

A note of clarification regarding the difference between *morality* and *ethics*: Although these terms are often used interchangeably, morality generally involves the ways in which humans value actions within particular cultural settings, whereas the field of ethics studies the nature of value as it may apply throughout all cultures. As well, we need to realize that ethics distinguishes itself from other fields of study by *prescribing* what actions ought to be done (i.e., those actions believed to be the best or most valued course of human action under specific circumstances). In this way, philosophers have separated the field of ethics from the sciences by maintaining that the function of science is to *describe* what is found in nature. The popular belief since the time of David Hume is that there is nothing in describing the facts of nature that could tell us anything about prescribing actions for human behavior. Of course, this idea has been contested recently,[1] and we shall find that the sciences do have a lot to say about the limits of our ethical actions and behavior. Finally, we must always keep in mind the context or setting in which the circumstances surrounding any particular action or set of actions take place. It would be unfair to judge someone's behavior too rashly or quickly without fully appreciating the context in which those actions occurred.

THE NATURAL RESPONSE

In recent history—say, the last five thousand years or so, ethics and morality stemmed largely from mythological and religious beliefs. That is, deities were defined, and rules and regulations for social behavior were dictated according to a set of supernatural statutes and beliefs. Many believe the invention and development of religions was perfectly consistent with human evolution. As the human brain evolved and grew larger, and language capacity increased and consciousness became more fully developed, it is not surprising to see our ancestors explain natural phenomena and answer the Big Five in terms of supernatural explanations. In many ways, mythologies and ancient religions provided very crude systems of science and ethics—that is, they had explanatory power and provided social cohesion, but they were (and still are) extremely limited. Our ancestors simply did not possess the conceptual or methodological capacity to understand the world in purely mechanistic and natural ways.

Socialization

One of the central conditions for bringing about ethics and morality in human evolution was socialization: the banding together of individuals for the purposes of group survival. Pooling resources and survival strategies simply had higher survival value than going it alone. We can see this pattern repeatedly in other species, for example, herd animals, schools of fish, and flocks of birds. The idea here is that there is strength in both numbers and camouflage. The more there are of you, the less likely it will be that you will be a predator's next meal—unless, of course, you become isolated through injury, old age, mutation, and the like. A species carrying a gene that expresses a trait that does not allow it the capacity to recognize predators will be quickly selected out, thus disallowing that particular individual to pass on its genetic material to its offspring. Those species with survival-promoting DNA successfully make such distinctions; they stay with the pack and stand a better chance of reproducing. But it is not as though zebras simply were determined to grow stripes and consciously decided that hanging around in herds was a good idea. Evolution has no such direction. It just so happened that the mutants with stripes that hung out in herds tended to survive better than those that did not. So there were more or them around to pass on their genetic material. The camouflage/strength-in-numbers eventuality was not a conscious strategy. It just happened. In this way, evolution is blind.

Human Evolution and Ethics

Humans, however, are quite a unique bunch. We did not develop fantastic camouflage, sharper teeth, faster legs, poisonous fangs, or any of the other defense mechanisms we see in other species. Instead, we developed large, bulbous brains. Staying together in groups, however, does not require big, bulbous brains. Birds, bees, and educated fleas do it, and they have tiny brains. We just happened to be social animals that developed bigger brains. But the fact that our brains got bigger fairly quickly has led to all sorts of interesting developments in how we treat one another. When talking about human evolution and ethics, we must never forget some very important constraints:

1. First, the two main motivating drives in all humans are, in no particular order, survival and sex. The rest is merely culture.
2. Second, in order to survive and reproduce, one must follow a subset of rules: Eat and don't get eaten.

Some evolutionists refer to these rules as the "Four Fs": fight, flight, food, and . . . procreation. We can really sum them up in three rules:

Eat.
Don't get eaten.
Make babies.

Successful survival strategies under such constraints led to the efficacy of human socialization. By way of analogy, ethologists, primatologists, and cognitive scientists look at animal behavior to better understand human behavior. Much of the work of people like Jane Goodall, Frans de Waal, Andrew Whiten, Robert Sapolsky, Christophe Boesch, and Richard Wrangham have shown the complex social systems that develop in various types of primates, our closest relatives. Within the last decade, an international team of chimpanzee experts established the most comprehensive survey of social behavior ever conducted. The researchers found no less than thirty-nine chimpanzee patterns of behavior that could be labeled as cultural variations involving tool use, grooming techniques, courtship rituals, and more.[2] In such societies, there are often but not always[3] alpha males—those males that dominate the pack. We see this in other species as well (e.g., wolves, lions). There are right and wrong ways to behave in such groups, and there is a clearly defined pecking order. For instance, in groups of larger chimpanzee species (*Pan troglodytes*), the alpha male has his harem. He alone gets to pass on his genetic material when the females are in estrus. Ah, but our chimp cousins resemble us in embarrassingly similar ways. Those male chimps down a few rungs on the ladder of dominance have developed mating techniques requiring neither physical strength nor size. Some have developed the capacity for deception and intelligence—in other words, sneakiness. In several cases, film crews have actually caught on film a secret tryst between a younger male and a female from an alpha male's harem. In what can only be described as a premeditated rendezvous, the two chimps meet, look around, and quickly engage in intercourse, before returning to the group as though nothing had happened (see fig. 11.1).

In colloquial terms, some evolutionary psychologists have branded such procreators with a rather unflattering title: "sneaky fuckers."[4] This colloquial but accurate term demonstrates how intelligence, creativity, and sneakiness sometimes trumps size and strength. Should the female conceive from her sneaky fucking partner, this may proliferate more sneaky fucking genes into the chimpanzee gene pool to make little sneaky fucking chimp offspring. Film crews have also captured a chimp *in flagrante delicto*: the alpha male's spies witnessed the act of infidelity and

Fig. 11.1. Chimp Rendezvous. Image created by Vanessa Tignanelli.

reported back to him. Let's just say it was not a good day for the daring young romancer. He was beaten quite severely. Here, where we see some acts being rewarded while others are punished, is evidence of social customs or rules in species other than our own.

What we see emerging in specific mammalian activities is a type of social contract. Members of a group develop rules that, when adhered to, promote survival. When a member violates a social contract or even a part of one, there are ramifications. Order is maintained when all members are cognizant of the most important macro rules for the group's survival.

Context

Environmental conditions can put terrific strains on group survival strategies and so may alter and upset currently accepted procedures. We must never ignore the very important aspect of context when it comes to considering ethics and morality. We live in a generally civilized country. We respect, for the most part, the beliefs and actions of others living in a pluralistic society. However, if the thin blue line were breached, and our legal and punitive institutions crumbled, and anarchy ensued, we might not be acting in the same civilized manner toward each other. If we were still alive, we would be concerned most with survival strategies of our own. Just insert the setting of any particular zombie movie here. Without laws, order, and appeals to those who have the power to enact punishment on wrongdoers, we face anarchy: the law of the jungle would surely prevail. But we would probably still try to make alliances with others to protect ourselves from those who might wish us harm, and this is because we know there is strength in numbers. Within our groups we might still appoint some as capable of ruling and others capable of enacting some form of control. But the bond between all of us is only as strong as our agreements. Should we decide to disagree with the macro beliefs of the group, we could always go it alone; or branch off and form our own group; or try to convince the current group that our way is better. But notice what is underlying all this hypothetical thought experimentation? It is human behavior understood within the context of cooperation, agreement, and enforcement. If you and your fifty people and me and my fifty people get together and decide not to fight each other, then we could pool our resources and protect ourselves from other marauding clans of one hundred or more. If not, and fighting should result, then regardless of who wins, there will still be the same system of cooperation within the smaller group—unless, of course, the group divides into still smaller clusters.

Science and Ethics Today

Today, scientific inquiry has led to a remarkable understanding of human development and behavior. Various fields in the physical and social sciences ranging from neurology and biology to the cognitive sciences, psychology, zoology, genetics, chemistry, and the ecological sciences have provided considerable insight into the varied ways in which we develop an understanding of the value of human actions. For example, knowing that our sun is a large accumulation of hydrogen under which gravitational pressures fuse these molecules into helium and then into more and more dense matter thus releasing extraordinary amounts of energy (in accordance with Einstein's $E = mc^2$), which in turn fuels the millions of forms of life on our planet, releases us from the burden of having to make human or other animal sacrifices to the Aztec god Huitzilopōchtli or the Egyptian god Ra, or any other sun god. The same can be said for understanding so-called miracles. Images of the Virgin Mary in grilled-cheese sandwiches or chocolate Jesus figures, or the Arabic word for Allah in clouds or anywhere else—all are simply cases of coincidence known as pareidolia (that is, if we look carefully and long enough, we will see patterns of identity emerging from almost anywhere).

Some of the truly great achievements that a natural account has given us in understanding values, morals, and ethics come from our knowledge of the constraints under which humans behave. The Onion Skin Theory of Knowledge illustrates how complex the physical and cultural worlds are in terms of cause-and-effect relationships. This also raises another very important question: How much free will do we actually have in apparently choosing between actions considered right or wrong? Many supernatural accounts maintain that we are free to choose between good and evil, and eternal rewards or punishments come with those choices. But scientific discoveries of the natural world have revealed a complex array of cause-and-effect chains that, at least at the level of human interaction, admits to very little choice.

Ethics and Free Will

Ask yourself how much free will you have. For example, did you freely decide to read this book? Did you freely decide to wear the types of clothes you do? Or eat chunky soup with a fork or a spoon? According to the OSTOK, we know a vast number of complex cause-and-effect relationships interact on physical and cultural levels. As such, we know that we attempt to manipulate these systems to the best of our abilities in an effort to attain the types of things we value. In so doing, have you given much thought to the level or extent to which you freely make these decisions? How much control do we really have over our lives and the choices we make? Basically, there are three schools of thought on this subject: There are those who believe that we have total freedom (the libertarians); there are those who believe we have absolutely no freedom (the hard determinists); and then there are those who believe that we have limited freedom (the soft determinists). When it comes to choosing between two or more alternative actions, how do we know when we have done so of our own "free will"?

I have devised a model as an analogy to try to make the question of free will and choice easier to understand. It's based on an old logic problem called the sorites paradox (or heap paradox) and it goes something like this: In making a heap of rice, if I were to begin with one grain, we would admit that, by itself, this does not make a heap. And if I put another grain next to it, this would also not make a heap. So the the paradox goes, by adding additional grains of rice, no matter how many I add (for example, ten million grains of rice), because I am only increasing the number of grains in the pile one at a time, I will never make a heap. Now, clearly, we can see that this type of thinking is going to fail at some point in the process of adding grains of rice because we know that one grain of rice does not make a heap but ten million grains of rice certainly would (see fig. 11.2). To make this so-called paradox useful, we can use the gradual accumulation of grains of rice to represent the amount of control or lack of control we might have over our wills, volitions, desires, actions, and so on. In this way, we can figuratively understand total lack of control over ourselves as one grain of rice and total control over ourselves as a heap. In this way, we can better understand incremental gradations of change between a state of Not-X (no control) to Becoming-X (or some control) to X (or total control).

Not-X . . . . Becoming-X X
(No Control)   (Some Control)   (Total Control)

This can be applied to other states of being as well, like height (when is someone tall or short?), to baldness (how many hairs does a man have to lose or retain to be considered bald?), to age, to weight, and so on. For our purposes, we are discussing control over our choices and decisions. When, exactly, are we in control of them and when are we not?

Fig. 11.2. Rice and Tweezers. Photograph by Matthew DiCarlo.

It would seem that the most interesting aspect that concerns us in ethics is the fuzzy area in between the extremes of noncontrol and total control. I refer to this area as *the umbra of becoming*. This is the shadowy world in which, to use our rice example, we are well on our way to making a heap. So exactly who or what is in control or lacking in control when it comes to making ethical decisions? For supernaturalists, there is the position of dualism (i.e., an immaterial substance residing within the physical substance that is largely responsible for making such decisions). For naturalists, there is no such substance but only the physical matter.[5] Most laws of the land assume that we can either choose to abide by them or, in choosing not to, must pay a penalty or price. When you run a red light and an officer of the law gives you a ticket, he or she is assuming that you chose to drive through the red light. You were not forced, but it was a decision over which you had full control. The same is true for moral actions. When you tell a lie and are caught, it is assumed that you could have done otherwise. For the supernaturalist, it was the soul or spirit—the ghost in the machine—that was responsible for such behavior. However, for a naturalist, the fault lies not in a soul but in the manner in which our natural systems are functioning. What if those natural systems are not functioning properly? Wherein lies the blame, the guilt, or the innocence? At what point along the sorites chain within the umbra of becoming do we make such a determination? In other words, how many grains of rice of causality within our natural and cultural systems does it take for us to hold someone accountable for his or her actions? For example, on July 30, 2008, Vince Li was acting under the constraints of a serious mental health ailment, schizophrenia, when he stabbed and decapitated Tim McLean on a Greyhound bus in Manitoba.[6] The psychiatrist for the case, Stanley Yaren, told the court that Li did not understand his actions were wrong and that Li believed God had instructed him to carry out the murder. Based on this defense, Li was not sentenced to serve his time in prison for first-degree murder but was instead sent to a mental health facility. On August 11, 2000, Dr. Suzanne Killinger-Johnson, a successful psychiatrist, walked into a Toronto subway station and, with her six-month-old son, Cuyler, jumped into the path of an oncoming train.[7] They were both killed. She had been diagnosed with severe postpartum depression. To what extent would we say that Li and Killinger-Johnson were acting within their control and could have chosen otherwise? Were they acting immorally or unethically as defined by myths, religions, or philosophies? Or were their actions beyond their natural abilities to choose, or to will, or to gain control over? How many grains of rice shy were they from possessing the control necessary to refrain from such actions?

Within the vast causal complexities and randomness of the Byzantine networks within the Onion Skin Theory of Knowledge, wherein lies moral blame or praise? In terms of the Relations of Natural and Cultural Systems, are we nothing more than a conglomerate of complex matter influenced by the indefinite numbers of constraints acting in accordance to random chance? This seems rather bleak to some. Yet it may be the case. And if it were? What then? Is there anything we can do about it? Can we somehow magically transcend beyond the physical constraints under which we all must act and defy the very physical laws that influence our behavior? The evolved capacity for consciousness in *Homo sapiens* allows us to examine the behavior of ourselves and others as no other species can. As such, our lives are a constant struggle between considering what our societies value and recognizing that we all act under the vast constraints of the networks within the OSTOK. So what would happen if science eventually reveals that we have very little (if any) control over our actions? How would our systems of governance change? Politics, law, education, and the like, would all need to account for randomized behavior under current known constraints. Concepts of "good" and "evil" will become purely matters of chance and luck. To admire the creativity of an accomplished violinist would be to appreciate his or her luck (i.e., the right genes, temperament, environment, etc.). To attribute blame to a criminal would involve the realization of a series of unfortunate natural and cultural incidents. The possibility that we may be heading in this direction is, I believe, the single greatest fear of the social sciences, religion, politics, and law. For if choice and free will are no longer factors that influence human behavior and action, wherein lie our accounts of value for good and evil?

A natural understanding of how we should behave must develop an ambitious model that synthesizes the knowledge of the sciences with the analytic rigor of philosophy. We must look honestly at the constraints under which we all act and develop a means by which to understand the umbra of becoming in an effort to determine the extent of our control and accountability. An example that demonstrates the need for this concern involves the laws of some US states to execute criminals who are mentally challenged or possess what has been described as an "intellectual disability."[8] According to the OSTOK, if a person is without the capacity to know that what he or she is doing or has done is wrong or unlawful, to what degree can we hold the person accountable for those actions? This is not to say that we do not need to address the issue of crime in such cases, but it does mean we have to redefine and restructure our judicial systems in an effort to acknowledge that the old system incorporating a dualist understanding of human behavior must be revised. This is not a license to behave relativistically in whatever manner we choose. We cannot simply act in any manner we so desire and then claim to be faultless simply because of the complexities of the OSTOK. It is simply a more honest model of understanding value in light of a much broader account of influencing constraints. And so now the really hard work begins. (Hurray! Jobs for philosophers!) We need to try to understand the level at which these individuals were or were not in control of their capacities with regard to the treatment of themselves and others. To a significant degree, we have become cognizant of what makes us tick. The human machine has a good understanding of the complexities of its evolved properties. In understanding ourselves in this way, we can gain a better understanding of the contexts and constraints in which we are more and less likely to be in control of our actions.

A Naturalized Understanding of Ethics

The better science can understand the constraints under which people develop and behave, the better we will be able to act with compassion and care toward them and toward those whose lives they affect. To be in a responsible position by which to judge the value of human actions, a naturalist might argue that we should begin with a comprehensive understanding of the many constraints involved in the context of a given situation. In other words, before we can begin to label goodness/badness or rightness/wrongness of actions, we need to understand the heavily layered contextual, physical, and social constraints under which people behave. We must be attentive to the various causal forces at work in any given ethical situation. This returns us to an understanding of our limits to knowledge and information. And so we can develop something like the Onion Skin Theory of Knowledge to better conceptualize just how complex the universe is and how many factors are involved when we attempt to make value judgments about the actions of ourselves and others. We must realize that we can no longer praise or condemn others for their actions because we assume that they have freely chosen to do so. We may not be as free as we think we are. But knowing more about the constraints that influence our behavior and actions will provide us with a more responsible outlook of accountability. For example, if I greatly dislike the taste of all alcoholic beverages and do not consume them at all, should I be considered as virtuous as an alcoholic who abstains? Is this not simply a matter of coincidence and chance? I might choose to drink alcoholic beverages if they tasted differently. But since they all offend my sense of taste to such a degree, is it me or my taste buds that deserve moral praise? A naturalized ethics must take into account many factors when judging the value of human actions. Perhaps the greatest fear that stands in the way of a naturalized ethics is the fear of losing personal control. The fear of losing choice, volition, and freedom implies for some the fear of losing responsibility, accountability, and trust.

> People like to exercise control over their environment, which is why many of the same people who drive a car after consuming half a bottle of scotch will freak out if the airplane they are on experiences minor turbulence. Our desire to control events is not without purpose, for a sense of personal control is integral to our self-concept and self-esteem. In fact, one of the most beneficial things we can do for ourselves is to look for ways to exercise control over our lives—or at least to look for ways that help us feel that we do.[9]

However strong the fear of losing control may be, there should be due diligence in our attempt to judge the actions of others with fairness, compassion, and care. For without such diligence, we may be guilty of a greater injustice against humankind: giving praise or blame where it is not due.

> Obviously it can be a mistake to assign brilliance in proportion to wealth. We cannot see a person's potential, only his or her results, so we often misjudge people by thinking that the results must reflect the person. The normal accident theory of life shows not that the connection between actions and rewards is random but that random influences are as important as our qualities and actions. . . . We are inclined, that is, to see movie stars as more talented than aspiring movie stars and to think that the richest people in the world must also be the smartest. . . . Alas, as all of those who dress for success know, we are all too easily fooled by the money someone earns.[10]

The same may be said when we observe the poor and the homeless. A supernaturalist might say, "There, but for the grace of God, go I." But a naturalist understands the causal complexities of the OSTOK and recognizes that much of what happens in our lives is due to physical and social constraints with a healthy dose of randomness that lie beyond our power of control. So we must be prudent in assigning values of good and bad, right and wrong, to the decisions and actions of others.

Commonalities in Ethics

Even in the face of acknowledging the causal complexities of networks represented by the OSTOK, there seem to be some common rules among societies throughout the world. Many of the cultural rules around discouraging bad behavior stem from what many have called the Golden Rule, which generally states the ethical precept: "Do unto others what you would have them do unto you."[11] To put this into practical terms, it really means, "Think before you act by considering the fairness of your actions with respect to yourself." This ethical principle has been found in ancient philosophies and religions from the Code of Hammurabi in ancient

Babylon to the Torah, through ancient Egypt and Greece, and it is present in one formulation or another in most world faiths and religions of today. It puts forth perhaps the oldest ethical principle of fairness ever recorded. We have spoken a good deal about fairness in this book, and we have noticed that many people can only accept so much of it. This is unfortunate because fairness as a guiding principle for behavior will actually benefit the greatest number of people involved in an ethical dilemma. By being unfair, you can essentially harm another person for your own personal benefit. In philosophy, this is known as the no harm principle. We know there will always be harm in the world. But what we generally want to avoid is unnecessary harm. By harming so many people in so many different ways, we could make a good case that ruthless dictators throughout history violated both the Golden Rule and no harm principle.

One of the tools that has emerged from understanding ethics naturalistically is the Tolerance-Harm Inverse Proportion law (or T-HIP law). This is the idea that we should be allowed to believe and act in ways desired, provided that we are not needlessly harming our own or any other species (see fig. 11.3).

The way the tolerance-harm inverse proportion law works is simple: the beliefs and actions of any person or group will be tolerated provided they are not generating unwanted or unnecessary harm to others. However, once the actions of a person or group generate harm, then others have the right to lower their tolerance and act against it. There will be an intersecting point at which the level of harm perceived by one person or group meets the level of tolerance by another person or group. Of course, the really difficult part of all this is in deciding what "harm" is and when it breaches one's tolerance levels. This leads us to consider how we would be able to determine where these intersecting points are. On its most basic level, when considering how we should behave, a fundamental principle might be that the more we generate unnecessary harm according to our beliefs, the greater we can expect intolerance by others who may actively attempt to stop our behavior. We are going to have disagreements regarding what qualifies as harm and when tolerance levels have been breached. And it is going to be very difficult to measure harm and tolerance and

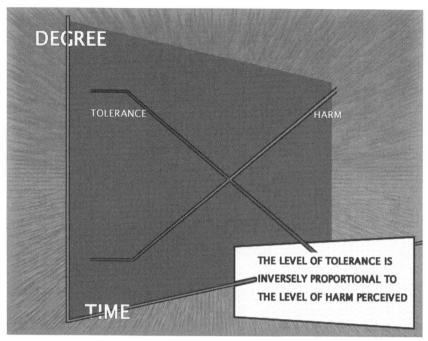

Fig. 11.3. The Tolerance-Harm Inverse Proportion (T-HIP) Law.
Image created by Robert Loucks.

attempt to standardize ethical behavior in this way. Nonetheless, it appears in principle that we might be able to appreciate this inverse proportional relationship between tolerance and harm so that we can better see and understand what our beliefs and actions may be doing to others, and what others' actions are doing to us.

The important point to note here is that the T-HIP law demonstrates the relationship we all have to the views and actions of others. We could probably attain agreement that in principle, this relationship does demonstrate when we are more warranted in accepting beliefs and actions and when we feel obligated to act against them. In terms of tolerance and harm, people can believe anything they like. But they should not be able to cause unnecessary or unwanted suffering to humans or other species based on their either natural or supernatural views. Let's consider an example. Would every adult sentient person alive today be able to agree with the following proposition?

Unwanted torture and harm of another person or species for no reason but to cause unprovoked suffering for the sake of deriving personal pleasure is wrong.

Is this proposition something upon which we could universally agree? Would we really see nothing inherently wrong with the idea of actively seeking out unwanted personal suffering for the purposes of our own amusement? There were plenty of societies throughout history that engaged in this type of activity. But this fallacious appeal to popularity and antiquity does not necessarily make either the above proposition or the action itself right. This seems to contain the notion of the Golden Rule, in other words, that we really should only act toward others in ways that we would want to be treated. But the Golden Rule by itself works only with a number of conditionals. The first conditional is that you cannot bring about unwanted suffering and justify it by saying you would wish or would not mind if the same were done to you (e.g., you cannot be a mass murderer and justify your behavior by saying that you would also want to be a victim of a mass murderer). This is where the Golden Rule breaks down; murderers, thieves, rapists, and general jerks could still justify their horrific actions. To account for this shortcoming, we need to introduce a second conditional that disallows unwanted and/or unnecessary harm—in other words, a no harm principle. Combining the Golden Rule with the T-HIP law provides a working ethical framework that may not be perfect but will make it quite difficult for anyone to unjustifiably harm others.

The more we embrace and develop a synthetic model like the OSTOK for understanding causality, actions, volitions, and will, the better enabled we shall become in assigning responsible measures of value on human behavior. As a final natural response to the question "How should I behave?" I would like to mention a radio competition that took place on the Canadian Broadcasting Corporation (CBC) in 1972. The radio host, Peter Gzowski, held a contest for listeners to come up with a saying which was roughly the equivalent of the saying "As American as apple pie." The winner was a seveteen-year-old music student named

Heather Scott, who submitted the saying, "As Canadian as possible under the circumstances." It captures rather nicely the self-deprecating politeness with which Canadians are often characterized, eh? And it is also a nice analogy for the way in which naturalists would respond when asked how we should behave: *as ethically as possible under the circumstances*. The best we can do is to understand the very complex number of constraints and random circumstances that govern our lives and try as best we can to live according to those ethical principles upon which we can agree. These represent some of the more pertinent factors involved in a serious discussion of ethics in light of our understanding of complex natural and cultural elements (represented in the OSTOK). A naturalist gives serious consideration to what science can bring to the table in humanity's discussions of ethics and morality. In light of the Golden Rule and the T-HIP law, naturalists would anticipate a need to further develop the OSTOK model for use as a facilitator of discussion on numerous aspects of culture that relate to social policies regarding the management of both human and natural resources.

THE SUPERNATURAL RESPONSE

It would not be difficult to make a case that for every set of supernatural beliefs, there exists a set of rules, regulations, commandments, or dictates to follow in accordance to those beliefs. And as we shall see, it is not always necessary for there to actually be an existing deity to make some of the supernatural ethical principles good or warranted. Some ethical concepts seem to overlap in pragmatic ways in both the natural and supernatural responses.

In reference to Hinduism, many believe in the ideas of *dharma* and *karma*.[12] Dharma is a concept that refers to order, proper conduct, morality, religion, law, duty, righteousness, justice, and norm, and is believed to be the element that puts things in their proper place and maintains order. According to more traditional views of Hinduism, dharma is a code of conduct that varies according to the caste in which one finds oneself. The caste system, which was traditionally practiced in Hindu beliefs, includes Brahmin (priestly caste), Kshatriya (traditionally the warrior caste), Vaishya (traditionally the caste of merchants and farmers), and Shudra (manual laborers). The caste in which one finds oneself will determine the ways in which one is to act. So there is a contextual element to ethical behavior. In reference to a value like charity, for example, someone in a priestly caste might act differently than a manual laborer or a warrior, depending on the action and the context in which it's placed. Karma is the idea that the manner you behaved in past lives directly affects the way you are living now, which will in turn affect you in future lives. For every action, there is an immediate form of justice in determining reward or retribution. So your present state of being is the direct result of the manner in which your past selves acted toward others.[13] Perhaps the most important ethical precept that results from both dharma and karma is *ahimsa* or nonviolence. Taken from ancient Hindu texts such as the Mahabharata, the idea of ahimsa is said to generate positive karma. Underlying the concept of ahimsa is the idea that all living beings are karmically interconnected. So any action that would harm another being—no matter how large or small—will affect every other being. Whenever an animal is harmed or killed, this karmically affects not only the one who harms or kills it but also the animal that is harmed or killed and collectively all other beings as well. This has led to a schism or division within Hinduism between those who believe that it is only willful harming of another being that generates bad karma and those who believe *any* harming (willful or unintentional) that is done to another being will lead to bad karma. The followers of Jainism represent this latter form of ahimsa where extreme measures are taken to avoid the harm that could come to any living thing, including tiny insects, any plants, and even microscopic entities. What I find compelling in such supernatural views is the inherent no harm principle that we see in more secularized or natural views of ethics and morality. The ideas of the Golden Rule and the no harm principle seem to be repeated in various forms throughout many different natural and supernatural responses to the question of human conduct.

In the Abrahamic faiths, we see guidelines of behavior found in various texts, including the Torah, the Bible, and the Koran. According to Islamic scholars, the prophet Muhammad said, "I have been sent to perfect the morals." By far, the most important megarule of the Koran is to abide by Allah. Or else. Whatever Allah says goes. It's Allah's way or the highway . . . to hell, literally. But there are many references made to various activities ranging from the care of children, to charity, to divorce, to oppression, to suicide, and so on. In regard to charity, we find at 2:271 the following passage: "If you give alms openly, it is well, and if you hide it and give it to the poor, it is better for you; and this will do away with some of your evil deeds; and Allah is aware of what you do." Notice how Allah is always watching. So don't think you're going to get away with anything. In this respect, he's a lot like Santa Claus. At 6:151 of the Koran, we find this passage in reference to murder: "Do not kill the soul which Allah has forbidden except for the requirements of justice; this He has enjoined you with that you may understand." So capital punishment is allowed in the name of justice. This begs the question somewhat on what is meant by justice or that it can be determined unequivocally. In relation to adoration of false idols, we see at 29:17: "You pray only to idols that are created by Allah, instead of praying to Allah, the creator, and you only invent a lie when you say that these creations can hear prayer. These creations whom you pray to instead of praying to Allah, the creator, own no provision for you. Seek your provision from Allah, the creator of everything and everyone, and pray to Allah and give thanks to Allah. To Allah you shall return in the Hereafter."[14] Much like we find in the Torah, Allah, like Yahweh, is a god who needs constant praise and obedience. In terms of war, peace, and oppression, at 60:8 we find that "Allah does not forbid you respecting those who have not made war against you on account of your religion and have not driven you forth from your homes, that you show them kindness and deal with them justly; surely Allah loves the doers of justice." This is an interesting passage insofar as it seems to express a fundamental respect for tolerance under the no harm principle, in other words, as long as people are not oppressing you or warring against you because of your religion, they should be respected. Taken as a maxim, it seems to incorporate the T-HIP law. It appears to say that all Muslims should be tolerant of those who have not harmed them. It then states, however, that such people who are not of the Muslim faith will be treated kindly and justly but only according to the justice that is approved by Allah. So again, actions must be approved by the head office first. In terms of taking your own life, we are told to do the following: "And spend in the way of Allah and cast not yourselves to perdition with your own hands, and do good [to others]; surely Allah loves the doers of good" (2:195). Again, you don't want to perform or refrain from performing actions for their own sake, but because Allah approves or disapproves of the action. This again raises the question-begging problem Socrates raised with Euthyphro: are the acts Allah approves of good in themselves or are they good because Allah's approval makes them so? It would seem the latter. And so we can rightly ask what is it about Allah that his approval or disapproval rating makes actions good or bad? In relation to war and peace, we see the following: "Permission [to fight] is given to those upon whom war is made because they are oppressed, and most surely Allah is well able to assist them" (22:39). This appears to be a statement of self-defense. So any Muslim would be justified in defending himself or herself against oppressors. This seems to be embedded in most civil and human rights claims. But the interesting question to determine here is when does "harm" according to the term "oppressed" become apparent? At what point in the umbra of becoming do Muslims decide that they are being oppressed and have every right to defend themselves? George W. Bush continues to argue that a preemptive strike on Iraq was justifiable based on the information he had regarding weapons of mass destruction. Clearly, Bush's application of the intersection of tolerance and harm (the T-HIP law) was different from those who decided not to back his decision to invade. Upon reflection, perhaps even those who believed they were justified in such a military action might consider things differently in hindsight.

It is not my intention to castigate or find overwhelming fault in any one particular set of supernatural beliefs. My purpose is to demonstrate inherent problems with specific supernatural responses to the Big Five. Specific interpretations by many people of the texts of these various religions focus on values that most would consider acceptable, good, or right. As we shall see, the problem of lacking a Reality Measuring Stick will just not go away. Since we are still without such a device, we can really measure the value of the supernatural responses to human conduct only on a small t or practical level of truth. In this regard, we will see many values that are shared by most, if not all, schools of thought.

In turning to Judaism, we find in the Torah a character, Moses, who descends from a mountain with two tablets, each containing five commandments that were dictated to him by God (see fig. 11.4). The first tablet refers to the reverence that should be given to God, while the second tablet is more concerned with things humans should not be doing. From Exodus 20:2–17 we get a list that may differ in slight degrees depending upon interpretation but generally goes something like this:

1. I am the Lord your God, who brought you out of the land of Egypt, out of the house of bondage. You shall have no other gods before Me.
2. You shall not make for yourself a carved image, or any likeness of anything that is in heaven above, or that is in the earth beneath, or that is in the water under the earth; you shall not bow down to them nor serve them. For I, the Lord your God, am a jealous God, visiting the iniquity of the fathers on the children to the third and fourth generations of those who hate Me, but showing mercy to thousands, to those who love Me and keep My Commandments.
3. You shall not take the name of the Lord your God in vain, for the Lord will not hold him guiltless who takes His name in vain.
4. Remember the Sabbath day, to keep it holy. Six days you shall labor and do all your work, but the seventh day is the Sabbath of the Lord your God. In it you shall do no work: you, nor your son, nor your daughter, nor your male servant, nor your female servant, nor your cattle, nor your stranger who is within your gates. For in six days the Lord made the heavens and the earth, the sea, and all that is in them, and rested the seventh day. Therefore the Lord blessed the Sabbath day and hallowed it.
5. Honor your father and your mother, that your days may be long upon the land which the Lord your God is giving you.
6. You shall not murder.
7. You shall not commit adultery.
8. You shall not steal.

9. You shall not bear false witness against your neighbor.
10. You shall not covet your neighbor's house; you shall not covet your neighbor's wife, nor his male servant, nor his female servant, nor his ox, nor his donkey, nor anything that is your neighbor's.

So the first four rules appear to be fairly narcissistic for an all-loving God. For such a powerful deity, He seems awfully needy, self-conscious, neurotic, and insecure. A bit of an omnipresent stalker, if you will. The fifth rule sounds decent enough. I'm not sure if we could all agree on total, unconditional honor for our parents. For example, if mom or dad were extremely harmful to their children, to what extent should the kids continue to "honor" them? It could probably stand some qualification, like, "All things considered, if your parents are relatively decent and have sacrificed a great deal for the continuation of your survival and success, it's not a bad idea to honor them." The last five rules are really just negative restrictions telling people what not to do. For the most part, they cover some of the really important stuff in life: avoid theft, murder, infidelity, and lying. But nowhere in these ten rules does it mention anything of helping the poor, caring for the sick and indigent, or preventing child abuse. You would think that an all-knowing God would know that these types of things

Fig. 11.4. Moses and the Ten Commandments. Image created by Vanessa Tignanelli.

are going to happen and that we should consider how it is we're going to deal with them.

In the New Testament, the figure of Jesus Christ compresses these ten commandments into two:

1. Love God with all one's heart and soul and mind (Matthew 27:37/Luke 10:27).
2. Love thy neighbor as thy self (Mark 12:31).

From the Sermon on the Mount (Matthew 5–7), Jesus Christ reportedly diverges from the Old Testament commandments, which bring about justice with "an eye for an eye and a tooth for a tooth"(Leviticus 24:19–21, Exodus 21:22–25, Deuteronomy 19:16–21). Here, Christ speaks more of a forgiving demeanor by suggesting that we love our enemies and, when assaulted, do not retaliate. A similar sentiment attributed to Mohandas Gandhi is the statement, "An eye for an eye makes the whole world blind." These are very interesting ethical doctrines because they introduce the notion of passive nonaggressive resolutions to power, domination, and violence and the concept of *forgiveness.* Even though we do not possess a Reality Measuring Stick to measure the extent to which such supernatural ideas are absolutely certain, we might agree that there is still practical, humane value to be found in some of the writings of supernatural doctrines. In other words, in relation to the general increase in benefit or reduction in harm specific actions may generate, it may not matter that we are unable to determine the certainty with which any supernatural doctrine of ethics professes. But that does not preclude the fact that some of the moral aspects of such doctrines may still work well within a natural or secular context. So there are overlapping moral principles found in both the natural and the supernatural responses to the question of how we should behave. The most obvious example of overlapping principles of value in supernatural and natural belief systems are the concepts of the Golden Rule and the no harm principle.[15] These have been stated in one form or another in the following world religions:

African Traditional Religions: One going to take a pointed stick to pinch a baby bird should first try it on himself to feel how it hurts (Yoruba Proverb: Nigeria).

Bahá'í Faith: Ascribe not to any soul that which thou wouldst not have ascribed to thee, and say not that which thou doest not (Bahá'u'lláh).

Christianity: All things whatsoever ye would that men should do to you, do ye so to them; for this is the law and the prophets (Matthew 7:12).

Confucianism: Zi Gong asked, saying, "Is there one word which may serve as a rule of practice for all one's life?" The Master said, "Is not *reciprocity* such a word?" (Confucius, Analects 15.24). Never impose on others what you would not choose for yourself (Confucius, Analects).

Buddhism: Hurt not others in ways that you yourself would find hurtful (Udana-Varga 5,1).

Hinduism: This is the sum of duty; do naught onto others what you would not have them do unto you (Mahabharata 5,1517).

Islam: Hurt no one so that no one may hurt you (Muhammad, the Farewell Sermon).

Jainism: A man should wander about treating all creatures as he himself would be treated (Sutrakritanga 1.11.33).

Judaism: What is hateful to you, do not do to your fellowman. This is the entire Law; all the rest is commentary (Talmud, Shabbat 3id). You shall not take vengeance or bear a grudge against your kinsfolk. Love your neighbor as yourself: I am the Lord (Leviticus 19:18).

Native Spirituality: We are as much alive as we keep the world alive (Chief Dan George).[16]

Sikhism: The truly enlightened ones are those who neither incite fear in others nor fear anyone themselves (Guru Granth Sahib, *Slok*, tr. Patwant Sing, p. 1427).

Taoism: Regard your neighbor's gain as your gain, and your neighbor's loss as your own loss (Tai Shang Kan Yin P'ien, 213–18).

Zoroastrianism: Do not do unto others whatever is injurious to yourself (Shayast-na-Shayast 13.29). That nature alone is good which refrains from doing to another whatsoever is not good for itself (Dadisten-I-dinik, 94,5).[17]

Regardless of the motivation for acting in accordance to ethical precepts like the Golden Rule or the no harm principle, the effects may still be the same. A Christian may abide by such a rule because in so doing he believes he will attain salvation and everlasting immortality in an afterworld called heaven. A Hindu may abide by such a rule because in so doing she believes she will be reborn into a better life the next time around. Whatever the motivation, there seems to be a basic fundamental soundness to the Golden Rule—especially in conjunction with the no harm principle.

But if we were to consider the main differences between the natural and supernatural responses to how humans should behave, we would see that the natural account does not require the need for a supposed deity in which to ground the value of these principles. The ethical precepts of the naturalist in this regard comply better to Occam's razor than do those of the supernaturalist. The naturalist has less criterial baggage and acts for the sake of the benefit or the reduction of harm such actions bring about, rather than for some type of eternal reward. We must remember that one of the central motivating factors involved with many supernatural beliefs regarding human behavior is the idea of reward and punishment. Acting in a morally valued manner may be done by a supernaturalist not simply because the act itself generates a desired end or eliminates harm in some way; it may be done predominantly because by acting in such a way, one will be rewarded in an afterlife rather than punished. This is evident in both Eastern supernatural beliefs like Hinduism, Sikhism, and Buddhism, which offer reincarnation cycles of reward and punishment, as well as the Abrahamic faiths, which focus more on singular lives with the concepts of heavenly or hellish afterlives. The supernaturalist may not act only because of the practical benefits of increasing benefit or reducing harm but also for the anticipated reward that comes from the approval of a supernatural agent or agents. In a recent article we find that these beliefs run quite deeply throughout communities of various supernaturalists:

> One potential means of implementing fairness norms is via culturally postulated supernatural agents, in particular "full-access strategic agents" such as omnipotent, omniscient, moralizing gods. Individuals who believe that behavioral norms are policed by an all-knowing supernatural agent with the power and inclination to inflict terrible retribution for norm violations will have a strong incentive to comply with those norms.[18]

So there is a considerable difference in terms of motivation and expectation within the various supernatural responses to how we should behave. The difficult task for us to consider involves the complexities of actions related to each supernatural response. For example, when Sikhs act according to the Golden Rule or no harm principle, do they do so because they think that all people in their position would want the types of eternal rewards that may come to them if they abide by their god's particular rules? This is going to differ drastically from a Christian or Muslim perspective. When Muslims abide by the Golden Rule or no harm principle, are they doing so because they believe that all people would want the types of eternal rewards that will befall them if they act according to the will of Allah? But what if I don't happen to be Muslim? Or Sikh? Or Christian? Or a member of any other supernaturalist group?

In considering the question "How should I behave?" there are many more instances of overlapping values between naturalists and supernaturalists. We have just considered two of the so-called megaprinciples in this chapter: the Golden Rule and the no harm principle. It is in response to this particular question that we have seen the most amount of agreement between the naturalists and supernaturalists. We note a considerable difference in the ways in which both sides are motivated to act in ethical situations. The concept of reward and punishment by supernatural agents plays quite prominently in world religions and becomes the subject of our next chapter and final question of the Big Five: "What is to come of me?" It is to this question that we now turn our attention.

CHAPTER 12
WHAT IS TO COME OF ME?

I don't believe in the afterlife, although I am
bringing a change of underwear.

—WOODY ALLEN

I am ready to meet my Maker. Whether my
Maker is ready for the ordeal of meeting me is
another matter.

—WINSTON CHURCHILL

I am about to take my last voyage. A great leap
in the dark.

—THOMAS HOBBES

The question of what is to come of us has two distinct references. On
the one hand, we can consider this question in light of what will
happen to us now, while we are currently alive. Will I get the job I've
always wanted? Will I be happy? Will I find someone to love? Will I lose
ten pounds? And so on. For many, these outcomes are dependent on planning properly, being industrious and resourceful, and seeking out realistic
opportunities for success. For supernaturalists, however, success in life is
directly related to the manner in which we have appeased the desires,
intentions, rules, or commandments of a particular deity or deities. Many
supernaturalists believe in the concept of divine intervention through the
work of a god, lesser gods, angels, saints, intervening deceased relatives,

and so on. Many sports teams still take part in a pregame prayer as though somehow a specific deity will see to it that either the conditions are right for that particular team on that particular day or that the deity will intervene during the game to direct the eventual outcome of the game. Of course, only one team will be victorious. This raises a few questions: Which deity was prayed to? If in fact it was the same one for both teams, there are going to be some pretty elaborate *ad hoc* reasons for why the particular deity intervened or refrained from intervening during the game to favor the one team over the other.

In getting back to the question at hand, the other, perhaps deeper manner in which we can answer this question is to consider what will come of us after we die. I have left this question for last because it literally is the last question any of us will consider. The way in which humans have answered this question has differed in many imaginative ways throughout recorded history. Due to the emotional context of this particular question, it has become extremely problematic when we try to discuss the responses rationally. But try we must. For the way in which people answer this question—as they have with the previous four questions—has profound effects on the way in which people currently conduct their lives and act toward others.

THE NATURAL RESPONSE

In response to the first part of this question: "What is to come of me during my lifetime?" the naturalist sees the world in a manner represented—at least by some approximation—by the Onion Skin Theory of Knowledge (OSTOK), which is bound up in vastly complex linear and nonlinear relationships between natural and cultural systems. Within this incredibly complex universe, the naturalists do their best to manipulate systems in an effort to attain the types of things that they value. But we are still very limited in our understanding of the vast network of complexities that affect our lives. For example, consider the developing field of *epigenetics*. Basically, the field of epigenetics examines the ways in which environmental factors may influence gene behavior in animal and human development. The prefix *epi-* is Greek for "above," so the field examines properties that operate above the DNA. Imagine genes as switches that can either be expressed (turn on) or remain dormant (turn off). The concept of epigenetics looks at activities called methylation and acetylation, processes that act like dimmer switches on genes. These environmental influences do not disrupt DNA but influence the manner in which genes express or do not express. Some geneticists have found that what distinguishes the development of specific types of cells within our bodies is not simply our DNA but also the manner in which the genes of those cells are regulated (i.e., switched on or off through epigenetic processes). Very small changes in developing fetuses, for example, can result in dramatically different developmental characteristics later in life. In one study, researchers found that if a gene that regulates a specific protein is disrupted during fetal development, it can lead to problems of diabetes, growth retardation, cardiovascular disease, obesity, and neurodevelopmental delays later in life.

"Our study emphasizes that maternal-fetal health influences multiple healthcare issues across generations," said Robert Lane, professor of pediatric neonatology at the University of Utah, and one of the senior researchers involved in the study. "To reduce adult diseases such as diabetes, obesity, and cardiovascular disease, we need to understand how the maternal-fetal environment influences the health of offspring." The scientists made this discovery through experiments involving two groups of rats. The first group was normal. The second group had the delivery of nutrients from their mothers' placentas restricted in a way that is equivalent to preeclampsia. The rats were examined right after birth and again at 21 days (21 days is essentially a preadolescent rat) to measure the amount of a protein, called IGF-1, that promotes normal development and growth in rats and humans. They found that the lack of nutrients caused the gene responsible for IGF-1 to significantly reduce the amount of IGF-1 produced in the body before and after birth.[1]

So what a mother eats during her pregnancy can drastically affect the growth and development of her offspring. If this is taken into the context of a cultural system like economics, we can better understand how poor nutrition, which usually occurs in lower-income families, may actually increase the likelihood of future health problems decades and perhaps even generations into the future. Answering the first part of the question of what is to come of me depends to a considerable degree on factors that are entirely out of your control—like what Mom ate (or did not eat) during her pregnancy with you.

Similar results are being found in studies that look at the parental effects of stress and psychological trauma on offspring—sometimes several generations later. Some researchers have found that early-life stressful experiences induced depressionlike behaviors and altered behavioral responses to aversive environments in mice. Even though the offspring of stressed males were raised in an environment without stress, they exhibited behavioral alterations similar to their parents.

> "It is fascinating that clinical observations in humans have suggested the possibility that specific traits acquired during life and influenced by environmental factors may be transmitted across generations. It is even more challenging to think that when related to behavioral alterations, these traits could explain some psychiatric conditions in families," said Dr. Mansuy, lead author on this project. "Our findings in mice provide a first step in this direction and suggest the intervention of epigenetic processes in such phenomenon."[2]

What is becoming more and more apparent is that in many important respects, we are not only what our mothers and grandmothers ate but also what they experienced under stressful conditions.

> "The idea that traumatic stress responses may alter the regulation of genes in the germ-line cells in males means that these stress effects may be passed across generations. It is distressing to think that the negative consequences of exposure to horrible life events could cross generations," commented Dr. John Krystal, editor of *Biological Psychiatry*. "However, one could imagine that these types of responses might prepare the offspring to cope with hostile environments. Further, if envi-

ronmental events can produce negative effects, one wonders whether the opposite pattern of DNA methylation emerges when offspring are reared in supportive environments."[3]

It is important to keep in mind that the field of epigenetics is young and, like all sciences, ongoing. It will be interesting to see what types of causal connections are made between other complex elements of systems in the future (see fig. 12.1).

It still makes me wonder, though, the influence the Spanish Armada may have had on the development of world politics in the Western Hemisphere. On April 5, 1588, Thomas Hobbes was born in Malmsbury, England. Hobbes was a brilliant political and ethical theorist who wrote extensively on human nature and the ever-presence of fear in our political developments. He was so concerned with fear that he developed the concept of the social contract, a provocative idea that has had considerable influence on law and politics in numerous countries. Hobbes recounts in his autobiography that his mother went into labor early and gave birth to him prematurely when she learned that the Spanish Armada was on its

Fig. 12.1. Epigenetics.
Image created by
Vanessa Tignanelli.

way to attack England: "Fear and I were born twins. My mother hearing of the Spanish Armada sailing up the English channel gave premature birth to me."[4] It is interesting to consider what effects the environments of Hobbes's parents and grandparents had on him. Although we may never know the answer, epigenetics has become cross-disciplinary by opening up avenues in the interpretation of historical events. Historians and psychologists can now consider figures like Hobbes and others in a new dimension by piecing together relevant epigenetic constraints that could have played significant roles in the history of their progenitors.

Understanding the vast complexities of the world in which we interact, there are many new and diverse ways by which to better understand what some of the network of complexities are as they relate to us and our health. At Kent State University, for example, there is the Center for Complexity in Health, where researchers examine causal elements of the OSTOK concerning "complex systems thinking, computational modeling, network analysis, data mining, and qualitative and historical approaches to complexity."[5] By examining such complexities, the hope is to make connections between both natural and cultural systems in an effort to better understand and treat specific illnesses. Numerous agencies, universities, and affiliates are concerned with the complex manner in which so many natural and cultural systems overlap.[6] I would be willing to make the noncontentious prediction that much of the future of scientific understanding will come from an interdisciplinary approach to understanding the various causal clusters of the OSTOK. By understanding the interconnectedness of the OSTOK in its various levels of complexity, we can better manage human and natural resources by manipulating to our advantage the various natural and cultural systems that affect our lives and the lives of other species.

The complexities of the OSTOK have revealed that when a naturalist considers what is to come of us while we are still alive, the best answer so far is: luck (see fig. 12.2).

It was lucky that Orville Delong did not get hit in the head by a meteorite on a Kitchener golf course. It was lucky that some people missed their flights that eventually ended in devastating crashes. It was unlucky

Fig. 12.2. Coin Toss.
Photograph by Matthew DiCarlo.

for those who made such flights. And it is largely a matter of luck that you have the genes you do, the environment in which you were raised, the family that raised you, the culture you now find yourself in, the politics of your current country of residence, and so on.

Before the twentieth century, the incidence of infant mortality worldwide was fairly high. You may not know this (because families rarely discuss this topic), but your mother may have had miscarriages before or after becoming pregnant with you. It is quite an act of luck that your mother did not miscarry you. It will also be entirely a matter of luck and chance whether the bacteria and viruses with which you come in contact throughout your life will be destroyed by your immune system or will manipulate your biological systems in such a way as to produce various forms of disease to which you will have no defense. Perhaps this is not the most reassuring of prospects, but it's necessary to understand if we wish to stay healthy. So in answering what is to come of us while we are still alive, we need to understand to what extent luck plays a part in our lives and to what extent we can exercise control over the many complex causal elements of the OSTOK. What we attempt to do through our various methods of understanding is to recognize when, where, and how we have control over particular systems within the OSTOK and to manipulate them to our advantage in an effort to survive and reproduce. Do not forget that control is itself an issue. How will we be able to determine within the umbra of becoming when we do have control in manipulating the networked systems of the OSTOK?

When responding to the second part of the question regarding what is to come of us after we die, the naturalist will respond with an overall skeptically safe answer: I don't know. This does not mean that the naturalist cannot fathom some educated guesses about what will happen to us after death. As David Hume pointed out, when we consider the death of other species, we generally do not attribute a separately existing entity like souls or spirits dwelling within them. In reasoning by analogy, Hume is suggesting that the same fate that befalls all living organisms—plant or animal—will befall us. In other words, nothingness: a total lack of consciousness.

The field of neuroscience has established that the consciousness by which we understand this world, the recognition of ourselves by others that gives us our identity, and the manner in which we plan for the future, reflect upon the past, and live our lives, are all products of neural activity. Without such activity, we can experience none of these things. As so many cases of head injury and trauma have demonstrated, once the capacity for neural activity is gone, much of who we are is gone as well. This does not mean that we cannot rewire our neural circuitry to overcome various forms of trauma; on the contrary. Dr. Norman Doidge, among others, has done exceedingly provocative work in this area by demonstrating how plastic and malleable the human brain actually is. The point to note here is that without the function of our brains, there is really very little in terms of a conscious understanding and interaction with others in the world. For example, when my mother experienced a heart attack that deprived her brain of oxygen for an extended period of time, she was resuscitated and kept alive on life support systems for more than a week. Our neurologist met with my family and me to inform us that she had not responded to several neurological assessments. He basically said that our mother as we knew and loved her was "gone." With this news it made it somewhat easier to stop her life support and allow her to die. Upon her death, she was surrounded by her family. Where our mother "went" after her death will differ greatly depending upon whom you ask. For a supernaturalist, a soul remains conscious and leaves the physical body to enter into some otherworldly realm. I witnessed no such transgression with my mother (notwithstanding the lack of a body scale to measure the loss of 21 grams, which is the mass that Dr. Duncan MacDougall believed a soul might occupy).[7] But a supernaturalist will say that the soul is invisible and can be seen only by other souls, perhaps angels, god(s), and the like. As we saw in chapter 10, defining the soul or spirit in this way leads to all kinds of problems. So naturalists tend not to believe in such things. What a naturalist might consider is that, based on the argument from ignorance, since we do not know all the properties of the various forces of the physical universe including quantum factors, field theory, string theory, quantum loop gravity, holographic projection theory, and so on, there is the possibility that the information that has composed our lives somehow "lives on" in other realms or quantum dimensions hitherto unknown by us. So in terms of an afterlife, there exists the possibility for a purely physical dimension to allow for a continuance of some currently unfathomable realm. But this is certainly not the typical conception of an afterlife most commonly depicted in various supernatural belief systems. At best, such a hypothetical description provides a fanciful hope in the realm of possibility that some continuance of human consciousness is somehow possible. But it is highly dependent upon an appeal to the argument to ignorance. Since we do not yet know of the various properties of the physical universe, there exists a chance that such an afterlife exists. This is by no means a guarantee, nor is it anything like any of the more common references to an afterlife found in most supernatural proposals.

So what is the alternative to an afterlife? Well, nothingness. But what would that be like? Many have difficulty imagining what it would be like without an afterlife. If this applies to you, you can try this thought experiment: Do you remember what your existence was like fifty years before you were born? You would experience the afterlife just like that. In other words, we have no way of knowing exactly what nothingness feels like because we would have to be nothing in order to experience it. But in being nothing, there can be no consciousness to comprehend or feel this. So the best we can do is to try to imagine what that state of nothingness was like prior to being conceived. Now, for many, this is an absolutely horrific thought. The idea that there is nothing more to life than, well, this life, is a thought that is so disturbing many cannot bear to accept it. And to some degree, this is understandable (see fig. 12.3).

For billions of people, there seems to be a great need to believe that there really is something more than just this life. These people have a strong metaphysical yearning for meaning and purpose and truth. To think that this is it is just too much to bear. For if there is absolutely nothing forever and for all time after we depart from this wonderful Earth, then life and the universe, and you and me, and the music of Bach and Mozart, the cathedrals of St. Paul and Westminster Abbey, the sunsets from Bombay, the majesty of the Andes, the splendor of the Great Barrier Reef—all these things will, in the grand scheme of things, have meant nothing. The millions who died in wars fighting for what they believed to be valiant and dignified causes will have been for nothing. The love that you feel, have felt, and will feel for those you care most deeply about, "all those moments . . . will be lost in time . . . like tears in rain."[8] Billions of people on this planet find this prospect so terrifying that they are willing to sacrifice reason, humility, and understanding in an effort to flee from it. They believe that a universe without purpose is one without sense and devoid of meaning or hope. A naturalist does not take this view, however. Instead, a naturalist sees this realization as liberating and attempts to create the best possible world for himself or herself and all other species on this planet in the limited time available while occupying this world. For this is not *all for nothing*. If this is all there is, then *this is everything*.

Fig. 12.3. Tombstone.
Image created by Sarah Sienna.

Let's think about this carefully. If it turns out that all current conceptions of an afterlife are false and we have only one life and, upon death, we will forever lose consciousness, why is this such a bad thing? We have come full circle from our lessons from Socrates. While facing his executioners, Socrates said more than 2,400 years ago what is equally true today. In death, either one of two things will happen: either consciousness somehow continues or it does not. This is a genuine dichotomy. If the former turns out to be true, then due to our current facticity, this is something that a naturalist has absolutely no way of determining at this point in our history. If the latter turns out to be true, then this is the best sleep we are ever going to get because it's going to last forever. There are literally no wake-up calls ever, because there is no *ever*; there is nothing—the same kind of nothing as existed prior to the Big Bang. As Socrates said, "If death is like this, then, I call it gain; because the whole of time, if you look at it in this way, can be regarded as no more than one single night."[9] If the latter is the case, why is that such a bad state? Why is sleeping forever such a bad thing? First of all, you won't be around to piss and moan that you're not around. Second, everyone could catch up on some sleep. Just think of how rested we'll all feel when never comes around again. And finally, it's the great equalizer. No special afterlife club where chosen ones get VIP treatment. No eternal bliss. No reward for all the sacrifices made in this life. No seventy-two virgins (where applicable; see manual for details). There is just . . . nothing. So many supernaturalists are counting on an afterlife; it is just too tantalizing to give up. For many, it is a form of metaphysical pension. True believers contribute to it all their lives (or at least they believe they are); so it follows that upon retirement from life, one should get a self-perpetuating and eternal supernatural annuity in the form of infinite happiness. There could be no greater interest on one's capital investment than this. This does sound awfully appealing, doesn't it? Why would anyone give up such beliefs? They are too comforting. How, then, does a naturalist manage to be content with what is knowable at the small t level of truth and withhold judgment on matters such as an afterlife and focus more on the current (and perhaps only) life? They do so, just as they have for the previous four questions, by responding in an epistemically responsible fashion that has been influenced by the doctrines of Socrates and the ancient Skeptics. In conjunction with the ABCs of critical thinking, naturalists try to structure their arguments in a valid and consistent manner, while keeping in mind their biases and the context of the responses. Providing evidence attained in a reliably sufficient manner, acknowledging a lack of nonarbitrary criteria by which to measure supernatural claims (i.e., a Reality Measuring Stick), and avoiding various logical fallacies also contribute to the naturalist's humbled stance in response to the Big Five.

I have argued elsewhere[10] that the fear of death and the realization that your loved ones have died would have instilled in our ancestors a genuine psychological and communal need to deal with these experiences. Recognizing by way of analogy that we, too, must some day part from this world does not make it any easier. So creating concepts of an afterlife is an evolved, conscious way to lessen the stress of losing people about whom we care deeply. But we are at the stage of our cultural evolution where we can actually consider that death may simply be the complete end to all our experiences. We generally don't like the good times to end. We want the party to keep going. And so we want life to be the same. Many find it difficult to realize that when a mother or father or brother or sister dies, he or she is gone forever. Read most obituaries in any major newspaper in the world and you will find constant references to how the departed are now happier and waiting for us to eventually join them. Psychologically, we can understand this need, even if our rationality says otherwise. You can see why I left this question for last. If you are a naturalist, the evidence would seem to suggest that this may be our only life. This then puts much more importance on our current lives, which in turn makes us more aware of how it is we should behave not only toward each other but also toward other species that occupy this planet. For those supernaturalists who believe that there is something greater beyond our death, they will perhaps have different agendas regarding not only how they see the world but also how they behave in it. It is to their responses that we now turn our attention.

THE SUPERNATURAL RESPONSE

When we consider the supernatural responses to the first part of this question—"what is to become of me during my lifetime?"—we should note that many supernaturalists believe in the concept of free will, which allows them to choose various paths between perceived acts of good and evil. Although we may live in a world that is seemingly governed by various natural laws of physics, chemistry, biology, and so on, supernaturalists believe that we possess the capacity to *choose* how it is we wish to live our lives. But many supernaturalists also believe that within those governing natural laws are agents at work who intervene and either prevent atrocities from occurring or bring about great fortunes for others. In a poll conducted in February 2010 by the Pew Forum on Religion and Public Life, findings indicate that around 79 percent of Americans believe in miracles defined as some form of supernatural intervention, similar in some ways to alleged miracles discussed in the Bible.[11] In a Gallup poll from 2004, 78 percent of Americans claim to believe in angels[12] as intervening entities that affect activities and personal lives in the physical universe—specifically, on our planet. Among those who believe in such supernatural beings and the miracles they perform, some believe that each person is born with a guardian angel who watches over him throughout his life, while others believe angels act as messengers and sometimes interveners for and against specific types of activities on Earth. It would appear that a significant number of supernaturalists literally believe that what happens to them while they are alive on this planet is not simply the result of blind natural forces and luck but in some ways results from the deliberate intervention of invisible nonempirical beings. Again, we can see some of the psychological reasons why someone might believe in spiritual or otherworldly interventions; unexplainable specific phenomena might be one reason. The argument to ignorance has been fallaciously used to justify such supernatural agents as intervening messengers of divinity for millennia because there seems to be no other way to explain a particular series of events. Since we lack the ability to rationally explain a given event, many will jump to a conclusion by stating that it had to be some

Fig. 12.4. Gray Squirrel. Photograph by Robert Loucks.

supernatural force. I recall a colleague of mine once stating that a squirrel ran into the road under his vehicle while he was driving, yet it managed to escape from what he thought was certain death for the poor rodent (see fig. 12.4).

As luck would have it, the pace of the squirrel's legs timed perfectly with the momentum of the vehicle, and the squirrel escaped unscathed between the four wheels to happily continue on with its daily chores of finding sustenance and tormenting dogs. This all took place within a split second, to which my colleague jokingly exclaimed, "It's a miracle!" The point he was trying to make is that it really was not a miracle at all but just bloody fortunate for the squirrel that timing was on its side that day. But should the same luck have befallen a young child, we could see how some would interpret such an unlikely survival as miraculous. Appealing to ignorance is a common fallacy when dealing with things like miracles, angels, saints, and so on.

But rational, intelligent people don't subscribe to such nonnatural and unscientific explanations as miracles, do they? Apparently some do. One example that comes to mind involves the work of Dr. Jacalyn Duffin, a practicing hematologist and internist and Hannah Professor of the history of medicine at Queen's University in Kingston, Ontario, Canada. Dr. Duffin is author of the 2009 book, *Medical Miracles: Doctors, Saints, and Healing in the Modern World*, which is published by Oxford University Press. In her book, Duffin examines 1,409 Vatican-documented miracles from the year 1588 to the present. Dr. Duffin apparently became interested in the subject when she was asked to take part in a blind evaluation of bone marrow samples from an acute leukemia patient.[13] She later found out that the study was commissioned by the Grey Nuns and that her work contributed to the canonization by the Roman Catholic Church in 1990 of Saint Marie-Marguerite D'Youville. She later attended the canonization ceremony and was able to meet with Pope John Paul II. At this point, we might be thinking that her work could be subject to a number of fallacies. For example, examining Vatican-documented "miracles" from the sixteenth century to the present is probably going to contain some level of bias in the selection process. As well, the concept of "miracles" is question-begging, in other words, it assumes that such things as miracles already in fact exist. Finally, if there is any predisposition to believe in such things as miracles, we need to be extremely cautious to recognize and limit confirmation bias. Duffin herself refers to her work in the Vatican archives and library as a "miracle feeding frenzy." In a review of *Medical Miracles* in the *New England Journal of Medicine*, reviewer Iona McCleery states:

> There can be no miracle if there has been no attempt at medical treatment, and rejection of medicine on pious grounds has always been frowned upon by the Catholic Church. The result is that over the centuries, healing miracles have become increasingly medicalized, the medical testimony—even by non-Catholics and atheists—is still crucial to canonization.... Duffin argues that religion and medicine are remarkably similar belief systems, with the same attention to evidence and standards of proof, and that both exist as ways of people to deal with suffering and dying.[14]

Now to some degree, we might want to say that, historically, it is interesting to see how one culture considered healing to have been brought about by some form of divine intervention. It is quite another, however, to say that this was actually the case in those so-called miracles that currently lack medical or natural explanation (see fig. 12.5).

Apparently a "self-professed atheist," Duffin believes that both medicine and religion are looking at the same stories of illness, suffering, and recovery:

> And in the absence of any concrete evidence in a particular case, said Duffin, the belief that a person was healed by divine intervention through the intercession of a saint, or the belief that some unexplained biological phenomenon deserves the credit are both simply beliefs. "Medicine is a belief system, just like religion," she said. Duffin later said she does believe in a "spiritual side of living" and that, in fact, she does believe in miracles.[15]

I find this particular passage of considerable interest due to its marvelous demonstration of inconsistency. First of all, Dr. Duffin states that when

concrete or empirical evidence is lacking regarding the healing process of a particular individual, it is just as legitimate to maintain that an invisible saint was the cause of the recovery as any natural cause. Based on this same reasoning, I should be able to say that not only was a specific healing due to an invisible gnome or a fairy or a witch but that these should be accepted with the same conviction of possibility or likelihood as any methodical natural explanation. The second problem with Duffin's statements is that, at last count, there are currently more than

Fig. 12.5. Stethoscope and Crucifix. Image created by Sarah Sienna.

ten thousand saints in the Catholic Church. This makes it rather difficult to know precisely when each saint is intervening in the natural world to bring about various miracles. What system could possibly exist, what Reality Measuring Stick is available for anyone on this planet to actually attempt to confirm such supernatural claims? Third, Duffin makes the erroneous claim that medicine is a belief system, just like religion. On one hand, we would agree that although the two are both belief systems, we must also admit that they are extremely different in the manner and methods by which they attain information in developing such belief systems. To put it analogously, it's like me saying that belief in the function of the human circulatory system is just like belief in the existence of saints and angels. Medicine *is* a belief system, but it is *nothing* like religion. Medicine is empirical; religion is not. Medicine withstands the rigors of the scientific hypothetico-deductive method; religion does not. Medicine makes predictions and confirms or falsifies these on the basis of reliably attained data; religion does not. Medicine is based on scientific reason, mathematics, advanced technology, and empirical studies. Religion is not. And finally and most blatantly obvious is the inconsistency with Duffin's statement that she is a "self-professed atheist" and then shortly thereafter states that she believes in "a spiritual side of living" and that she does, in fact, believe in miracles. Unless she is equivocating on the term "miracles" to mean something other than what she has been examining in her book, Dr. Duffin is being quite inconsistent in her statements. This is a most obvious breach of the law of noncontradiction—maintaining that she can simultaneously both be an atheist and believe in invisible spiritual entities that cause miracles. She can either eat her cake or have it. Maybe this is somehow possible at the quantum level, but not here. Her final comment commits a fallacious appeal to ignorance:

"I believe that there are things that we can't explain," said Duffin, adding that, if someone should choose to frame such things in religious terms, and there is no better explanation, she is in no position to dismiss such beliefs.[16]

But of course there *are* better explanations. Time and time again, science has demonstrated how so called miracles from the Bible, the Torah, the Koran, and elsewhere have occurred and can be explained within a natural context.[17] Based on Dr. Duffin's reasoning, there is no better explanation for the image of the Virgin Mary to appear on a grilled-cheese sandwich, so I should not dismiss anyone's beliefs in such a happening as a genuine miracle. The same would be true for the nun bun, which looks like Mother Teresa in the form of a cinnamon bun, or the fishstick, dumpling, or potato chip bearing the apparent images of Jesus Christ.[18] For such a highly educated person, I am bewildered by Dr. Duffin's lack of intellectual rigor in her research. Her fallacious appeal to ignorance echoes the age-old defense that simply because we do not currently have a natural explanation for X, the cause must therefore be supernatural. The same line of reasoning has been used by modern-day creationists who maintain that simply because science has not been able to demonstrate that life could have arisen from inanimate matter, it must have been the result of an intelligent designer.

For many supernaturalists, answering the first part of the question regarding what is to come of me is dependent on the will of supernatural entities in conjunction with natural forces. If supernaturalists act in particular ways and ask for things either to happen or not to happen through activities like prayers, or involvement with specific types of ritualistic behavior like attending mass, facing east and praying five times a day, wailing at a wall, making pilgrimages, fasting, spinning prayer wheels, performing puja (Hindu gift giving) at home or in a temple, handling rattlesnakes, or cutting foreskins off of male baby penises, and so on, good or bad fortune may befall them. When supernaturalists are faced with a difficult problem in their reasoning—for example, when bad things happen to good people—appeals can be made to ignorance in the form of not possessing the capabilities to understand a specific deity's plan. "God must have a plan" has often been used to explain why such powerful supernatural beings would allow devastating events like tsunamis and widespread disease to kill hundreds of thousands of innocent children (see fig. 12.6).

Let's consider the consistency of the line of reasoning behind a divine plan, prayer, and divine intervention in the form of an argument.

Fig. 12.6. God's Plan. Image created by Vanessa Tignanelli.

(P1)   If God has a plan, then his plan will be known to him from beginning to end (since God is all-knowing).

(MP1) So God must know in advance which miracles he is going to perform.

(MP2) If MP1 is true, it follows that no amount of prayer is going to change things.

(C)   So it follows that prayer is useless.

What emerges from this argument is that if God is all-knowing and all-powerful, then no matter what you do or don't do, it's not going to matter, because things are going to turn out exactly as he knows they are going to. One way around this of course is to admit that God doesn't have a plan. Then he might intervene all the time. This is based on the idea that God created an imperfect universe that has so many problems that he has to fix them through miraculous intervention after hearing prayers. But this makes him a lesser god. And many supernaturalists are not willing to limit the power of their deity. So the supernaturalist has some homework to do here. Consider the following example: If God has a plan, and two sports teams pray to this god, but only one team can win, it would have to follow that such a god must have a specific plan, which would be able to explain why the one team was successful while the other was not. So there is an obvious inconsistency here (unless God is a huge Lakers fan).

1. If God has a plan, forget about the power of prayer and the existence of miracles. It ain't happening. What happens, happens. That's just the way it is. And nothing is going to change it.
2. If God allows for miracles through divine intervention acting on prayer, then he does not have a plan, and his choices for miracles are completely arbitrary; on some days, an arbitrary number of children get to live, while on other days, an arbitrary number of children die.

For many supernaturalists, it just seems easier to give in to ignorance than to accept inconsistencies such as this. Earlier we discussed the psychological motivation for this type of behavior. The appeal of the supernatural to people touches a very old and very tenacious part of the brain—the limbic system. This is the emotional center of the brain, and it has been around in our ancestors' heads a lot longer than have our developed abilities to reason and to think logically. So it should not come as much of a surprise to see so many people on this planet accept supernatural claims even in the face of logically and empirically inconsistent evidence. This was seen when President Barack Obama commented on the recovery of a US diplomat, Richard Holbrooke, who underwent a twenty-hour surgery for a life-threatening tear in one of his arteries:

> US President Barack Obama gave a hint of the seriousness of the situation, saying in a statement that he and First Lady Michelle Obama were praying for Holbrooke's recovery.[19]

While discussing the matter on CNN's *State of the Union*, Obama adviser David Axelrod said,

Anyone who knows [Holbrooke], and I was with him Friday morning before this happened, knows how tough and resilient he is, and we're all praying that that quality sees him through now.[20]

This does not really make sense. Axelrod is praying that Holbrooke's qualities of toughness and resilience will make him survive this ordeal. How does God intervene miraculously in this regard? Does he somehow magnify Mr. Holbrooke's characteristics of toughness and resilience? Isn't Mr. Holbrooke simply tough and resilient enough to have these qualities see him through this ordeal? If this is the case, then what does prayer really have to do with anything? Axelrod's statement is rendered meaningless.

But let's consider Mr. and Mrs. Obama's situation. Here we see the president of the United States and his wife stating how they are asking for help from what they believe to be a supernatural agent who, because of their best wishes, is going to affect the survival of Richard Holbrooke. Does the president of the United States literally believe this? If so, he too has some homework to do. But we might just think that Obama and others are saying this to be politically sensitive to those who have deeply religious faith. As a political maneuver, we could understand this (in a Machiavellian way). Unfortunately for Mr. Holbrooke, he succumbed to his circumstances and died the following day. From all media accounts, he seemed to be an extremely adept diplomat in foreign policy. His death came at a great loss to his friends, family, and country, and most likely to the efforts of sustaining world peace. Why wouldn't God intervene and generate a miracle for Mr. Holbrooke's life? If this was part of God's "plan," then all the praying in the world was not going to save him. This means that God needed him to die to help fulfill his plan. But for those who loved and appreciated this man, it had better be a pretty good plan if you're going to allow one of the world's best diplomats to be "called home."

Because supernatural beliefs are often highly emotionally motivated and sustained, prayer becomes a powerful form of wishful thinking, which is really a manifestation of hope in the face of adversity. Recent studies indicate that there is value to be found in prayer as a form of therapy and hope. For some people who are involved in abusive relationships, prayer has been a powerful coping mechanism not only in allowing them to vent their anger and pain but also in seeing themselves as they believe God perceives them. This abstraction allowed them to increase their sense of self-esteem and worth, which counteracts the abuser's hurtful words and actions. There has been a considerable amount of work in this area that shows a strong link between the limbic or emotional center of the brain and the need to answer the Big Five with supernatural responses.[21] This is perhaps the strongest reason why supernaturalists can be resistant to arguments that demonstrate inconsistencies in their reasoning. Perhaps the strongest motivating factor behind the supernaturalists' responses to the Big Five is the fear of death—not simply death in and of itself as a believed passage to another dimension, another world, or another shot at life. It is fear of never being again. It is fear of nothingness, of forever being lost to the ravages of time, like tears in rain. It is to this final response that we now turn our attention.

In responding to the second part of the question in reference to what will become of us after we die, supernaturalists might state that this is entirely dependent upon the manner in which they chose to answer the fourth question of the Big Five regarding how we should behave. For those supernaturalists who believe that a deity or deities require subservience to specific rules on pain of eternal punishment and ruin, or the reward of everlasting life, it would seem that as long as they act according to the believed doctrines of their particular faith, they are guaranteed a better situation either in the afterlife or when they are reincarnated back into this world. There have existed hundreds of descriptions of a so-called afterlife penned in various religions and spiritual movements, and depicted on stage, on screen, and in all other manner of media. These range widely in name and description; here are examples of just a few: Elysium (Greek mythology), Heaven (Abrahamic), Valhalla (Norse), Niflhel (Norse), Gehenna (Greek, Hebrew/Yiddish), Paradise (most), Kingdom of the Dead (Greek mythology), the Fields of Aaru (Egyptian mythology), Hades (ancient Greek underworld), Erebus (Greek mythology), Tartarus (Greek mythology), Asphodel Fields (Greek mythology), Spirit Prison (Latter-Day Saints), Jannah (Muslim: heavenly), Jahannam (Muslim:

hellish), Nirvana (Hindu, Buddhist, Jain), Punarjanma (Hindu), Sukhā-vatī (Buddhist), Abhirati (Buddhist), Ghanavyūha (Buddhist), Aakāvatī (Buddhist), Mount Potala (Buddhist), the Copper-Colored Mountain (Buddhist), Tuita (Mahayana Buddhist), Sukhavati (Mahayana Buddhist), the eternal home (most), astral projection (New Age), Land of the Dead (Australian Aboriginal), eternal rest (secular), eternity (most), the great unknown (agnostic), the Happy Hunting Ground (cliché for North American Aboriginal), the hereafter (most), the Eternal Dreamland (Australian Aboriginal), immortality (most), God's kingdom (Abrahamic), the Other Side Camps (Native American: Crow), kingdom come (Abrahamic), life everlasting (most), life to come (most), the next world (New Age), Metnal (Mayan hell), Tlalocan (Mayan heaven), the next plane of existence (New Age), the Dance Hall of the Dead (Native American: Navajo), the pearly gates (Christian), Mictlan (Aztec), the promised land (Abrahamic), and of course, hell (Abrahamic, folk, and others).[22]

In a 2004 Gallup poll, about 81 percent of Americans surveyed believed in an afterlife.[23] That is a fairly high number. And yes, I realize that I have been using statistical data to support my analysis; so you have every right to scrutinize my data (as you should) by using the criteria regarding the examination of the value of scientific studies in chapter 5. If, as a conditional, we can accept this figure to be reflective of the percentage of Americans who believe in an afterlife, the recurring problem the supernaturalist faces is that there are so many different versions of an afterlife we have no way of determining which, if any, represent the Big T Truth. Without a Reality Measuring Stick there is simply no way to confirm or falsify such claims. I can therefore make similar claims that the afterlife consists of an eternal bisexual orgy in the land of infinite dildos, and nobody will be able to prove me otherwise. According to the law of non-contradiction, it is logically and physically *impossible* for all accounts of the afterlife to be true. They just differ far too drastically. But logically, it is possible for every account of an afterlife to be false. For as naturalists would contend, there may simply be no afterlife at all. Given the vast diversity of afterlife accounts, what meaningful discourse can be brought to light on this subject?

Some supernaturalists have made claims that there are, in fact, empirical methods for confirming the reality of the afterlife. These have been studied scientifically for decades. They are called near-death experiences (NDEs). When I was a precocious high school student, I happened to come across a book called *You Cannot Die*. It was written by a professor named Ian Currie who was then at the University of Guelph (in the town in which I grew up). I became fascinated with the topic of death and the afterlife. Along with other luminaries in the field like Elisabeth Kübler-Ross[24] and Raymond Moody,[25] Currie seemed to offer a scientific approach to the study of the afterlife that I thought warranted further consideration. I quickly learned that his views of paranormal phenomena relied quite heavily on pseudoscience and personal testimonies. His book examined case histories of parapsychological phenomena that examined anecdotal testimonies of out-of-body experiences, deathbed visions, mediumship, apparitions, possessions, and hauntings. One of the aspects of this New Age version of death and the afterlife presented itself empirically by examining NDEs. It became quite popular to claim that empirical proof for the existence of things like souls, spirits, and the like, can be found in the natural world and experimentally confirmed. There is an enormous amount of literature on NDEs and the afterlife.[26] Some of these accounts are connected to organized religions, while others maintain a sort of New Age spirituality not connected with religion in any way. The pattern of an NDE is usually the same: a temporary loss of consciousness, followed by an out-of-body experience (OOB)—a feeling of floating above one's body, then the appearance of a tunnel, and then the appearance of a bright light. Many claim to feel quite calm and relaxed and at peace during an NDE. Some are met by apparent angels or deceased family members. Many have had similar experiences regardless of where they resided in the world or what religion they believed or did not believe. An organization known as the Horizon Research Foundation has put together the Human Consciousness Project. It is currently conducting the "first large-scale scientific study of what happens when we die and the relationship between mind and brain during clinical death."[27] Members of this group claim that between 10 and 20 percent of individuals who undergo cardiac arrest report detailed out-of-body-type experiences without any measurable brain activity during these periods.

> These studies appear to suggest that the human mind and consciousness may in fact function at a time when the clinical criteria of death are fully present and the brain has ceased functioning. If these smaller studies can be replicated and verified through the definitive, large-scale studies of the Human Consciousness Project, they may not only revolutionize the medical care of critically ill patients and the scientific study of the mind and brain, but may also bear profound universal implications for our social understanding of death and the dying process.[28]

So this surely must be proof of an afterlife, right? Actually, no. Several natural explanations have been put forward for people's experience of such events. These range from artificially induced electrical stimulation of the temporal lobe and hippocampus during neurosurgery to the presence of high carbon dioxide levels (hypercarbia), to ATP and ion stock depletion, which is really just your brain's gradual turning off; to decreased cerebral perfusion, which results in local cerebral hypoxia, which fighter pilots experience when they train in a centrifuge and all the blood drains from their brain and they suffer acute oxygen deprivation. As the centrifuge slows and the blood courses quickly back into the brain, they get a bit of a jolt in terms of endorphin/encephalin and serotonin activity, which momentarily gets them high and gives them a feeling of warmth and peace. Scientists like Barry Beyerstein maintained that what is actually happening during NDEs is that the brain is simply shutting down. When oxygen deprivation occurs as the brain is in its final stages, some people experience a dream state or complex hallucinations. During the 1980s and 1990s, Dr. James E. Whinnery, chief aeromedical scientist at the Naval Air Warfare Center, examined the behavior of more than 1,200 naval pilots during centrifuge training. He discovered that about 18 percent of all pilots went through experiences quite similar to those described in NDEs. Notice how this percentage matches that of the percentage of individuals who undergo cardiac arrest and report detailed out-of-body-type experiences without any measurable brain activity during these periods (as claimed by members of the Human Consciousness Project). During accel-eration experiments, many test pilots would experience gray-outs, tunnel vision, black-outs, loss of consciousness, and dreams, which were associated with the loss of consciousness due to cerebral blood loss and a lack of oxygen in the brain. Neuroscientist Christoph Koch claims to have similar experiences to NDEs and OOBs almost every evening; he calls it dreaming. To Koch, NDEs are really just another form of very vivid dreams. He predicts that the number of NDE claims will continue to rise as the rate of medical technology becomes better at pulling people back from the brink of death.

Of course, there will always be supernaturalists who will claim that such naturalist explanations are simply too skeptical. There are personal testimonies maintaining that the experience of death was a real, transcendent state and you "just have to experience it for yourself" to know that it is the real thing. To some degree, this is understandable. Such people have been pulled back from the point of death and are quite happy to be still alive. Experiencing feelings of warmth and comfort and a bright light and so on is bound to have a powerful impact on them. But we must not mistake the power of an experience with its potential reality. Otherwise, we would be inclined to admit that those who claim to experience powerful feelings of a spiritual presence in the form of a deity or angel or saint must also be having genuine or true experiences. We need to be wary of Occam's razor in this regard. Invoking supernatural agency into the physical world multiplies far more entities beyond necessity than does a natural explanation. Be that as it may, my emotional side is hoping that NDEs and OOBs are the real thing. I, too, would rather attend the "after party" and hang out for eternity with those I love. But wishing something doesn't make it so. And we need to have the courage to realize that if this is the only life we have, then we should reconsider how we should be treating one another as well as the planet itself.

CONCLUSION

We have covered quite a lot since this book began. From the ABCs of critical thinking to the Socratic and Skeptical methods of reasoning and analysis, we have used many important and powerful tools in considering the natural and supernatural means for answering the Big Five. There will be those who believe that naturalism has nothing to say about supernaturalism. They will say that supernatural content exists in another realm and cannot be completely understood in a natural context. We have seen how the claims of the naturalists clearly do not extend into the realm of the supernatural. And we have seen that when supernaturalists state claims that are testable empirically, the naturalists have every right to scrutinize their arguments. They do both rationally—through the use of logic and reason as well as with the Socratic method and the modes of the ancient Skeptics—and empirically—according to the hypothetico-deductive method of scientific analysis. Such testing was done in the interest of fairness, for we have seen that when supernatural explanations of any sort are given or presented as a means for expressing what is perceived to be absolute Truth, no account has yet demonstrated consistency or complied with the criteria used to warrant explanatory arguments in either rational or empirical fields of investigation. Whether in paranormal activity or spiritual or religious capacities, there has not been a single demonstration of supernatural phenomena capable of withstanding naturalistic scrutiny. This is not to say it is impossible; it merely points out a consistently bad track record for supernaturalists who may wish to seriously reexamine their premises and assumptions. This reminds me of a Tim Minchin song called "If You Open Your Mind Too Much, Your Brain Will Fall Out" (or "Take My Wife").[1] In this song, Minchin sings about what is required in terms of evidence for accepting supernatural phenomena. It goes like this:

> If anyone can show me one example in the history of the world of a single Psychic who's been able to prove under reasonable experimental conditions that they are able to read minds—
> And if anyone can show me one example in the history of the world of a single Astrologer who's been able to prove under reasonable experimental conditions that they can predict future human events by interpreting celestial signs—
> And if anyone can show me one example in the history of the world of a single Homeopathic Practitioner who's been able to prove under reasonable experimental conditions that solutions made up of infinitely tiny particles of good stuff dissolved repeatedly into relatively huge quantities of water have a consistently higher medicinal value than a similarly administered placebo—
> And if anyone can show me one example in the entire history of the world of a single Spiritual or Religious person who's been able to show either empirically or logically the existence of a higher power with any consciousness or interest in the human race or ability to punish or reward humans for their moral choices or that there is any reason—other than fear—to believe in any version of an afterlife—
> I will give you my piano, one of my legs, and my wife.

One of the main purposes of this book was to take a fair and honest look at the ways in which people not only answer the Big Five but also regulate their lives according to the ways they answer them. The hope is that maybe we can come to some agreement about what we can really talk about and say in terms of answering the Big Five. This is going to take a bit of work, because by believing in supernatural entities, one assumes not only that one possesses a level of certainty of information about the world, the universe, and oneself, but also that one has the ability to know this and can possibly demonstrate this to others. That is, one believes onself to be in possession of a Reality Measuring Stick. Those who use supernatural explanations as responses to the Big Five are sincere in their beliefs that they are in possession of information that is absolutely certain. When placed alongside the Reality Measuring Stick, supernaturalists believe that their views measure up 100 percent accurately, whereas the views of others do not quite measure up. Those who believe themselves to be in sole possession of the absolute Truth believe they have the best answers to the Big Five: the True answers. There is a bit of a problem though: supernaturalists answer the Big Five in extremely different ways. Naturalists use criteria of consistency, coherence, agreement, and universality as means by which to measure the value of their responses to the Big Five. With well over one thousand religions, sects, and so on in existence, it is impossible for all of them to be 100 percent accurate according to the Reality Measuring Stick. It would be interesting to ask various supernaturalists how they consider the views of others to measure up next to theirs. In terms of answering the Big Five, how would supernaturalists compare the supernatural views of others to their own? You would think a naturalist would measure quite lowly in comparison to the views of most supernaturalists. For example, if the Sunni Muslim worldview could be imagined to be the one worldview that, on the Reality Measuring Stick, measures up with 100 percent accuracy, how would the Christians, Jews, Hindus, Sikhs, Raelians, Scientologists, and all the others measure up? For as we have seen, if supernaturalists make the claim to possess absolute answers to the Big Five, it would also follow that they are somehow in possession of a means for measuring this (i.e., a Reality Measuring Stick). This device would also give them the ability to see how other supernatural views are lacking compared to theirs. In other words, Sunni Muslims would be able to demonstrate to other Muslim sects—like Shia or Ahmadiyya—why, in fact, they are wrong. They may be close in some regards but just don't quite have it right. I'm not sure I totally agree with Richard Dawkins that theists are just atheists with one more god. I don't think they take the all-or-nothing stance with other religions—just with atheists. It's sort of like a supernatural carnival where proponents of various religious and supernatural views step right up to the High Striker game and swing their hammers down onto the lever to see how high they can make the puck rise.

The one privileged striker who rings the bell wins the prize of attaining 100 percent absolute Truth of Reality. All others, of course, will make the puck rise only part of the way. This would mean there is the potential for overlapping truth between their worldviews and the one worldview that happens to ring the bell. When we give this some thought, the relationship supernaturalists have with one another is quite bizarre in the context of a Reality Measuring Stick. Overlapping commonalities would give other theistic worldviews credibility in some regards, but never 100 percent absolute Truth like the one, True supernatural worldview. It would also follow that in possessing a Reality Measuring Stick,

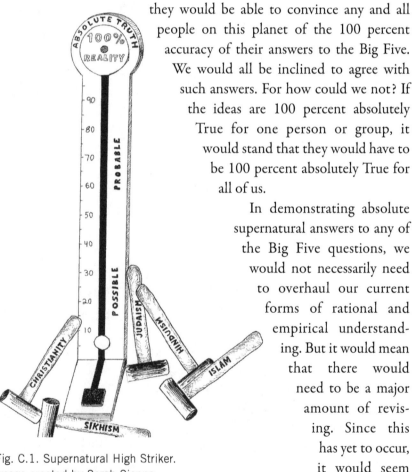

they would be able to convince any and all people on this planet of the 100 percent accuracy of their answers to the Big Five. We would all be inclined to agree with such answers. For how could we not? If the ideas are 100 percent absolutely True for one person or group, it would stand that they would have to be 100 percent absolutely True for all of us.

In demonstrating absolute supernatural answers to any of the Big Five questions, we would not necessarily need to overhaul our current forms of rational and empirical understanding. But it would mean that there would need to be a major amount of revising. Since this has yet to occur, it would seem

Fig. C.1. Supernatural High Striker.
Image created by Sarah Sienna.

the most responsible thing to do is approach the Big Five with a certain amount of humility. This is not to say that supernatural ways of answering the Big Five are not important to billions of people; clearly they are. But what we can now see is that since there is no way to extend beyond our ignorance of such supernatural responses, the most rational and responsible thing to do would be to set them aside while we figure out how we're going to get along. Based on our historical facticity, we are simply stuck with the ways and techniques that attain information in the most responsible ways we can come up with. So far, the rational techniques of Socrates and the ancient Skeptics and the empirical techniques of the sciences seem to do this quite successfully and quite fairly. They may not be perfect, but they do provide us with very novel, interesting, fair, and wonderful ways of understanding ourselves, our world, and the universe. We just have to culturally grow up a little more as a species.

Now that you have learned many tools for helping you better understand why we answer the Big Five the way we do, please feel free to answer them again if so desired in the worksheet that follows.

1. What can I know?

_____

_____

_____

2. What am I?

_____

_____

_____

3. Why am I here?

_____

_____

_____

4. How should I behave?

_____

_____

_____

5. What is to come of me?

_____

_____

_____

We have seen that the ways we answer the Big Five have a direct influence over the manner in which we respond to and act on many other aspects of our lives. Think about some of the other very important issues facing us today: abortion, human rights, euthanasia, freedom of speech, crime and punishment, war, resource allocation, political theory, health and nutrition. In these and many more aspects, the way we answer the Big Five will influence our responses in significant ways. The following examples clearly illustrate this:

1. Republican Senator John Shimkus (19th District, Illinois) believes that we do not need to worry about global warming because it clearly states in the Bible (Genesis 8: 21–22) that God promised Noah that He would not flood the world again. "I believe that is the infallible word of God and that's the way it's going to be for His creation."[2]
2. Brand choice is affected by religiosity. In the latest study from Ron Shachar of Tel Aviv University, he demonstrates how a consumer's religiosity has a large impact on his likelihood for choosing specific brands.[3]
3. George W. Bush believed, to some degree, that his actions as president of the United States were directly influenced by the Evangelical Christian God. In Bob Woodward's 2002 book, *Bush at War*, he writes, "The President was casting his mission and that of the country in the grand vision of God's Master Plan."[4] Similarly, in the October 17, 2004, *New York Times Magazine*, Ron Suskind

quotes Bruce Bartlett, a former Reagan adviser, as saying that George W. Bush "truly believes he's on a mission from God."[5]

4. Beliefnet is an online service that offers its customers spiritual options for their consumer purchases: "Our mission is to help people like you find, and walk, a spiritual path that will bring comfort, hope, clarity, strength, and happiness. Whether you're exploring your own faith or other spiritual traditions, we provide you inspiring devotional tools, access to the best spiritual teachers and clergy in the world, thought-provoking commentary, and a supportive community."[6] Beliefnet is hailed as the largest spiritual website and is not affiliated with any particular spiritual organization or movement. It claims: "Our only agenda is to help you meet your spiritual needs."

5. A Christian group called Fans of Family Radio Inc., a nationwide Christian Network in Tennessee, has placed a message on forty billboards in and around Nashville and in eight other states informing the public that the Rapture date has been set for May 21, 2011, and Jesus will be returning to this planet on that day. Here is the official story from its website:

> This website serves as an introduction and portal to four faithful ministries which are teaching that WE CAN KNOW from the Bible alone that the date of the rapture of believers will take place on May 21, 2011, and that God will destroy this world on October 21, 2011. Please take your time and browse through the teachings of Harold Camping, President of Family Radio. Visit EBible Fellowship, Bible Ministries International, and The-Latter-Rain to read and listen to many faithful teachers give scriptural insight on the doctrines that God is teaching His people.[7]

Notice this supernatural claim is measurable in the natural world. This means that it will be easy enough to either confirm or falsify empirically. Even though this book has come out after May 21, 2011, I will predict that you are still with us and reading along. Otherwise, you can collect one million dollars from the James Randi Foundation (though one million dollars won't be much use to you if there's no world left). When we witness that the world does not come to an end on October 21, 2011, the second claim will have been empirically falsified. Seems easy, right? But it's not going to work that way. These claims are actually set up to be a win-win for the four faithful ministries. For in the unlikely event that the Rapture occurs, they are vindicated and get to say "We told you so." But when it does not come, they will still be vindicated, for they will say that God is merciful and decided to call off the Rapture until a later time which, in turn, proves his love for all humankind. A considerable amount of work was done in this area by psychologist Leon Festinger who, in the 1950s, examined a similar scenario involving his infiltration of a cult that believed the world was coming to an end.[8] As Festinger predicted, when the destruction of the world did not come, members of the group had one of two responses: some saw that their views were false and began to question the soundness of their overall worldview, and some remedied their cognitive dissonance by using ad hoc propositions to justify why the end of the world did not occur. Festinger developed the concept of *cognitive dissonance* to explain some of the group members' tenacity to still believe, even in the face of countervailing empirical evidence.

Some other headlines from various world newspapers include ART TEACHER LOSES JOB AFTER KIDS SEE NUDE SCULPTURE: CHILDREN WERE ON SCHOOL-APPROVED FIELD TRIP; JUDGE: TEN COMMANDMENTS TO STAY ON OHIO COURTHOUSE LAWN; DOMINO'S PIZZA FOUNDER TO BUILD CATHOLIC TOWN. As well, one can put one's money into faith-based mutual funds—those mutual funds for which investors purchase shares in companies based on Christian or Islamic principles. This makes the idea of investment rather interesting, for it would seem to put a considerable amount of trust on those in charge of the investors' money. They could not commit any sins by acting in a non-Christian or non-Muslim way. Based on this reasoning, we should all invest in faith-based mutual funds. But it's not quite like this. The principles that such funds stress are negative rather than positive. Instead of focusing on values like not ripping off your fellow investor, faith-based funds tend to focus more on what investors *do not want* their money invested in: companies that support abortion, contraception, pornography, degradation toward the sacrament of marriage (i.e., homosexuality and/or same-sex marriage), embryonic stem-cell research, and even the packaging or processing of pork products. Ah, pork. The one you love.

Thousands of other examples are available online, in newspapers, on television, and elsewhere. These stories come from your neighbor, your grocer, your kid's teacher, your local cop, your boss, and anyone else, who collectively represent over 80 percent of the world's population, all of whom have deep and abiding conviction in their supernatural beliefs. Sometimes the ways people act in accordance with their supernatural responses to the Big Five are obvious and overt. But for the most part, they are hidden.[9]

We see the same trickle-down effect for those who answer the Big Five naturally. Views on same-sex marriage, abortion, euthanasia, breast-feeding in public, capital punishment, treatment of women, treatment of children, treatment of the environment, politics (how it should be run and by whom), and so on, will all be considered based on our particular biases and worldviews. Since we do not have a Reality Measuring Stick to determine absolutely who's right, we need to come up with some guiding principles that we can all agree on in a fair and equitable manner. In terms of acceptance of various responses to the Big Five, we can consider the Tolerance-Harm Inverse Proportion (T-HIP) law. This law maintains that all responses to the Big Five are tolerable provided that they do not generate perceived harm onto others. In the words of H. L. Mencken: "We must respect the other fellow's religion, but only in the sense and to the extent that we respect his theory that his wife is beautiful and his children smart."[10] In principle, there should be no conflict that all humans occupying this planet recognize they can answer the Big Five in just about any manner they want; and they can act in accordance with the manner in which they answer them as well. They just cannot harm others in the process. If they do cause harm, we would all, as equal inhabitants of this planet, have to admit that, because harm is undesirable and unwarranted, it should not be allowed, and we would be morally justified to take action to stop or prevent it.

This is about the best we can do under the circumstances. We have the tools by which to reason. We have the sciences by which to understand the natural world. The rest is up to us. You are now equipped with tools that I hope will assist you in answering the Big Five in a responsible and consistent manner. I wish you the very best of luck in this regard.

ACKNOWLEDGMENTS

One does not become a really good pain in the ass without the help and assistance of so many friends, family members, colleagues, and dissenters. To my editor, Steven L. Mitchell at Prometheus Books, I want to express my appreciation for his patience and dedication in encouraging me to complete this book. My thanks also goes out to other staff at Prometheus Books, including Catherine Roberts-Abel in Production and Traffic, Jade Zora Ballard for proofreading, Jill Maxick in Publicity, and Jen Durgan, who skilfully copyedited the manuscript.

I would also like to extend my thanks to my brother-in-law Robert Loucks for his photographic assistance and wonderful illustrations. I would also like to thank two of Guelph's finer up-and-coming artists: Sarah Sienna and Vanessa Tignanelli. In what seemed to be an impossible deadline, they were able to produce some wonderful illustrations for this book. I hope their artwork continues to provide enjoyment and appreciation for many in the years to come.

My appreciation also extends to so many friends and colleagues with whom I have had the pleasure of discussing so many of life's questions. From the mundane to the sublime, in all walks of life, my time with you has been invaluable; and this of course extends to the various esteemed members of the 14½ Mercer Street Debating Society. Decades of Thursday-night discussions and debates have contributed to a great deal of good-natured banter on many a diverse and interesting topic. My gratitude is extended for both your input and tolerance.

A note of thanks must also go out to my past professors: for those who were good professors, thank you for your encouragement and insight into pedagogy, research, and academic integrity. For the bad professors, thank you for demonstrating what does not work very well in these respects. My only hope is that you have come to recognize into which category you fit. To my past students who have asked so many searching questions and demanded properly supported answers, you have kept me as honest as a critical thinker can be. We all know that in education, as in all other aspects of life, we are all hypocrites who just vary by degree. But your inquisitiveness has held a mirror up to me in this regard and forced me to try to become a more responsible thinker and educator. My hope is that I have been able to comply with this on an acceptable level.

To organizations such as the Society for Ontario Free Thinkers, with Kathy and Chris Meidell whose advice, technical support, and friendship has served me well, to the Center for Inquiry, the Council for Secular Humanism, Humanist Canada, and many others, I greatly appreciate the invitations to speak at various events throughout the world.

And to science fiction author Robert Sawyer, my appreciation goes out to you for your advice on authorship and organization.

To Tim Minchin, whose wit and humor have given me and so many others great joy and appreciation, I owe many thanks for the permission to use your song lyrics. Keep up the great work.

To my friend and often debating combatant, Elizabeth McLeod, thank you for all of your support in so many ways as well as the support of your family. You have always given us reason to visit Illinois.

To my dearly departed parents, Marge and Ernest DiCarlo, I owe considerable gratitude and respect for having to put up with such a precocious and self-important know-it-all son. They endured much in my developing years as a young Socratic skeptic. The same may be said of my siblings Brad DiCarlo and Marti Valeriote, who have had to tolerate the inquisitiveness and ponderings of a sometimes all-too-philosophically relentless younger brother. To my brother Mark DiCarlo, whom we best know as 'Mink,' your insight, wit, and encouragement have kept me in this game for longer than I should have sensibly stayed. Your greatest and most enviable gift will always be the fact that you genuinely care about what others think and you make them feel as though they are the most important person in the world.

And finally, to my family, I owe immeasurable thanks and gratitude. To my sons, Jeremy and Matthew, thank you for teaching me more about critical thinking than any book I could ever write. And a personal thanks to Matt for his wonderful photographic work in the book and to Jeremy for his modelling abilities. To my wife, Linda, thank you for your dedication, feedback, and support throughout some very pressing times. When Steven L. Mitchell asked me if I would be able to complete my manuscript for the 2011 release, Linda said to tell him that she would give me all the support needed to do so. And for this I will be forever grateful.

I am sorry if I have neglected to thank anyone who has influenced me in the development and completion of this book. This oversight is due not to lack of appreciation but the inevitable constraints under which my weary brain is influenced.

NOTES

CHAPTER 1. A IS FOR ARGUMENT

1. See, for example, Mighty Magic Tricks at http://www.mightytricks .com/ or "David Blaine's Magic Tricks Revealed!" at http://www.freeinfo society.com/pdfs/misc/david_blaines_magic_revealed.pdf. There are plenty of other sites to consider.

CHAPTER 2. B IS FOR BIASES

1. A study is currently being conducted by James Allan Cheyne and Fred Britton that covers, among other aspects, the reasons behind why atheists, humanists, agnostics, skeptics, and so on, came to be the way they are. I recently received the preliminary findings from the study's authors, and there is quite a similarity among nonbelievers in this regard. Most "conversions" to nonbelief occurred between the ages of sixteen and twenty.

2. Russell A. Barkley, *ADHD: And the Nature of Self-Control* (New York: Guilford Press, 1997). Also see L. Misener, P. Luca, O. Azeke, J. Crosbie, I. Waldman, R. Tannock, W. Roberts, M. Malone, R. Schachar, A. Ickowicz, J. L. Kennedy, and C. L. Barr, "Linkage of the Dopamine Receptor D1 Gene to Attention-Deficit/Hyperactivity Disorder," *Molecular Psychiatry* 9 (2004): 500–509. doi:10.1038/sj.mp.4001440 (published online October 21, 2003). See also Anita Thapar, R. Harrington, and P. McGuffin, "Examining the Comorbidity of ADHD-Related Behaviours and Conduct Problems Using a Twin Study Design," *British Journal of Psychiatry* 179 (2001): 224–29.

3. Sergey Gavrilets and William R. Rice, "Genetic Models of Homosexu-

ality: Generating Testable Predictions," *Proceedings of the Royal Society* 273, no. 1605 (December 2006): 3031–38.

4. Nedalee Thomas, "Deliverance and Exorcism Books," 2007, http://deliveranceandexorcism.com (accessed June 3, 2011).

5. J. D. Watson and F. H. C. Crick, "A Structure for Deoxyribose Nucleic Acid," *Nature* 171 (1953): 737–38.

6. Matt Ridley, *Nature via Nurture: Genes, Experience, and What Makes Us Human* (Toronto: HarperCollins, 2003).

7. David Sapsted, "Mother Jumped to Her Death with Child in Her Arms," *Telegraph*, June 5, 2004, http://www.telegraph.co.uk/news/uknews/1463691/Mother-jumped-to-her-death-with-child-in-her-arms.html (accessed June 3, 2011).

8. Scott Tracey, "Guelph Infanticide Case Goes to Appeal Court," GuelphMercury.com, September 1, 2010, http://www.guelphmercury.com/news/article/315897—guelph-infanticide-case-goes-to-appeal-court (accessed June 13, 2011).

9. Wolfgang Retz, Petra Retz-Junginger, Tillmann Supprian, Johannes Thome, and Michael Rösler, "Association of Serotonin Transporter Promoter Gene Polymorphism with Violence: Relation with Personality Disorders, Impulsivity, and Childhood ADHD Psychopathology," in "Serial and Mass Homicide," special issue, *Behavioral Sciences and the Law* 22, no. 3 (May/June 2004): 415–25.

10. Atsushi Mochizuki, Koji Yahara, Ichizo Kobayashi, and Yoh Iwasa, "Genetic Addiction: Selfish Gene's Strategy for Symbiosis in the Genome," *Genetics* 172 (February 2006): 1309–23.

11. Norman Doidge, *The Brain That Changes Itself* (New York: Penguin, 2007).

12. These are sometimes referred to as the basic eight emotions.

13. A more complete list might include the following: acceptance, amusement, anger, anticipation, apprehension, avarice, awe, calmness, comfort, contentment, confidence, cool, courage, depression, disappointment, disgust, desire, elation, embarrassment, envy, fear, folly, friendship, grief, guilt, glee, gladness, hate, happiness, honor, hope, humility, joy, jealousy, kindness, love, modesty, nervousness, pain, patience, peace, phobia, pity, pride, rage, remorse, repentance, sadness, shame, shyness, sorrow, shock, suffering, surprise, terror, unhappiness, vulnerability, and worry.

14. The term *fan* is an abbreviation for *fanatic*.

15. Robert Sapolsky, "Taming Stress," *Scientific American* 289, no. 3, Sep-

tember 2003, pp. 86–95; and Robert Sapolsky and R. Mitra, "Effects of Enrichment Predominate over Those of Chronic Stress on Fear-Related Behavior in Male Rats," *Stress* 12, no. 4 (2009): 305–12.

16. Anne Moir and David Jessel, *Brain Sex: The Real Difference between Men and Women* (New York: Dell, 1992).

17. M. E. Frederikse, A. Lu, E. Aylward, P. Barta, and G. Pearlson, "Sex Differences in the Inferior Parietal Lobule," *Cerebral Cortex* 9, no. 8 (1999): 896–901.

18. M. L. Collaer and M. Hines, "Human Behavioural Sex Differences: A Role for Gonadal Hormones during Early Development?" *Psychological Bulletin* 118, no. 1 (1995): 55–77.

19. These represent just some of the findings in brain differences among males and females. Plenty of sources are available online to corroborate these differences. See, for example, "Male/Female Brain Differences," Medical Education Online: The Student–Teacher Interface, October 25, 2006, http://www.medicaleducationonline.org/index.php?option=com_content&task=view&id=46&Itemid=69 (accessed June 3, 2011); Lise Eliot, "Girl Brain, Boy Brain? The Two Are Not the Same, but New Work Shows Just How Wrong It Is to Assume That All Gender Differences Are Hardwired," *Scientific American*, September 8, 2009, http://www.scientificamerican.com/article.cfm?id=girl-brain-boy-brain (accessed June 3, 2011); Robin I. M. Dunbar, "Male and Female Brain Evolution Is Subject to Contrasting Selection Pressures in Primates," BMC Biology 5 (2007): 21, doi: 10.1186/1741-7007-5-21 (published online May 10, 2007), http://www.ncbi.nlm.nih.gov/pmc/articles/PMC1876205/ (accessed June 3, 2011); and Carina Dennis, "Brain Development: The Most Important Sexual Organ," Nature 427 (January 29, 2004): 390–92, doi:10.1038/427390a, http://www.nature.com/nature/journal/v427/n6973/full/427390a.html (accessed June 3, 2011).

20. For a more complete description, see Christopher diCarlo, "How Problem Solving and Neurotransmission in the Upper Paleolithic Led to the Emergence and Maintenance of Memetic Equilibrium in Contemporary World Religions," in "Contemporary World Religions," in "Bioculture: Evolutionary Cultural Studies," special evolutionary issue, *Politics and Culture* no. 1 (April 27, 2010). http://www.politicsandculture.org/2010/04/27/how-problem-solving-and-neurotransmission-in-the-upper-paleolithic-led-to-the-emergence-and-maintenance-of-memetic-equilibrium-in-contemporary-world-religions/ (accessed June 3, 2011).

21. Richard Dawkins, *The Selfish Gene* (New York: Oxford University Press, 1976), p. 192.

22. Elizabeth D. George, Kelly A. Bordner, Hani M. Elwafi, and Arthur A. Simen, "Maternal Separation with Early Weaning: A Novel Mouse Model of Early Life Neglect," *BioMed Central Neuroscience* 11 (September 26, 2010): 123.

23. Maude Beauchemin, Berta González-Frankenberger, Julie Tremblay, Phetsamone Vannasing, Eduardo Martínez-Montes, Pascal Belin, Renée Béland, et al., "Mother and Stranger: An Electrophysiological Study of Voice Processing in Newborns," *Cerebral Cortex* (December 13, 2010). doi:10.1093/cercor/bhq242.

24. "Mom's Voice Plays Special Role in Activating Newborn's Brain," Physorg.com, December 16, 2010, http://www.physorg.com/news/2010-12-mom-voice-special-role-newborn.html (accessed June 3, 2011).

25. Ibid.

26. Aryn Baker, "The Taliban: Friend to Education?" *Time*, January 22, 2007, http://www.time.com/time/world/article/0,8599,1581119,00.html (accessed June 3, 2011).

27. Stated by George Wendt as the character Norm Peterson on the US situation comedy *Cheers*.

CHAPTER 3. C IS FOR CONTEXT

1. The original *Dragnet* series starred Jack Webb as Sgt. Friday and first appeared on radio from June 3, 1949, to February 26, 1957. The series then debuted on television (NBC) from December 16, 1951, to August 23, 1959, and from January 12, 1967, to April 16, 1970.

2. Tony Long, "Oct. 13, 1972: Survival Instincts Put to the Test," *Wired*, October 13, 2009, http://www.wired.com/thisdayintech/2009/10/1013 cannibalism-plane-crash-andes/ (accessed June 3, 2011).

3. Fox News, "Andrew Breitbart on *Hanity*: 'This Is Not about Shirley Sherrod,'" July 21, 2010, http://www.foxnews.com/story/0,2933,597324,00 .html (accessed June 3, 2011).

4. Ibid.

5. "Shirley Sherrod: The FULL Video," YouTube video, 43:15, from a speech broadcast in March 2010 on DCTV in DeKalb County, Georgia, posted

by "naacpvideos," July 20, 2010, http://www.youtube.com/watch?v=E9NcCa _KjXk (accessed June 3, 2011).

6. NAACP, "NAACP Statement on the Resignation of Shirley Sherrod," July 20, 2010, http://www.naacp.org/press/entry/naacp-statement-on-the -resignation-of-shirley-sherrod1/ (accessed June 3, 2011).

7. I cannot begin to provide anywhere near the amount of data available. But I would suggest the reader look in the bibliography for further suggestions.

CHAPTER 5. E IS FOR EVIDENCE

1. I think Steven Spielberg did an excellent job in showing how a disturbed mind would attempt to reconcile such a dilemma. The commandant can both be near the woman and have contact with her through occasional beatings while still maintaining the Nazi ideology of hatred for Jews. A consistently demented reconciliation of conflicting beliefs.

2. Carl Sagan, interview by *NOVA*, 1996, http://www.pbs.org/wgbh/ nova/aliens/carlsagan.html (accessed June 6, 2011).

3. Originally published in *Contemporary Review*, January 1877. Reprinted in *Lectures and Essays by the Late William Kingdon Clifford, F.R.S.*, ed. Leslie Stephen and Frederick Pollock, with an introduction by F. Pollock, 2nd ed. (London: Macmillan, 1886), p. 344.

4. From Latin *prōpositiō*, *prōpositiōn*, setting out in words, from *prōpositus*, past participle of *prōpōnere*, to set forth (http://www.bartleby.com).

5. I usually refer to this as: No proposition without presupposition. But they both mean the same thing.

6. This saying has been attributed to Mark Twain, British prime minister Benjamin Disraeli, and Charles Wentworth Dilke.

7. Deborah J. Bennett, *Logic Made Easy* (New York: Norton, 2004), p. 29.

8. Of course, understanding many of the facets of Einstein's theory requires extremely complex forms of mathematics. But the equation itself is quite elegantly and simply stated.

CHAPTER 6. F IS FOR FALLACIES

1. Don Lindsay, "A List of Fallacious Arguments," Don Lindsay Archive, March 15, 2011, http://www.don-lindsay-archive.org/skeptic/arguments.html (accessed June 6, 2011); Bradley Dowden, "Fallacies," Internet Encyclopedia of Philosophy, December 31, 2010, http://www.iep.utm.edu/fallacy/ (accessed June 6, 2011).

2. "Clinton, 'I Did Not Have Sexual Relations with That Woman,'" YouTube video, 0:26, posted by "forquignon," August 30, 2006, http://www.youtube.com/watch?v=KiIP_KDQmXs (accessed June 6, 2011).

3. This echoes Saul of Tarsus, the founder of Christianity, who said, "Do not do as I do, but do as I tell you." Parents effectively do the same with their children sometimes.

4. In Canada, three of the most famous cases of wrongly accused people include Steven Truscott, Guy Paul Morin, and David Milgard.

5. "Jean Chretien 'Face Ad,'" YouTube video, 3:02, posted by "llehman84," October 22, 2008, http://www.youtube.com/watch?v=PikszBkfTHM (accessed June 6, 2011).

6. Havard Gould, "Attack Ad Backfires on Kim Campbell," CBC News, October 15, 1993, http://archives.cbc.ca/clip.asp?IDLan=1&IDClip=12983 &IDDossier=0&IDCat=335&IDCatPa=260 (accessed June 7, 2011).

7. Mike Godwin, "Godwin's Law of Nazi Analogies (and Corollaries)," Electronic Frontier Foundation, January 12, 1995, http://www.eff.org/Net _culture/Folklore/Humor/godwins.law (accessed June 7, 2011).

8. James Randi Educational Foundation, "The Case of the Cottingley Fairies," http://www.randi.org/library/cottingley/index.html (accessed June 6, 2011).

9. From "Fairies, Phantoms, and Fantastic Photographs," Arthur C. Clarke's World of Strange Powers, ITV, presented by Arthur C. Clarke and narrated by Anna Ford, May 22, 1985, season 1, no. 6, at the 8:25 mark: "World of Strange Powers Fantastic Photographs 2 of 3," YouTube video, 7:13, posted by "junmn77," January 21, 2008, http://www.youtube.com/watch?v=Jk6QJJMS3 -U&feature=related (accessed June 6, 2011).

10. Ibid.

11. See Michael Shermer, Why People Believe Weird Things (New York: Henry Holt, 2002).

12. Hands down, Florence Henderson.

13. Physorg.com, "We Believe Experts Who Confirm Our Beliefs," December 13, 2010, http://www.physorg.com/print211474112.html (accessed June 6, 2011).

14. "Homer at Bat," *The Simpsons*, season 3, episode 17, February 20, 1992.

15. Beg the Question: Get It Right, "What Is Begging the Question?" http://begthequestion.info/ (accessed June 6, 2011).

16. The 23 Enigma is actually considered by some to be a corollary of a book called the *Principia Discordia*, which contains the idea that "all things happen in fives, or are divisible by or are multiples of five, or are somehow directly or indirectly appropriate to 5." Also see http://www.ology.org/principia/body.html for further information.

17. I intentionally use the pronoun *her* because, on average, most psychics are female.

18. Obviously, love deals also with relationships, but more specifically the type of love of a partner rather than family, friends, and so forth.

19. JREF staff, "Challenge Info: One Million Dollar Paranormal Challenge," October 30, 3008, http://www.randi.org/site/index.php/1m-challenge.html (accessed June 6, 2011).

20. The USA network broadcasts a detective comedy-drama called *Psych*, which stars James Roday as a crime consultant working for the Santa Barbara Police Department. Roday's character possesses "heightened observational skills" that allow him to help solve cases. This fools people into believing that he possesses true psychic abilities.

21. William Paley, *Natural Theology*, edited with introduction and notes by Matthew D. Eddy and David M. Knight (New York: Oxford University Press, 2006).

22. "The Nose Job," *Seinfeld*, season 3, episode 9, November 21, 1991, written by Peter Mehlman, Seinfeld Scripts, http://www.seinfeldscripts.com/TheNoseJob.html (accessed June 7, 2011).

23. *Dictionary.com*, s.v. "theory," http://dictionary.reference.com/browse/theory (accessed June 7, 2011).

24. "The Parrot Sketch," YouTube video, 5:28, posted by "MontyPython," December 3, 2007, http://www.youtube.com/watch?v=npjOSLCR2hE (accessed June 7, 2011).

25. This example is taken from an old friend and past professor of mine, Bill Hughes.

26. Net Industries, "Euthanasia—Oregon's Euthanasia Law," http://law.jrank.org/pages/6602/Euthanasia-Oregon-s-Euthanasia-Law.html (accessed June 7, 2011).

CHAPTER 7. THE METHOD OF SOCRATES AND THE MODES OF THE ANCIENT SKEPTICS

1. See *Euthyphro, Apology, Crito,* and *Phaedo.*

2. On a personal note, it was during my second semester as an undergraduate student that I took my first philosophy course at the University of Guelph with Professor Jakob Amstutz. We covered "The Apology," and at that point I changed my major from English to philosophy. I am very grateful for having the privilege of learning from such a wonderful and learned man as Jakob, and though I shall never possess either his grace or eloquence I shall try my best to convey the passion and power of this seminal philosophical work.

3. John R. Hale, Jelle Zeilinga de Boer, Jeffrey P. Chanton, and Henry A. Spiller, "Questioning the Delphic Oracle," *Scientific American*, July 15, 2003, p. 67.

4. Plato, "The Apology," in *Readings in Ancient Greek Philosophy: From Thales to Aristotle*, 2nd ed. (Indianapolis, IN: Hackett, 2000), p. 115.

5. Plato, "Apology," p. 116. An interlocutor is anyone engaged in a dialogue or conversation.

6. Ibid., p. 122.

7. Ibid., pp. 129–30.

8. Ibid.

9. Ibid., p. 127.

10. Ibid., pp. 128–29.

11. Ibid., p. 129.

12. June 19, 2001.

13. July 4, 2000.

14. Philip P. Hallie, *Sextus Empiricus: Selections from the Major Writings on Scepticism, Man, and God* (Indianapolis, IN: Hackett, 1985), p. 12.

15. Christopher DiCarlo, "The Roots of Skepticism: Why Ancient Ideas Still Apply Today," *Skeptical Inquirer* 33, no. 3 (May/June 2009): 51–55.

16. These were called *phantasiai kataleptikai*.

17. Hallie, *Sextus Empiricus*, p. 19.

18. William Shakespeare's *Julius Caesar*, act 1, scene 2, Literature Network, http://www.online-literature.com/shakespeare/julius_caesar/3/ (accessed June 8, 2011).

19. Robert M. May, "How Many Species Inhabit the Earth?" *Scientific American* 267, October 1992, pp. 42–48.

20. Thomas Nagel, "What Is It Like to Be a Bat?" *Philosophical Review* 83, no. 4 (October 1974): 435–50; and Thomas Nagel, *The View from Nowhere* (New York: Oxford University Press, 1986).

21. In the first episode of the second season of a situation comedy called *The Big Bang Theory*, reference is made to the Münchhausen Trilemma by a character named Sheldon, who uses it to avoid providing any reason for moving out of an apartment he shares with a friend.

22. In 1988, Terry Gilliam of Monty Python fame made a movie called *The Adventures of Maron Munchausen*, starring Eric Idle, John Neville, and Sarah Polley.

PART 3. ANSWERING THE BIG FIVE: PREAMBLE

1. The technical term for such people is Intrinsic Methodological Naturalists (IMN).

2. The technical term for this group of people is Provisory or Pragmatic Methodological Naturalists (PMN). See Maarten Boudry, Stefaan Blancke, and Johan Braeckman, "How Not to Attack Intelligent Design Creationism: Philosophical Misconceptions about Methodological Naturalism," *Foundations of Science* 15, no. 3 (2010): 227–44, for a very good description of both schools of thought.

3. Russell Blackford, "NAS on the compatibility of Science and Religion," Metamagician and the Hellfire Club, May 3, 2009, http://metamagician3000 .blogspot.com/2009/05/nas-on-compatibility-of-science-and.html (accessed June 8, 2011).

4. J. M. Bennett and C. W. Hollister, *Medieval Europe: A Short History* (New York: McGraw-Hill, 2006), p. 326.

5. Bruce Flamm, "The Columbia University 'Miracle' Study: Flawed and Fraud," *Skeptical Inquirer* 28.5, September/October 2004, Committee for Skep-

tical Inquiry, http://www.csicop.org/si/show/columbia_university_miracle_study_flawed_and_fraud/ (accessed June 8, 2011).

6. *Canadian Press*, "Virgin Mary Statue Removed from Windsor Home," November 6, 2010, TheStar.com, http://www.thestar.com/news/canada/article/887053—virgin-mary-statue-removed-from-windsor-home (accessed June 8, 2011).

7. See Richard White, "Dating Methods in Science: Strata, Fossils and Age of the Earth," Darwiniana and Evolution, April 22, 2011, http://darwiniana.org/datingmethods.htm (accessed June 8, 2011); or Roger C. Wiens, "Radiometric Dating: A Christian Perspective," American Scientific Affiliation, revised 2002, http://www.asa3.org/ASA/resources/wiens.html (accessed June 8, 2011).

CHAPTER 8. WHAT CAN I KNOW?

1. There were nine until we kicked Pluto out of the club.

2. There is a great debate happening in the theoretical physics community regarding such things as superstrings and whether they can explain what their proponents believe they can explain.

3. Personally, I believe that this is not only possible but that such agreement will, in turn, produce the type of global literacy that will lead to a more responsible and equitable management of human and natural resources.

4. You can visit the online version of the RNS at http://www.relationsofnaturalsystems.com.

5. There are many excellent books on the subject of randomness. My favorite at this time is Leonard Mlodinow's *The Drunkard's Walk* (New York: Random House, 2008).

6. George Aghajanian, Benjamin S. Bunney, and Philip S. Holzman, "Patricia Godman-Rakic, 1937–2003," Neuropsychopharmacology 28 (2003): 2218–20, doi:10.1038/sj.npp.1300325, http://www.nature.com/npp/journal/v28/n12/full/1300325a.html (accessed June 8, 2011).

7. Bertrand Russell, "Is There a God?" commissioned but not published by *Illustrated Magazine*, 1952.

CHAPTER 9. WHY AM I HERE?

1. United States Geological Service, "Radio Metric Time Scale," June 13, 2001, http://pubs.usgs.gov/gip/geotime/radiometric.html (accessed June 9, 2011); for a very good Christian old earth account, see Roger C. Wiens, "Radiometric Dating: A Christian Perspective," American Scientific Affiliation, revised 2002, http://www.asa3.org/ASA/resources/wiens.html (accessed June 8, 2011).

2. Ibid.

3. Marcus Chown, "Our World May Be a Giant Hologram," *New Scientist* 2691, January 15, 2009, pp. 24–27.

4. Please refer to Stephen Hawking and Leonard Mlodinow's latest book, *The Grand Design* (New York: Bantam, 2010).

5. A Planck length is $1.616252(81) \times 10^{-35}$ meters. In other words, a really short length.

6. "'A Universe from Nothing' by Lawrence Krauss, AAI 2009," YouTube video, 1:04:52, posted by "richarddawkinsdotnet," October 21, 2009, http://www.youtube.com/watch?v=7ImvlS8PLIo (accessed June 9, 2011).

7. Ibid.

8. Ibid.

9. The term *Khnum* means "the Molder."

10. Holy Bible, King James Version (Nashville: Royal Publisher, 1971).

11. University of Calgary, "Canada's First Nations," 2002, quoting James Axtell, ed., "The Indian Peoples of Eastern America: A Documentary History of the Sexes" (Oxford: Oxford University Press, 1981), http://www.ucalgary.ca/applied_history/tutor/firstnations/earth.html (accessed June 9, 2011).

12. Stanford Encyclopedia of Philosophy, "Ontological Arguments," first published February 8, 1996, substantively revised July 12, 2007, http://plato.stanford.edu/entries/ontological-arguments/ (accessed June 9, 2011).

13. In this disjunct, U refers to the Universe; i refers to intended; v refers to the logical notation "or"; and the tilde ($\sim$) is the negation sign.

14. Christopher DiCarlo, "The Co-Evolution of Consciousness and Language and the Development of Memetic Equilibrium," *Journal of Consciousness Exploration and Research* 1, no. 4 (2010): 410–28. This article provides a more complete analysis behind the neurological basis of supernatural beliefs.

CHAPTER 10. WHAT AM I?

1. For further reference regarding the biochemical origins of life, that is, life from nonlife, please see the Harvard University Origins of Life Initiative at http://origins.harvard.edu/.

2. Upon hearing this at a conference, Dr. Rob Buckman said to me that it must have happened on a Saturday night.

3. Carl Zimmer, *Evolution: The Triumph of an Idea* (New York: Harper-Collins, 2001).

4. For a concise account of migratory trends during this time, see Christopher DiCarlo, "We Are All African! Can a Scientific Understanding of Our Commonality Save Us?" *Free Inquiry* 30, no. 4 (2010): 18–22.

5. Much of this information is taken with permission from Christopher DiCarlo, "We Are All African! Can a Scientific Understanding of Our Commonality Save Us?" *Free Inquiry* 30, no. 4 (2010): 18–22.

6. The term *hominin* refers more strictly to human ancestry distinguishing bipedal activity, whereas *hominid* includes all great apes (including humans). So *Australopithecus, Ardipithecus, Kenyanthropus,* and *Homo* would fall into the classification (tribe) of hominin. See an excellent article on this distinction: Lee Berge, "Viewpoint: Is It Time to Revise the System of Scientific Naming?" *National Geographic,* December 4, 2001, http://news.nationalgeographic.com/news/2001/12/1204_hominin_id.html (accessed June 9, 2011).

7. NZEDGE.com, "Allan Wilson: Revolutionary Evolutionist," http://www.nzedge.com/heroes/wilson.html (accessed June 9, 2011).

8. Geoffrey Carr, "The Proper Study of Mankind," *Economist,* December 20, 2005, http://www.economist.com/node/5299220 (accessed June 9, 2011).

9. Spencer Wells, "The Genographic Project," National Geographic Society, https://genographic.nationalgeographic.com/genographic/index.html (accessed June 14, 2011).

10. Carr, "Proper Study of Mankind."

11. William D. Hamilton, "The Evolution of Altruistic Behavior," *American Naturalist* 97 (1963): 354–56.

12. Dennis Drayna, "Founder Mutations," *Scientific American,* September 26, 2005, p. 85.

13. Whether or not it arose unassisted by latent extraterrestrial simple biotic forms.

14. David Hume, *Essays on Suicide and the Immortality of the Soul*, unauthorized ed., 1783, also available at http://ethics.sandiego.edu/Books/Hume/Essays/Hume_Essays_Suicide.htm (accessed June 14, 2011).

15. Ibid.

16. See Daniel C. Dennett, *Consciousness Explained* (Boston: Little, Brown, 1991), p. 36.

17. Either the cartoon or the movies.

CHAPTER 11. HOW SHOULD I BEHAVE?

1. Christopher DiCarlo and John Teehan, "On the Naturalistic Fallacy: A Conceptual Basis for Evolutionary Ethics," *Evolutionary Psychology* 2 (2004): 32–46; and Sam Harris, *The Moral Landscape* (New York: Free Press, 2010).

2. Andrew Whiten and Christophe Boesch, "The Cultures of Chimpanzees," *Scientific American*, January 2001, pp. 60–67.

3. For example, in Bonobo cultures there is less dimorphism and more cooperation among males and females. See Frans de Waal, *Our Inner Ape* (New York: Penguin, 2005).

4. Steven Rose, "Terms of Endowment," review of *Y: The Descent of Man*, by Steve Jones, *Guardian*, September 14, 2002, http://www.guardian.co.uk/books/2002/sep/14/featuresreviews.guardianreview18 (accessed June 14, 2011).

5. The official names of these two schools of thought are dualism and monism.

6. Mike McIntyre, "Vincent Li Found Not Criminally Responsible for Murder," *Winnipeg Free Press*, March 5, 2009, http://www.winnipegfreepress .com/breakingnews/Vincent-Li-found-not-criminally-responsible—40781652 .html (accessed June 14, 2011).

7. "Mother Who Killed Son on Subway Dies of Injuries," CBC News, November 10, 2000, http://www.cbc.ca/news/canada/story/2000/08/20/subway_000820.html (accessed June 14, 2011).

8. Death Penalty Information Center, "Intellectual Disability and the Death Penalty," last updated February 23, 2011, http://www.deathpenaltyinfo .org/intellectual-disability-and-death-penalty (accessed June 9, 2011).

9. Leonard Mlodinow, *The Drunkard's Walk* (New York: Vintage Books, 2008).

10. Ibid., pp. 210–11.

11. There are many different formulations of this ethical principle. For a good overview, see, Harry J. Gensler, "A Short Essay on the Golden Rule," Golden Rule, http://www.jcu.edu/philosophy/gensler/goldrule.htm (accessed June 9, 2011).

12. Patheos, "Hinduism Principles of Moral Thought and Action," 2011, http://www.patheos.com/Library/Hinduism/Ethics-Morality-Community/Principles-of-Moral-Thought-and-Action?offset=1&max=1 (accessed June 9, 2011).

13. It should be noted that neither the idea of *karma* (reward/punishment based on actions in past lives) nor *samsara* (transmigration of souls) appears in the original writings of Hinduism known as the *Vedas*. Instead, they appear in commentaries called the *Upanishads*, which are philosophical commentaries by Hindu sages developed from approximately 300 BCE to 100 CE.

14. Radio Somalia, "29a. Al Quran Surah 29 and Muslims, Christians and Jews Have the Same Allah (Arabic)," June 2011, http://sites.google.com/site/radiosomalia/muslims-christians-and-jews-have-the-same-allah (accessed June 9, 2011).

15. See R. M. Hare, *Freedom and Reason* (London: Oxford University Press, 1963); Jeff Wattles, *Golden Rule* (New York: Oxford University Press, 1996); and Harry J. Gensler, *Ethics: A Contemporary Introduction* (New York: Routledge, 1998).

16. Paul McKenna, "How to Order the Golden Rule Poster," Scarboro Missions, http://www.scarboromissions.ca/Golden_rule/poster_order.php (accessed June 9, 2011).

17. Some definitions from TeachingValues.com, "The Universality of the Golden Rule in the World Religions," 2009, http://www.teachingvalues.com/goldenrule.html (accessed June 9, 2011).

18. Ryan McKay, Charles Efferson, Harvey Whitehouse, and Ernst Fehr, "Wrath of God: Religious Primes and Punishment," *Proceedings of the Royal Society B*, November 24, 2010. doi:10.1098/rspb.2010.2125.

CHAPTER 12. WHAT IS TO COME OF ME?

1. Physorg.com, "The New 'Epigenetics': Poor Nutrition in the Womb Causes Permanent Genetic Changes in the Offspring," April 13, 2009,

http://www.physorg.com/news158856122.html (accessed June 10, 2011). See also Qi Fu, Xing Yu, Christopher W. Callaway, Robert H. Lane, and Robert A. McKnight, "Epigenetics: Intrauterine Growth Retardation (IUGR) Modifies the Histone Code along the Rat Hepatic IGF-1 Gene," *Federation of American Societies for Experimental Biology Journal* 23, no. 8 (2009): 2438–49. doi:10.1096/fj.08-124768.

2. Ibid.

3. Ibid.

4. John Rogers, "Thomas Hobbes: Balancing Dominion and Liberty," BBC, last modified February 17, 2011, http://www.bbc.co.uk/history/british/civil_war_revolution/hobbes_01.shtml (accessed June 10, 2011).

5. Center for Complexity in Health, "Center Updates," http://cch .ashtabula.kent.edu/ (accessed June 10, 2011).

6. See, for example, the New England Complex Systems Institute, the Santa Fe Institute, the Northwestern Institute on Complex Systems (NICO), Centro de Ciencias de la Complejidad, UNAM, the Complexity Complex at the University of Warwick, the Center for Social Dynamics & Complexity (CSDC) at Arizona State University, the Southampton Institute for Complex Systems Simulation, the Center for the Study of Complex Systems at the University of Michigan, the Center for Complexity in Health at Kent State University, the Center for Complex Systems and Brain Sciences at Florida Atlantic University, the ARC Centre for Complex Systems–Australia, the Center for Social Complexity at George Mason University, the York Centre for Complex Systems Analysis at University of York, and the Complexity Science Group at University of Calgary.

7. See Duncan MacDougall, "Hypothesis concerning Soul Substance Together with Experimental Evidence of the Existence of Such Substance," *Journal of the American Society for Psychical Research* 1, no. 5 (May 1907): 237–75.

8. These are the final lines stated by character Roy Batty (played by actor Rutger Hauer) in the 1982 movie *Blade Runner*, directed by Ridley Scott.

9. Plato, *The Last Days of Socrates* (Penguin: New York, 1984), p. 75.

10. See Christopher DiCarlo, "How Problem Solving and Neurotransmission in the Upper Paleolithic Led to the Emergence and Maintenance of Memetic Equilibrium in Contemporary World Religions," in "Contemporary World Religions" in "Bioculture: Evolutionary Cultural Studies," special evolu-

tionary issue, *Politics and Culture* no. 1 (April 27, 2010), http://www.politics
andculture.org/2010/04/27/how-problem-solving-and-neurotransmission-in
-the-upper-paleolithic-led-to-the-emergence-and-maintenance-of-memetic
-equilibrium-in-contemporary-world-religions/ (accessed June 3, 2011).

11. Pew Research Center's Forum on Religion and Public Life, "Religion
among the Millennials: Less Religiously Active Than Older Americans, but
Fairly Traditional in Other Ways" [Pew Poll], February 17, 2010, http://pew
forum.org/Age/Religion-Among-the-Millennials.aspx (accessed June 10, 2011).

12. Albert L. Winseman, "Eternal Destinations: Americans Believe in
Heaven, Hell," Gallup, May 25, 2004, http://www.gallup.com/poll/11770/
Eternal-Destinations-Americans-Believe-Heaven-Hell.aspx (accessed June 10,
2011).

13. Ronald Zajac, "Most Miracles of Medical Variety, Historian Tells Hospital's AGM," *Recorder & Times*, 2010, http://www.recorder.ca/Article
Display.aspx?archive=true&e=1626114 (accessed June 10, 2011).

14. Iona McCleery, review of *Medical Miracles: Doctors, Saints, and Healing
in the Modern World*, by Jacalyn Duffin, *New England Journal of Medicine* 360
(2009): 2261–62.

15. Zajac, "Most Miracles of Medical Variety, Historian Tells Hospital's
AGM."

16. Ibid.

17. Ibid.

18. FunnyPictures.net.au, "Religious Figures in Food," March 23, 2009,
http://www.funnypictures.net.au/religious-imagery/ (accessed June 10, 2011).

19. Josef Hebert, "US Diplomat Holbrooke in Critical Condition after
Long Surgery," *Guelph [Ontario] Mercury*, December 13, 2010, p. B9.

20. Ibid.

21. See DiCarlo, "How Problem Solving and Neurotransmission in the
Upper Paleolithic"; Christopher DiCarlo, "The Co-Evolution of Consciousness
and Language and the Development of Memetic Equilibrium," *Journal of Con-
sciousness Exploration and Research* 1, no. 4 (2010): 410–28; Pascal Boyer, *Reli-
gion Explained: The Evolutionary Origins of Religious Thought* (New York: Basic
Books, 2001); Scott Atran, *In Gods We Trust: The Evolutionary Landscape of
Religion* (New York: Oxford University Press, 2002); Lionel Tiger and Michael
McGuire, *God's Brain* (Amherst, NY: Prometheus Books, 2010).

22. Personally, the funniest depiction of an afterlife for me comes from

Demetri Martin's television show *Important Things*, where people must endure the bad electric guitar solos of an angry-looking clown for eternity. In this support group for NDE survivors, all members eventually realize the commonality of their experience and go on to describe in great horror how much they now fear death.

23. Winseman, "Eternal Destinations: Americans Believe in Heaven, Hell."

24. Elisabeth Kübler-Ross, *Death and Dying* (New York: Simon and Schuster, 1969).

25. Raymond Moody, *Life after Life: The Investigation of a Phenomenon: Survival of Bodily Death* (San Francisco: Harper, 2001).

26. See Near-Death Experiences and the Afterlife, http://www.near -death.com (accessed June 10, 2011).

27. Horizon Research Foundation, "Human Consciousness Project," http://www.horizonresearch.org/main_nav_pages.php?cat_id=10 (accessed June 14, 2011).

28. Ibid.

CONCLUSION

1. See TimMinchin.com, "Videos," http://www.timminchin.com/media/ (accessed June 10, 2011).

2. See "Global Warming vs. Congressmen of the US," posted by "SoLiOZuZ," Ninja Forums, April 5, 2009, http://www.theninjaforums .com/showthread.php?t=7934 (accessed June 10, 2011).

3. Ron Shachar, Tülin Erdem, Keisha M. Cutright, and Gavan J. Fitzsimons, "Brands: The Opiate of the Nonreligious Masses?" *Marketing Science* 30, no. 1 (January–February 2011): 92–110. doi:10.1287/mksc.1100.0591.

4. Glenn Weiser, "What Does the President Believe?" October 28, 2004, http://www.celticguitarmusic.com/Mland_Rapture.htm (accessed June 10, 2011).

5. Ibid.

6. Beliefnet, http://www.beliefnet.com (accessed June 10, 2011).

7. Fans of Family Radio Inc., "Judgment Day—May 21, 2011," http://www.wecanknow.com (accessed June 10, 2011).

8. Leon Festinger, Henry Riecken, and Stanley Schachter, *When Prophecy*

Fails: A Social and Psychological Study of a Modern Group That Predicted the Destruction of the World (New York: Harper-Torchbooks, 1956).

9. Christopher DiCarlo, "The Veneer of Tolerance: The Covert 'Ism' against Unbelievers," *Secular World* 16, no. 4 (2010): 15–24.

10. BrainyQuote, "H. L. Mencken Quotes," http://www.brainyquote.com/quotes/quotes/h/hlmencke101720.html (accessed June 10, 2011).

BIBLIOGRAPHY

Alper, Matthew. *The "God" Part of the Brain*. New York: Rogue Press, 2001.

Amos, William, and Andrea Manica. "Global Genetic Positioning: Evidence for Early Human Population Centers in Coastal Habits." *Proceedings of the National Academy of Sciences* 103, no. 3 (2006): 820–24.

Atran, Scott. *In Gods We Trust: The Evolutionary Landscape of Religion*. New York: Oxford University Press, 2002.

Aubert, Maxime, Sue O'Connor, Malcolm McCulloch, Graham Mortimer, Alan Watchman, and Marc Richer-LaFlèche. "Uranium-Series Dating Rock Art in East Timor." *Journal of Archaeological Science* 34, no. 6 (June 2007): 991–96.

Barnes, Jonathan, ed. *The Complete Works of Aristotle*. Rev. Oxford trans. 2 vols. Princeton, NJ: Princeton University Press, 1984. [See "De Interpretatione" and "Prior Analytics."]

Barnett, Bronwyn. "Genetics May Help Solve Mysteries of Human Evolution." Stanford News Service, February 19, 2003. http://news.stanford.edu/news/2003/february26/aaasklein-226.html.

Bar-Yosef, Ofer, and David Pilbeam, eds. *The Geography of Neandertals and Modern Humans in Europe and the Greater Mediterranean*. Peabody Museum Bulletin 8. Cambridge, MA: Harvard University, Peabody Museum Press, 2000.

Beauchemin, Maude, Berta González-Frankenberger, Julie Tremblay, Phetsamone Vannasing, Eduardo Martínez-Montes, Pascal Belin, Renée Béland, et al. "Mother and Stranger: An Electrophysiological Study of Voice Processing in Newborns." *Cerebral Cortex* (December 13, 2010). doi: 10.1093/cercor/bhq242.

Behar, Doron M., Saharon Rosset, Jason Blue-Smith, Oleg Balanovsky, Shay

Tzur, David Comas, R. John Mitchell, et al. "The Genographic Project Public Participation Mitochondrial DNA Database." *Public Library of Science Genetics* 3 no. 9 (2007): e104. doi:10.1371/journal.pgen.0030104.

Bennett, Deborah J. *Logic Made Easy.* New York: W. W. Norton, 2004.

Bennett, J. M., and C. W. Hollister. *Medieval Europe: A Short History.* New York: McGraw-Hill, 2006.

Berger, Lee. "Viewpoint: Is It Time to Revise the System of Scientific Naming?" December 4, 2001. http://news.nationalgeographic.com/news/2001/12/1204_hominin_id.html.

Bolton, Brian, John T. Chibnall, Michael A. Cerullo, and Joseph M. Jeral. "God, Science, and Intercessory Prayer." *Archives of Internal Medicine* 162, no. 12 (2002): 1422–23.

Boudry, Maarten, Stefaan Blancke, and Johan Braeckman. "How Not to Attack Intelligent Design Creationism: Philosophical Misconceptions about Methodological Naturalism." *Foundations of Science* 15, no. 3 (2010): 227–44.

Boyer, Pascal. *Religion Explained: The Evolutionary Origins of Religious Thought.* New York: Basic Books, 2001.

Brown, Andrew. "I Wanted to Show How Niceness Evolves." Interview with David Sloan Wilson. *Guardian*, July 24, 2003. http://www.guardian.co.uk/science/2003/jul/24/scienceinterviews.research.

Canadian Institute for Stress. 2011. http://www.stresscanada.org/research.htm.

Cann, R. L., M. Stoneking, and A. C. Wilson. "Mitochondrial DNA and Human Evolution." *Nature* 325 (January 1, 1987): 31–36. doi:10.1038/325031a0.

Carr, Geoffrey. "The Proper Study of Mankind." *Economist*, December 20, 2005. http://www.economist.com/node/5299220.

Chown, Marcus. "Our World May Be a Giant Hologram." *New Scientist*, no. 2691 (January 15, 2009): 24–27.

Collaer, M. L., and M. Hines. "Human Behavioural Sex Differences: A Role for Gonadal Hormones during Early Development?" *Psychological Bulletin* 118, no. 1 (1995): 55–77.

Darwin, Charles. *The Illustrated Origin of Species.* Abridged and introduced by Richard Leakey. New York: Hill and Wang, 1982.

Davis, H. "Prediction and Preparation: Pavlovian Implications of Research Animals Discriminating among Humans." *Institute for Laboratory Animal Research Journal* 43, no. 1 (2002): 19–26.

Davis, H., and R. Perusse. "Numerical Competence in Animals: Definitional Issues, Current Evidence, and a New Research Agenda." *Behavioral and Brain Sciences* 11 (1988): 561–615.

Dawkins, Richard. *The Selfish Gene.* New York: Oxford University Press, 1989.

Deacon, Terrence W. *The Symbolic Species: The Co-Evolution of Language and the Brain.* New York: W. W. Norton, 1997.

Dennett, Daniel C. *Consciousness Explained.* Boston: Little, Brown, 1991.

de Waal, Frans. *Our Inner Ape.* New York: Penguin, 2005.

DiCarlo, Christopher. "The Co-Evolution of Consciousness and Language and the Development of Memetic Equilibrium." *Journal of Consciousness Exploration and Research* 1, no. 4 (2010): 410–28.

———. "Critical Notice: A Review of Anthony O'Hear's *Beyond Evolution: Human Nature and the Limits of Evolutionary Explanation.*" *Biology and Philosophy* 16, no. 1 (2001): 117–30.

———. "The Evolution of Morality." *Humanist in Canada*, no. 143 (2002–2003): 12–19.

———. "How Problem Solving and Neurotransmission in the Upper Paleolithic Led to the Emergence and Maintenance of Memetic Equilibrium in Contemporary World Religions." In "Contemporary World Religions." In "Bioculture: Evolutionary Cultural Studies." Special Issue. *Politics and Culture*, no. 1 (April 27, 2010). http://www.politicsandculture.org/2010/04/27/how-problem-solving-and-neurotransmission-in-the-upper-paleolithic-led-to-the-emergence-and-maintenance-of-memetic-equilibrium-in-contemporary-world-religions/.

———. "The Influence of Selection Pressures and Secondary Epigenetic Rules on the Cognitive Development of Specific Forms of Reasoning." *Journal of Consciousness Studies: Consciousness Research Abstracts* (2000): 137.

———. "The Roots of Skepticism: Why Ancient Ideas Still Apply Today." *Skeptical Inquirer* 33, no. 3 (2009): 51–55.

———. "The Veneer of Tolerance: The Covert 'Ism' against Unbelievers." *Secular World* 16, no. 4 (2010): 15–24.

———. "We Are All African! Can a Scientific Understanding of Our Commonality Save Us?" *Free Inquiry* 30, no. 4 (2010): 18–22.

DiCarlo, Christopher, and John Teehan. "On the Naturalistic Fallacy: A Conceptual Basis for Evolutionary Ethics." *Evolutionary Psychology: An International Journal of Evolutionary Approaches to Psychology and Behavior* 2 (2004): 32–46.

DiRienzo, A., and A. C. Wilson. "Branching Pattern in the Evolutionary Tree for Human Mitochondrial DNA." *Proceedings of the National Academy of Sciences* 88 (1991): 1597–1601.

Doidge, Norman. *The Brain That Changes Itself.* New York: Penguin, 2007.

Drayna, Dennis. "Founder Mutations." *Scientific American*, September 26, 2005. http://www.scientificamerican.com/article.cfm?id=founder-mutations.

Dunbar, Robin. *Grooming, Gossip, and Language.* Cambridge, MA: Harvard University Press, 1998.

Festinger, Leon, Henry Riecken, and Stanley Schachter. *When Prophecy Fails: A Social and Psychological Study of a Modern Group That Predicted the Destruction of the World.* New York: Harper-Torchbooks, 1956.

Frederikse, M. E., A. Lu, E. Aylward, P. Barta, and G. Pearlson. "Sex Differences in the Inferior Parietal Lobule." *Cerebral Cortex* 9, no. 8 (1999): 896–901.

Gavrilets, Sergey, and William R. Rice. "Genetic Models of Homosexuality: Generating Testable Predictions." *Proceedings of the Royal Society* 273, no. 1605 (December 2006): 3031–38.

Genographic Project. 2011. https://genographic.nationalgeographic.com/genographic/index.html.

George, Elizabeth D., Kelly A. Bordner, Hani M. Elwafi, and Arthur A. Simen. "Maternal Separation with Early Weaning: A Novel Mouse Model of Early Life Neglect." *BioMed Central Neuroscience* 11 (September 26, 2010): 123. doi:10.1186/1471-2202-11-123.

Goodman, Felix. *The Evolution and Function of Cognition.* Mahwah, NJ: Lawrence Erlbaum, 2003.

Grine, F. E., R. M. Bailey, K. Harvati, R. P. Nathan, A. G. Morris, G. M. Henderson, I. Ribot, and A. W. G. Pike. "Late Pleistocene Human Skull from Hofmeyr, South Africa, and Modern Human Origins." *Science* 315, no. 5809 (January 2007): 226–29. doi:10.1126/science.1136294.

Hale, John R., Jelle Zeilinga de Boer, Jeffrey P. Chanton, and Henry A. Spiller. "Questioning the Delphic Oracle." *Scientific American*, July 15, 2003. http://www.scientificamerican.com/article.cfm?id=questioning-the-delphic-o.

Hallie, Philip P. *Sextus Empiricus: Selections from the Major Writings on Scepticism, Man, and God.* Indianapolis, IN: Hackett Publishing, 1985.

Hamilton, W. D. "The Evolution of Altruistic Behavior." *American Naturalist* 97 (1963): 354–56.

Hamm, Robert M. "No Effect of Intercessory Prayer Has Been Proven." *Archives of Internal Medicine* 160, no. 12 (2000): 1872–73.

Hammerschmidt, Dale E. "Ethical and Practical Problems in Studying Prayer." *Archives of Internal Medicine* 160, no. 12 (2000): 1874–75.

Hare, R. M. *Freedom and Reason.* London: Oxford University Press, 1963.

Harris, Sam. *The Moral Landscape.* New York: Free Press, 2010.

Hawking, Stephen, and Leonard Mlodinow. *The Grand Design.* New York: Bantam Books, 2010.

Hebert, Josef. "U.S. Diplomat Holbrooke in Critical Condition after Long Surgery." *Guelph [Ontario] Mercury,* December 13, 2010, p. B9.

Heminway, John, and Michelle Nicholasen, producers. "The Mind's Big Bang" [episode 6]. *Evolution* [series]. WGBH, Public Broadcasting Service, 2001.

"Homo Sapiens Get Smart in Africa." *All Things Considered.* National Public Radio. January 10, 2002. http://www.npr.org/programs/atc/features/2002/jan/modernhumans/020110.modernhumans.html.

Hume, David. *Essays on Suicide and the Immortality of the Soul.* Unauthorized ed. 1783.

———. *An Inquiry concerning Human Understanding.* New York: Macmillan, 1989.

Jakobsson, Mattias, Sonja W. Scholz, Paul Scheet, J. Raphael Gibbs, Jenna M. VanLiere, Hon-Chung Fung, Zachary A. Szpiech, et al. "Genotype, Haplotype, and Copy-Number Variation in Worldwide Human Populations." *Nature* 451 (February 21, 2008): 998–1003. doi:10.1038/nature06742.

Jerison, Harry. *Brain Size and the Evolution of Mind.* James Arthur Lecture Series on the Evolution of the Human Brain. No. 59. New York: American Museum of Natural History, 1991.

Johanson, Donald, and Maitland Edey. *Lucy: The Beginnings of Humankind.* New York: Simon and Schuster, 1981.

Karis, Robert, and Dirk Karis. "Intercessory Prayer." *Archives of Internal Medicine* 160, no. 12 (2000): 1870.

Kellert, Stephen R., and E. O. Wilson, eds. *The Biophilia Hypothesis.* Washington, DC: Island Press, 1993.

Kübler-Ross, Elisabeth. *Death and Dying.* New York: Simon and Schuster, 1969.

Kurzban, R., and S. Neuberg. "Managing Ingroup and Outgroup Relationships." In *The Handbook of Evolutionary Psychology,* edited by D. Buss, 653–75. Hoboken, NJ: Wiley, 2005.

Leakey, Richard. *The Origin of Humankind.* New York: Basic Books, 1994.

Levitt, Steven, and Stephen J. Dubner. *Freakonomics: A Rogue Economist Explores the Hidden Side of Everything.* New York: William Morrow/HarperCollins, 2005.

Lewis, Ricki. "Human Origins from Afar: Sands and Sediments in One Corner of Ethiopia Provide a Time Machine to Revisit Whence We Came." *Scientist* 18, no. 7 (April 12, 2004): 18–22.

Lieberman, P. *The Biology and Evolution of Language.* Cambridge, MA: Harvard University Press, 1984.

———. *On the Origins of Language: An Introduction into the Evolution of Human Speech.* New York: Macmillan, 1975.

Linz, Bodo, François Balloux, Yoshan Moodley, Andrea Manica, Hua Liu, Phillippe Roumagnac, et al. "An African Origin for the Intimate Association between Humans and *Helicobacter pylori.*" *Nature* 445, no. 7130 (February 22, 2007): 915–18.

Loefler, I. "Health, Science, and Religion in Contemporary American Culture." *Mayo Clinic Proceedings* 78, no. 7 (July 1, 2003): 893–95.

Lumsden, Charles L., and E. O. Wilson. *Genes, Mind, and Culture.* Cambridge, MA: Harvard University Press, 1981.

MacDougall, Duncan. "Hypothesis concerning Soul Substance Together with Experimental Evidence of the Existence of Such Substance." *Journal of the American Society for Psychical Research* 1, no. 5 (May 1907): 237–75.

Manica, Andrea, William Amos, François Balloux, and Tsunehiko Hanihara. "The Effect of Ancient Population Bottlenecks on Human Phenotypic Variation." *Nature* 448 (July 19, 2007): 346–48.

May, Robert M. "How Many Species Inhabit the Earth?" *Scientific American* 267 (October 1992): 42–48.

McCleery, Iona. Review of *Medical Miracles: Doctors, Saints, and Healing in the Modern World,* by Jacalyn Duffin. *New England Journal of Medicine* 360 (2009): 2261–62.

McCrone, John. "Fired Up." *New Scientist* 166, no. 2239 (May 20, 2000). http://www.dichotomistic.com/mind_readings_fire.html.

McKay, Ryan, Charles Efferson, Harvey Whitehouse, and Ernst Fehr. "Wrath of God: Religious Primes and Punishment." *Proceedings of the Royal Society B.* November 24, 2010. doi:10.1098/rspb.2010.2125.

Mellars, Paul. "Going East: New Genetic and Archaeological Perspectives on the Modern Human Colonization of Eurasia." *Science* 313, no. 5788 (August 11, 2006): 796–800.

Mlodinow, Leonard. *The Drunkard's Walk: How Randomness Rules Our Lives.* New York: Random House, 2008.

Mochizuki, Atsushi, Koji Yahara, Ichizo Kobayashi, and Yoh Iwasa. "Genetic Addiction: Selfish Gene's Strategy for Symbiosis in the Genome." *Genetics* 172 (February 2006): 1309–23.

Moir, Anne, and David Jessel. *Brain Sex: The Real Difference between Men and Women.* New York: Dell, 1992.

Moodley, Yoshan, Bodo Linz, Yoshio Yamaoka, Helen M. Windsor, Sebastien Breurec, Jeng-Yih Wu, Ayas Maady, et al. "The Peopling of the Pacific from a Bacterial Perspective." *Science* 323, no. 5913 (2009): 527–30.

Moody, Raymond. *Life after Life: The Investigation of a Phenomenon: Survival of Bodily Death.* San Francisco: Harper, 2001.

Nagel, Thomas. *The View from Nowhere.* New York: Oxford University Press, 1986.

———. "What Is It Like to Be a Bat?" *Philosophical Review* 83, no. 4 (October 1974): 435–50.

News Briefs. *Archaeology* 55, no. 3 (May/June 2002). http://www.archaeology.org/0205/newsbriefs/index.html.

Olsen, Steve. *Mapping Human History.* New York: Houghton Mifflin, 2002.

Paley, William. *Natural Theology.* Edited with introduction and notes by Matthew D. Eddy and David M. Knight. New York: Oxford University Press, 2006.

Pande, Prakash N. "Does Prayer Need Testing?" *Archives of Internal Medicine* 160, no. 12 (2000): 1873–74.

Plato. "The Apology." In *Readings in Ancient Greek Philosophy: From Thales to Aristotle.* 2nd ed. Indianapolis, IN: Hackett, 2000.

Price, John M. "Does Prayer Really Set One Apart?" *Archives of Internal Medicine* 160, no. 12 (2000): 1873.

Retz, Wolfgang, Petra Retz-Junginger, Tillmann Supprian, Johannes Thome, and Michael Rösler. "Association of Scrotonin Transporter Promoter Gene Polymorphism with Violence: Relation with Personality Disorders, Impulsivity, and Childhood ADHD Psychopathology." In "Serial and Mass Homicide." Special Issue. *Behavioral Sciences and the Law* 22, no. 3 (May/June 2004): 415–25.

Ridley, Matt. *Nature via Nurture: Genes, Experience, and What Makes Us Human.* Toronto: HarperCollins, 2003.

Romero, G., A. Manica, J. Goudet, L. L. Handley, and F. Balloux. "How Accurate Is the Current Picture of Human Genetic Variation?" *Heredity* 102 (2009): 120–26.

Rosner, Fred. "Therapeutic Efficacy of Prayer." *Archives of Internal Medicine* 160, no. 12 (2000): 1875.

Sapolsky, Robert. "Taming Stress." *Scientific American* 289, no. 3, September 2003, pp. 86–95.

Sapolsky, Robert, and R. Mitra. "Effects of Enrichment Predominate over Those of Chronic Stress on Fear-Related Behavior in Male Rats." *Stress* 12, no. 4 (2009): 305–12.

Sarich, V. M., and A. C. Wilson. "Immunological Time Scale for Hominid Evolution." *Science* 158 (1967): 1200–1203.

Shachar, Ron, Tülin Erdem, Keisha M. Cutright, and Gavan J. Fitzsimons. "Brands: The Opiate of the Nonreligious Masses?" *Marketing Science* 30, no. 1 (January–February 2011): 92–110. doi:10.1287/mksc.1100.0591.

Sharp, Shane. "How Does Prayer Help Manage Emotions?" *Social Psychology Quarterly* 73 (2010): 417–37.

Shermer, Michael. *Why People Believe Weird Things.* New York: Henry Holt, 2002.

Sloan, Richard P., and Emilia Bagiella. "Data without a Prayer." *Archives of Internal Medicine* 160, no. 12 (2000): 1870.

Smithsonian Institution Human Origins Program. "What Does It Mean to Be Human?" 2011. http://anthropology.si.edu/humanorigins/ha/a_tree.html.

Stephen, Leslie, and Frederick Pollock, eds. *Lectures and Essays by the Late William Kingdon Clifford, F.R.S.* 2nd ed. London: Macmillan, 1886.

Sylvester, Robert. "How Emotions Affect Learning." *Education Leadership* 52, no. 2 (October 1994): 60–65.

Tattersall, Ian. *Becoming Human: Evolution and Human Uniqueness.* New York: Harcourt Brace, 1997.

———. "Once We Were Not Alone." In "New Look at Human Evolution." Special issue. *Scientific American*, June 2003, pp. 20–27.

———. "Out of Africa Again . . . and Again?" In "New Look at Human Evolution." Special issue. *Scientific American*, June 2003, pp. 38–45.

Van der Does, Willem. "A Randomized, Controlled Trial of Prayer?" *Archives of Internal Medicine* 160, no. 12 (2000): 1871–72.

Vincent, J. D. *The Biology of Emotions.* Cambridge, MA: Basil Blackwell, 1990.

Wade, Nicholas. "Geneticists Link Modern Humans to Single Band out of Africa." *New York Times*, May 12, 2005. http://www.nytimes.com/2005/05/12/science/12cnd-migrate.html.

Waterhouse, William C. "Is It Prayer, or Is It Parity?" *Archives of Internal Medicine* 160, no. 12 (2000): 1875.

Watson J. D. and F. H. C. Crick. "A Structure for Deoxyribose Nucleic Acid." *Nature* 171 (1953): 737–38.

Wattles, Jeff. *The Golden Rule.* New York: Oxford University Press, 1996.

White, Tim D., Berhane Asfaw, David DeGusta, Henry Gilbert, Gary D. Richards, Gen Suwa, and F. Clark Howell. "Pleistocene *Homo sapiens* from Middle Awash, Ehtiopia." *Nature* 423 (June 12, 2003): 742–47.

Whiten, Andrew. "Social Complexity and Social Intelligence." *Novartis Foundation Symposium* 233 (2000): 185–96.

Whiten, Andrew, and Christophe Boesch. "The Cultures of Chimpanzees." *Scientific American,* January 2001, pp. 60–67.

Wilson, David Sloan. *Darwin's Cathedral.* Chicago: University of Chicago Press, 2002.

Wittgenstein, Ludwig. *Tractatus Logico-Philosophicus.* London: Routledge, 1981.

Wrangham, R. W., J. H. Jones, G. Laden, D. Pilbeam, and N. Conklin-Brittain, "The Raw and the Stolen: Cooking and the Ecology of Human Origins." *Current Anthropology* 40 (December 1999): 567–94.

Yeh, Gloria Y., David M. Eisenberg, Roger B. Davis, and Russell S. Phillips. "Use of Complementary and Alternative Medicine among Persons with Diabetes Mellitus: Results of a National Survey." *American Journal of Public Health* 92, no. 10 (October 2002): 1648–52.

Zimmer, Carl. *Evolution: The Triumph of an Idea.* New York: HarperCollins, 2001.

INDEX